P9-DNL-360

The Compleat Cruiser

THE ART, PRACTICE AND ENJOYMENT OF BOATING

Other books by L. Francis Herreshoff

CAPTAIN NAT HERRESHOFF

AN INTRODUCTION TO YACHTING

THE
Compleat Cruiser

THE ART, PRACTICE AND
ENJOYMENT OF BOATING

By L. Francis Herreshoff

Illustrated by the author

SHERIDAN HOUSE

Published by
Sheridan House, Inc.
175 Orawaupum Street
White Plains, N.Y. 10606

© Copyright 1956 by L. Francis Herreshoff

Reprinted 1983

All rights reserved

ISBN 0 911378 05 7
Library of Congress Card Number 56 12511

Printed in the United States of America

Contents

List of Illustrations

Foreword

This little book is constructed on the lines of Izaak Walton's *The Compleat Angler* because the author feels that no better style for instructing (than carrying on a narrative) has been formulated since the famous writing of Honest Ike some 300 years ago. It is also believed that few, if any, books have achieved such universal popularity over as many years as *The Compleat Angler,* and that in itself would seem sufficient reason for imitation. Some book collectors say *The Compleat Angler* has been produced in more editions than any sporting book. And, if it came out in the troubled and confused times of the Commonwealth, the Dutch wars, and the fire of London, it would seem that a similar book which might also be diverting would be acceptable in these troubled times, for no doubt there are many who would appreciate a quiet evening of contemplation in reading about cruisers and cruising. While I have no hope of achieving the entertaining style of Walton, or even expect to create one-thousandth of his enthusiasm, still that might be fortunate for, as Washington Irving says in the entering paragraph of "The Angler" in *The Sketch Book:*

"It is said that many an unlucky urchin is induced to run away from his family, and betake himself to seafaring life, from reading the history of Robinson Crusoe; and I suspect that, in like manner, many of those worthy gentlemen, who are given to haunt the sides of pastoral streams with angle-rods in hand, may trace the origin of their passion to the seductive pages of honest Izaak Walton. I recollect studying his *Compleat Angler* several years since, in company with a knot of friends in America, and, moreover, that we were all completely bitten with the angling mania.

It was early in the year, but as soon as the weather was auspicious, and the spring began to melt into the verge of summer, we took rod in hand and sallied into the country, as stark mad as was ever Don Quixote from reading books of chivalry."

While the Dedicatory Epistle and Notice to The Reader of this Discourse are copied almost verbatim from *The Compleat Angler,* the reasons for this are twofold. First, I have desired to give the reader some of the feeling for the thing that is so aptly given in this section of the book, and because it has seemed to me that the wording of these parts coincided exactly with what I wished to say.

To the Right Worshipful

LLEWELLYN HOWLAND
of Hope's Garden, Padanarum, Massachusetts

My Most Honoured
Friend

Sir:

I have made so ill use of your former favours, as by them to be encouraged to intreat that they may be enlarged to the patronage and protection of this Book; and I have put on a modest confidence, that I shall not be denied, because 'tis a discourse of Cruisers and Cruising, which you both know so well, and love and practice so much.

You are assur'd (though there be ignorant men of another belief) that Cruising is an art; and you know that art better than any that I know: and that this is truth is demonstrated by the fruits of that pleasant labor which you enjoy when you purpose to give rest to your mind, and devest your self of your more serious business, and (which is often) dedicate a day or two to this recreation.

At which time, if common Cruisers should attend you, and be eye-witnesses of the success, not of your fortune, but your skill, it would doubtless beget in them an emulation to be like you, and that emulation might beget an industrious diligence to be so: but I know it is not atainable by common capacities.

Sir, this pleasant curiositie of Cruisers and Cruising (of which you are so great a master) has been thought worthy the pens and practices of divers in other nations, which have been reputed men of great learning and wisdome; and amongst those of this nation, I remember Starling Burgess (a dear lover of this art) has told me, that his intentions were to write a discourse of the art, and in the praise of Cruising, and doubtless he had done so, if death had not prevented him; the remembrance of which hath often made me sorry; for if he had lived to do it, then the unlearned Cruiser (of which I am one) had seen some treatise of this art worthy his perusal, which (though some have undertaken it) I could never yet see in English.

But mine may be thought as weak and as unworthy of common view: and I do here freely confess, that I should rather excuse myself then censure others, my own discourse being liable to so many exceptions; against which, you, Sir, might make this one, that it can contribute nothing to your knowledge; and lest a longer Epistle may diminish your pleasure, I shall not adventure to make this Epistle longer then to add this following truth, that I am really,

Sir,

Your most affectionate Friend, and most humble Servant

L. Francis H.
Marblehead, Massachusetts.

The
Compleat
Cruiser

1

Cruising in Company / The Cabin Stove
A Chowder / On Cruising in Canoes

VIATOR   Ahoy, aboard the *Piscator!* Where are you bound this beautiful June morning?

PISCATOR   I am bound for Smith's Cove to pick up an acquaintance. Where are you on the *Viator* headed?

VIATOR   We are making our way toward Annisquam through the 'Squam Canal. I have my young daughter with me and we are making a week-end cruise of it.

PISCATOR   If Annisquam is your destination for the night, sir, and with your permission, we on *Piscator* will join you at anchor there.

VIATOR   Do so, by all means, for I plan to have a fish chowder on the stove that should tempt true piscators.

We must now describe these people and their boats, for the latter could hardly be called "yachts." The *Piscator*, as one might well guess, was used mostly for fishing, and her owner, Coridon, swore she was the best combination ever worked out for amateur fishing, combined with a little cruising. She was rather a typical Cape Cod cat with a short bowsprit to hoist the anchor on, and there it was generally seen dangling back and forth or gyrating around so that the crown of the anchor described irregular circles just ahead of the bob stay. The *Piscator* had a neat hook on a pennant which would draw the crown and flukes of the anchor snugly against one side of the bow. Still, as Coridon knew many haunts of tautog among unfrequented rocky regions, he preferred to be always ready to anchor as he went sailing along. In fact, the anchor warp was carried coiled down in the cockpit so that the anchor could be cast loose within a few feet of the tiller at which time, whether Coridon was alone or had a guest, he would invariably call out: "Down killock!" For coming to anchor seemed to give him a very agreeable sensation, and although he had been doing it for years, it still gave him pleasure.

Although the *Piscator* was only about 24 feet long, she was nearly half as wide as she was long and as Coridon would say: "By golly, sir, she is roomy and shallow, comfortable and handy and you can't beat that combination."

Most of the *Piscator's* accommodations were used up by a large cockpit, but the cockpit's great width allowed some room around the box that covered the engine. Just forward of the engine, the rather large centerboard case commenced and this extended some way into the cabin. However, the forward part of the case was reduced in height so that it acted as the central part of a table that had folding leaves on each side, as is quite usual with Cape Cod cats of this size.

The cabin, or cuddy, was entered through swinging doors each side of the centerboard box. As these doors could be lifted off their hinges and slid into racks below the cockpit seats, the cuddy was cool and airy in hot weather and still could be made warm and snug quickly in a change of weather, for on the starboard side there was a good sized coal burning stove. Although it was somewhat rusty in places and was generally flanked with hanging socks and salty garments, nevertheless, Coridon thought it one of the best parts of the *Piscator* for it kept the whole forward region of the vessel dry in spring and fall sailing. He kept this stove burning almost as if it were a vigil light in a temple, although it gave off rather a spicy smell, no doubt caused by the slopping of many highly seasoned chowders, together with a

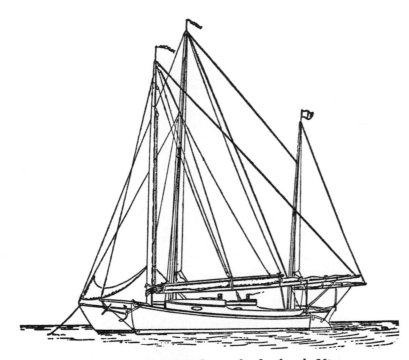

The catboat *Piscator* alongside the ketch *Viator*.

smell of many a baked haddock, and the spatterings of innumerable pans of bacon.

There was not much headroom in the *Piscator's* cuddy, but one could sit comfortably erect while eating, and at other times her crew usually sprawled out on two built-in berths or sleeping places. It must be admitted the crew of the *Piscator* always seemed happy, comfortable and contented, which is rarely the case on large yachts or boats. Some of this contentment may have radiated from Coridon's disposition for he was always full of enthusiasm and knew all the secrets of doing things easily and quickly, so that, in spite of the weather, each day passed as a pleasant adventure in which at times the *Piscator* may not have traveled five miles, but may have anchored two or three times.

Coridon was a middle aged bachelor who had spent most of his life in the insurance business and had owned many small yachts. He had, you might say, mastered the art of cruising simply, and of getting the most fun for the money that it was possible to do on the water.

The young man who joined the *Piscator* at Gloucester was named Briggs. He was in his twenties and, although he had sailed as crew on racing sail boats, this was his first experience in cruising. Briggs worked in the same office as Coridon and, as the latter's discourses on cruising had so interested him, he had requested Coridon to take him for a week-end cruise.

The other vessel, *Viator*, was quite a different craft, being an auxiliary ketch approximately 32 feet on deck and rather roomy for her size. She was a real single-hander, for her ground tackle was light and well arranged while her sail plan was moderate as she depended on her auxiliary motor in lighter airs. Her owner, Goddard, was a Boston lawyer and, although of moderate means, he had for years made a hobby of cruising. While his cruises had all been short ones, generally week-enders, his many years' experience at the game had made him nearly as skillful at it as Coridon. For several years, Goddard's wife had accompanied him on these cruises, but of late years she had acquired such an interest in gardening that she preferred to spend her week-ends at home with her relatives, who often visited her. Goddard's only child was his daughter, Primrose, who was nearly fifteen years old. Like many daughters of that age, she adored her father. Although Primrose was generally called Prim or Miss Prim by her friends, she was far from being prim and could rough it quite as well as most boys of her age. So, when she was allowed to accompany her father on these cruises, her enthusiasm was boundless. Thus she became very popular among Goddard's friends who visited the *Viator*, and if the truth were known it was Miss Prim's presence that made these cruises the pleasantest and most agreeable of any that Goddard had experienced. As he once said, "I hardly knew what cruising was until I took the young one along, for she enjoyed all of it, fair weather and foul."

Coridon and Goddard had become acquainted because the *Viator* and *Piscator* both hailed from Manchester Harbor in Massachusetts, where they anchored quite near each other, and where each had been attracted to the other from a mutual admiration of cruising skill. Perhaps Goddard admired Coridon's philosophy, and Coridon admired Goddard's real store of knowlege in the art of cruising. When they hailed each other this day, they were off Norman's Woe, both standing up Gloucester Harbor in a dying spring northwester which gave every promise of a pleasant day.

Goddard said to Prim: "I think we shall have a southerly breeze this afternoon."

"Why do you think that, Father?" asked Prim.

"Do you remember the heavy dew on the deck and rigging when we were getting under way this morning?"

"Yes, Father, I do."

"Well, Prim, a heavy dew almost always predicts a southerly wind in the following day, but if the decks had been dry this morning then we might expect a continuance of the northwest or northerly wind through the day. You are getting old enough now, Prim, to learn something about weather predictions so from time to time I will try to teach you some."

"I wish you would, Father, for it seems very interesting."

"Yes, Prim, and sometimes most useful. However, I have found on the whole that the very old predictions are best, and I will teach you these one at a time, perhaps a day or two apart, because I think you will remember them best that way. Some of the best predictions are in rhyme which makes them easier to remember."

By this time, the *Viator* and *Piscator* began to diverge in their courses, for one was headed for the Annisquam Canal entrance while the other bore off toward the inner harbor and Smith's Cove at Gloucester.

The distance around Cape Ann from Gloucester to Annisquam is a long way, but the *Piscator* with her shallow draft cut all the corners. She went inside Milk Island and Thatcher's, and even inside Straitsmouth Island at the Gap, which is generally only used by lobster boats, but Coridon was quite familiar with these shallow cuts. As he said, if there was a sea running, or the tide not more than half up, you wouldn't see the *Piscator* running the Gap. By these short cuts the distance was cut down to some sixteen nautical miles, and as a moderate southwester had sprung up, what with her motor going most of the time, the *Piscator* made good progress. In fact, the water boiled in her wake as if she were going two or three knots faster.

Coridon had cut Halibut Point close when young Briggs said to him:

"This is all a new experience to me, sir, and I like it immensely. All of my previous sailing has been on yachts whose draft has kept them outside all the buoys, and while that may be a safe way to go, still rounding Cape Ann that way seems a long drawn out affair, while these inside cuts of yours not only have given me a different view of Old Mother Ann but it is beginning to show me what fun cruising can be."

"Well," said Coridon, "a boat that can go anywhere you can't see bottom has its advantages, but I must tell you also that I have fished and anchored in many of these cuts—for instance, I am quite familiar with the rocks inside Thatcher's, which we passed close to. There is good fishing there for various kinds of small fish but there is danger of getting your anchor afoul of the cables that run to Thatcher's Island."

"Well, sir, what do you do in that case?"

"When I am on ground that may foul the anchor, Briggs, I make the anchor warp fast to the crown of the anchor with a clove hitch that is seized in place. Then the warp is led up by the shackle, or ring, and seized in place with a few turns of cod line. If you look way up in the eyes of *Piscator*, near the mast, you will see my fishing anchor is so arranged, and note carefully that there is some slack in the warp between the crown and the seizing at the ring. Otherwise the seizing won't always break to release or capsize the anchor when it's caught on bottom."

"Well, sir, I think that is very interesting, but tell me, will an anchor caught under a cable always free itself when secured that way?"

"Yes, nearly always," Coridon told him.

"Well, sir, suppose the cable or rock has caught on the fluke that is on the same side on which the warp passes the stock?"

"Then, young man, if the warp had been seized on without some slack between the crown and ring, the seizing will not break and the anchor will not free itself, and that is the common mistake made by many amateurs."

Briggs continued: "Now, sir, do you consider it safe to anchor overnight with the warp fastened in that way?"

"No, certainly not, for the light seizing at the ring can quickly be chafed through on some kinds of bottom, particularly where there are many oyster shells. While I never lay overnight with the warp made fast to the crown, still I must admit many people do, and some keep the anchor attached that way throughout the season, apparently preferring to drag rather than lose the anchor. When I come to anchor for the night, God willing, I hope to sleep soundly, so I have one anchor for fishing on rocky bottoms and the one forward on the bowsprit for all other occasions. The fishing anchor is quite light and could be called a kedge, but if the *Piscator* starts to drag when I am fishing it is of no consequence for, as I often say to myself, perhaps we will fetch up on better fishing ground."

The distance through the Annisquam River from Gloucester to Annisquam is only about four miles, but it was the practice of the *Viator's* owner to wait until the bridge was raised for some fisherman or dragger, for the crews that manned these vessels knew the best time to expect both the highway and railway bridges to open promptly. So, after the *Viator* lowered her sails and made a temporary furl with a stop or two, she cruised around the canal buoy with the engine at idling speed and Miss Prim at the helm. She was particularly alert and full of enthusiasm, for her father had promised that she could do the steering after they had passed the two bridges.

The tide was somewhat past the high water mark, but still not flowing hard, when along came a Gloucester dragger for which the bridges raised, so speeding up the motor the *Viator* followed her wake. It was exciting for a few minutes, for the canal is quite narrow, but fortunately quite straight in its first part with a little draft to spare for the *Viator* even at low tide. So, they went full speed until passing both bridges when the helm was turned over to Prim while her father carefully conned the navigation, for from here on the channel is crooked with many buoys and beacons.

"Father," said Prim, "I thought you told me it was correct to leave red buoys to starboard when entering a port."

"Well, so I did, Prim, but apparently the authorities considered Gloucester Harbor as the principal port to be entered through the Annisquam River and so have laid out their red and black buoys accordingly. In other words, we must consider that we are now leaving port and so should carry the red buoys and beacons to port Do you understand, Prim?"

"Yes, Father, I think I do, but it must be confusing sometimes."

"So it is, Prim, and when entering a strange port you must study the arrangements of the buoys and always keep the chart before you, for occasionally where the channel branches off in two directions, or leads to different ports, the red or black buoys are on the opposite side from what you might expect. But with a vessel of as moderate draft as the *Viator*, it is usually safe to pass on either side of a buoy provided you pass it closely. However, never go close to a middle ground buoy unless you know which side the shoal is on."

"What do you mean by a middle ground buoy, Father?"

"Why one that is black and red like the one off Ten Pound Island in Gloucester Harbor, which you remember we often go either side of."

"Yes, I remember, Father, but why do you suppose they call it Ten Pound Island?"

"Well, Prim, it is said that many years back, in Colonial times, the island was sold for ten pounds in English money, and Five Pound Island, the little one in the shallow water at the head of the harbor, sold for five pounds."

The *Viator* arrived at Annisquam well before lunch time and, finding a vacant place at a wharf near the bridge, they tied up and took a walk in this quaint part of the town. The place had always had a great fascination for Goddard, particularly before and after the summer season when the few people to be seen in the streets were residents. Many of the homes in Annisquam were very old and particularly snug looking. No doubt they had originally been built to withstand the northeast storms which sweep into Annisquam right out of the North Atlantic. Parts of the town, however, are sheltered by higher land, and as the small houses or cottages are clustered along the narrow streets, Annisquam is a remarkably good replica of colonial New England. In fact, its appearance in the winter time had so fascinated Goddard that he usually visited the old town by automobile about Christmas time. He tried to get there at dusk as the houses began to be lighted up, as there was something about the visual spirit of the place that was beneficial to his little family.

Goddard knew most of the lunch rooms that were within a short distance of the harbors he visited, so Prim and he were soon perched up on stools before a counter. After feeling restored, they sallied forth to stroll about the town. As it was a bit early in the season, the southeast wind which had sprung up in the afternoon felt rather raw, so they decided the cabin of the *Viator* would be a snug place under these conditions, and so they only stopped at the market to get some salt pork, haddock, onions and potatoes for the chowder they planned for supper.

When they arrived at the wharf where the *Viator* was tied up, one of the fishermen there told them that the place was generally occupied by two or three fishing boats which usually came in during the afternoon and tied up abreast of one another. Goddard told him that he was intending to anchor out in the stream and had only docked to make some purchases on shore. So they dropped out in the stream, which certainly is not very wide there. Goddard knew a place fairly close to the Lobster Cove bridge that had sufficient draft, but still little flow of tide.

After they had come to anchor, Goddard said to his daughter: "While it will perhaps be a little choppy here in the southwest wind that is blowing, this is a snug anchorage under most conditions, and I like it for its view of the town together with the distant marshes and creeks that lay all west and southwest of here, and we may see some Gloucester trawlers go up the river."

"Father," said Prim, "I think you pick out your anchorages mostly for the views they afford."

"Yes, Prim, that is so, and to be able to locate yourself or anchor in choice views is to me the most delightful part of cruising. Perhaps some people prefer the scene to be constantly changing, as it is when under way, but at such times I am so much occupied with the sailing (or piloting, if you prefer) that I cannot study the view. However, when at anchor I can look up at it from time to time like one who is painting a picture. But the southwest wind is a little raw this afternoon and under those conditions the cabin has charms."

Goddard had the custom of building a new fire when he cleaned the stove out, so now the fire box was filled with kindling made of rather small pieces of hard pine, placed with alternate layers at right angles to each other. He took pride in building his fires carefully for, as he said, if someone should fall overboard, or get wet from heavy rain, a good fire at once is one of the nicest things you can have.

So, as he opened up the ashpit door and touched a match to a little paper purposely sticking out through the grate, the fire kindled very rapidly. So rapidly, in fact, that the stovepipe and Liverpool head could not take all the smoke away, and each stove cover and crack in the stove gave off bluish gray wisps of smoke with pungent, acrid odors so that Prim began to sneeze and choke. But the stovepipe soon heated up from the bright fire merrily crackling in the stove and the draft suddenly became so strong that when Goddard lifted the stove cover to put in some coal there was no smoke. Goddard always carried his coal in paper bags, so to put coal on the fire he simply lifted the bag up and poured the coal in. In this way he kept the *Viator* much cleaner, for there were no coal bins and so no dust from transferring the coal in and out of the containers. He kept these paper bags of coal under the cockpit floor in a place that was both dry and easy to get at; thus doing away with one of the greatest nuisances of a coal burning stove. Incidentally, to remove the ashes with a minimum of dust, Goddard had adopted the scheme used on steam yachts. He used to wet down the ashpit, but from experience he knew better than to remove the ashes right after wetting down, which is certainly not satisfactory. Rather, he waited some five minutes until all the odor and dust from the combination of water and hot ashes had been drawn up through the fire. Then the ashes which had somehow become condensed were shoveled out in a damp and dustless condition.

The coal in the stove was now giving off very business-like crackles and snaps, the whole cabin seemed to radiate a comfortable feeling and it was time to think of preparing a chowder for supper.

First, Goddard sliced the salt pork they had bought into dice about half-an-inch square and set Prim to work peeling the potatoes. Then, while the pork was trying out on the stove for scraps, he peeled and sliced the onions, whereupon Miss Prim again had a coughing and sneezing spell, for that part of the cabin near the stove was giving off rather strong odors at this stage.

Although Goddard's pipe seemed to keep him immune, poor Prim finally said: "Goodness, Pa, can't you open up that hatch any wider?"

Now that the pork scrap was well tried out and the pieces that had originally been about half-an-inch square were now about three-sixteenths and nicely browned, Goddard used a fork and spoon in a certain way that picked them up and transferred them to a tea cup at the back of the stove. He then put the sliced onions in the skillet with the tried-out pork fat. Although it made a greasy looking mess, it certainly had an appetizing odor.

The sliced potatoes were boiling on the other side of the stove, so Goddard said to Prim: "Set the marker on the clock, for I think about fifteen minutes will be about right for potatoes sliced up this size."

"All right, Dad," said Prim, "but Mother gives potatoes more time to boil than that."

"Yes, I know, but these potatoes will get the last of their cooking in the chowder."

After the onions were well browned they were removed from the skillet and placed in a saucepan. Now, the pieces of haddock were slightly browned or singed in the skillet and then removed and put on top of the onions.

"Now, Prim, how is the time coming?"

"It wants about five minutes yet," said Prim, "but things begin to smell better in the cabin."

"I wish I had put the potatoes on first," said Goddard, "but he who makes no mistakes does nothing."

"Yes," agreed Prim, "and he who makes too many mistakes loses his job."

"Well, do you think I'll lose my job, Prim?"

"I guess not, Dad, for the captain and the cook are all one on the *Viator* so one cannot get along without the other."

"How's the time now, Prim?"

"Just right, Dad."

So Goddard poured the water the potatoes were boiling in into the pot the chowder was to be made in and then dried out the potatoes by putting the same pan in the oven for a few minutes. After that, he browned them in what fat was left in the skillet. There was hardly enough, so the potatoes stuck down and turned black in places.

"Now we are about ready to put the chowder together," said Goddard as he put a little more water in the pot and placed it on the stove until it started to boil. Then he added all of the ingredients except the pork dice and stirred them thoughtfully for a while, tasting them from time to time and adding now and then various spices, pepper and salt until it just suited his taste.

He was leaning against the companion ladder and had removed his hat to wipe his forehead with his handkerchief when Prim said: "You make harder work of cooking than Mother does."

"Yes, Prim, but I don't dirty as many dishes as she does and what's more I am having a good time."

"So am I, Father, and I think cruising is something like playing house: you know it is more fun when you don't have to do it but want to do it."

"That's it exactly, and if more people could learn to like to work or play around the cabin they would get much more fun out of cruising. As for me," continued Goddard, "I actually enjoy a spell of bad weather working around the cabin, for to hear the rain on the deck and the wind in the rigging makes the cabin a pleasant place to be in. To arrange everything below deck in the most handy manner seems as essential as good seamanship above deck. I wonder how they are getting along on the *Piscator*. I think they will be cold, and perhaps a little wet, for although they must have run before it on the outside of the Cape there will be some windward work from Halibut Point to Annisquam and it can be cold on the water here at this time of the year."

Not long after this, Prim stuck her head out of the companionway hatch and called: "Oh, Pa, here they come. They are under motor and have lowered the sail."

In a few minutes the *Piscator* was alongside and Coridon hailed them saying: "Sir, would you object if we lay alongside until after supper?"

"Certainly not, if you have good fenders," Goddard answered him, and so they were soon tied side by side. Goddard remarked: "It is interesting to see the two boats this way for while we seem to both have about the same sail area, the *Viator* is considerably the longer and deeper while she has the least beam. But come below, for I have something that, as they say, is good for the cockles of the heart."

So they went below, and after Coridon and Briggs had taken off their sou'westers and oilskin jackets, Coridon said, as he rubbed his hands together: "By Jove, I see something that looks good."

"How did you like the outside of the Cape?" asked Goddard of young Briggs.

"I liked it first rate, sir, but it seems rugged and dangerous-looking when seen at close hand."

"Yes," said Goddard, "the northeast side of Cape Ann is dangerous, particularly the part outside Sandy Bay, for there are many shoal spots where it breaks heavily in a gale and to me that barren clump of rocks called the Dry Salvages is particularly forbidding looking. They say that in early colonial times one of the small passenger ships, or immigrant boats, was wrecked there and, though most all hands succeeded in landing on the rocks, it was cold weather and they soon would have perished from the cold if someone on the mainland had not fortunately seen them and brought them ashore. Even then, it is said two or three of them died from exposure. The Dry Salvages certainly was a cruel place to strike after passing a month or so in fighting their way across the North Atlantic, and to think about it makes me feel thankful to be here in a warm cabin. What time is it now, Prim?"

"Six-thirty, Pa."

"All right, we will serve up the chowder now."

The *Viator* had a folding table in her main cabin and when the leaves were opened up they reached to the cabin transom seats. The table, besides having permanent racks in its central section, had racks along the edges of the folding leaves, and although it was smooth enough where they were anchored, still in all small craft now-a-days, if a power craft passes near, there may be an accident without the racks, so the racks were always kept in place.

"Now, Prim," said Goddard, "get four soup plates, four table spoons and four forks. Yes, and four saucers, and put them on the table where everyone can help himself. Then bring me the soup plates one at a time and don't forget the paper napkins."

Just before the chowder was served Goddard put a few hard water crackers in the pot and stirred them gently for a few seconds, and said: "All ready, Prim."

So she brought the plates one at a time to be filled, and after they were on the table Coridon remarked:

"It seems to me you are pretty stylish here with your soup plates, but we on the *Piscator* use pannikins for chowder. We tie them astern on a string after chow and let Father Neptune do the dishwashing, but I am going to watch how you do it later."

Goddard put some of the tried-out pork scraps on the saucers and said that some people put them on top of the chowder before serving, but as some like quite a lot and others very little he served them separately. He also had a few dry water crackers on the table and offered tea to anyone who wanted it, but he thought they would be pretty well wet down when they had finished their chowder. If not, perhaps they could find something to bowse up their jibs after supper.

For a while they ate in silence and Goddard could tell that the chowder was a great success by the way it was disappearing, when young Briggs spoke up:

"I never saw a chowder that looked like this one, for all the fish chowders I have seen were thick and white. But I must confess it is the tastiest chowder I ever have had."

"Well," said Goddard, "there are literally dozens of ways to make chowder, and while in Massachusetts they usually use milk in a chowder, still a little variety seems pleasant at times."

"Where did you learn to make chowder this way?" asked Coridon.

"It might be a long story," warned Goddard, "but once upon a time there was an old market gunner who lived on the shore south of Wickford in Narragansett Bay. He became famous for his chowders and generally served one every Sunday in the summertime. Perhaps his chowders were particularly good because they were cooked and served out-doors, but he claimed the secret of success was all due to the very old and rusty pot the chowders were cooked in and, in fact, his chowders were sort of a rusty, red color. While that might not sound attractive, it is a fact that a neighboring country doctor who often attended these chowders told us the iron in the mixture was one of the best things for most of us.

"I must also mention that the old boy made what he called a South Sea Mystery in the same iron pot. The first ingredient he put in was a round beach stone which rolled and gurgled around during the cooking. The other principal ingredient was water. This particular soup, or beverage, took several hours to mull along during which time most anything he had on hand like a chicken frame, beef bone, tomatoes, leeks, or a part of a cabbage went into it. It was a concoction that required a lot of seasoning, but the point of what I am telling is that it tasted remarkably good, which seems strange when it was started with a round beach stone."

"Well," said Coridon, "it only proves that some cooks can make something tasty out of most anything, while others only spoil expensive food. But when you made this chowder you made something, and don't forget it. Now, I want to see how you clean up afterwards."

"There's very little to it," said Goddard. "First Prim and I wipe every plate quite thoroughly with the paper napkins, and thus get rid of all the heavy grease. Then we put a hand basin or small dish pan in the sink, or if we are on a boat without a sink we put the dish pan on the table."

"Why," asked Briggs, "do you use a dish pan when you have a sink?"

"That, young man, is the very secret of the thing. If we had poured the hot water in the sink, the water at once would have become lukewarm, but where only a little water is to be used, it must be scalding hot and the small, light dish pan allows this. You will notice I carry a large hot water kettle on the stove all the time, for I like warm or hot water to wash and shave with any time of the day or night."

"That is a good looking kettle you have. I noticed it," said Coridon. "Where did you get it?"

"I got that at one of the Army-Navy surplus stores. It is one of the standard Navy coffee kettles made of heavy tin-lined copper and will last for years. Well, to proceed with the dish washing, first we rinse out the tumblers if we have any."

"Don't you use any soap powder?"

"No, or very seldom, for instead we use one of those dish washing brushes made by Fuller. Usually the brush alone, if the water is hot enough, does the job. But sometimes, as in the case of that sugar stuck in the bottom of this glass, I first dab the brush across a piece of Ivory soap. You see I do one glass at a time and, while quite hot, hand them to Prim who wipes them shining clean with a paper towel before they cool off. Next comes the silverware, and you might laugh at the word, but I have found solid silver and rustless steel is worth while on a small boat. There is so little of it, the cost is not great. You saw me wipe the knives, forks and spoons with paper napkins so the water in the dishpan is hardly soiled at all. But if it were, we would dump it in the sink and use some more scalding hot water. Now come the plates, which I take one at a time and dip in the hand basin, going over them quickly with the dish brush. Sometimes I hand them to Prim so hot that she has to lay them down for an instant, but so far she hasn't dropped one."

"I don't like this part of cruising," said Prim.

"But," said Coridon, "you've certainly done the dishes quickly and I can see now that doing them one at a time in very hot water has its advantages on a small boat where there are so few pieces to do. When I think of the mess I have seen some people make with a lot of dirty dishes in a large pail of cool water, I am amazed at how quickly this job has been done. When I think of the greasy dish towels I have seen drying back of galley stoves, I can see the great advantage of your paper towels which can be burnt at once in the stove. But how do you do in hot weather?"

"To tell you the truth," said Goddard, "there is hardly a summer night north of Cape Cod when a coal burning stove is disagreeably hot if all the hatches are open. Even on a hot, rainy night, if you can keep some distance from the stove, the dryness it affords is a comfort. However, the water south of the Cape is so very much warmer that when we cruise there we set a small alcohol stove on top of our Shipmate coal stove, and at times use Sterno canned heat. A friend of mine uses these Sterno cans in his regular stove by taking off the stove cover and placing in the hole a wire cage he has made which holds the Sterno cans a few inches below the cooking pans. This arrangement seems very satisfactory for bacon and eggs in the morning, or heating enough water for tea, or shaving. None of these arrangements, except possibly the burners of the Primus type, are satisfactory for keeping a good kettle of hot water warm all day, so when we cruise to the southward or westward we use paper plates and get most of our meals with a pressure cooker which can do its cooking in a few minutes. I must admit though that the cabin no longer seems homelike after the coal burning stove goes out."

"I agree with you," said Coridon, "but tell us now, are you one of those who builds a fresh fire every day, or can you keep the fire going continuously? I ask this because the fire box of my stove is so small that it will not go over night with enough life to catch green coal in the morning, and although I have tried it many times it always ends up with the fire going out just when I want to cook breakfast."

"Well," said Goddard, "I don't know your stove or the amount of draft it has, but I doubt if there is any need of its going out in the morning. I'll tell you how I run my stove on the *Viator*.

"Just before turning in I shake the stove down well and, if the fire looks as if it needed it, I rake it in spots with the poker. Then I open the damper and lower draft until the fire is burning brightly, adding a little coal at a time until the whole fire box is full up to about an inch and a half of the top. Then I let her go with the upper draft open to help burn off the gas, as they say. After this is done and the fire has turned to glowing coals with no flame, I close the lower draft and also the damper about half way. The fire seems to keep very steady all night and even some of the coal at the top is black in the morning. The first thing I do in the morning is to get out of bed very early and close the upper draft, open the stack damper and lower draft all the way. Then I go back to bed for ten or fifteen minutes or else use that time in dressing. At this stage, the fire seems to have become a whole hot mass of glowing embers and I put on a little green coal which at once crackles and starts to burn. After the fresh coal is burning well, I shake her down and seem to have a good bright fire which can be added to as required during the day.

"The mistake that most people make with a fire that has died is to shake it down first. Then, usually the whole thing will go out or take so long to nurse back to life that it is no good for breakfast, and it is a fact that some people really require hot coffee first thing in the morning. But if you let the old, undisturbed fire burn up brightly by opening the drafts you can invariably start the new coal going. And, best of all, you can be cooking breakfast without interruption during this time. No, sir," concluded Goddard, "the fire on the *Viator* never goes out if I intend to spend the night aboard."

"Hm-m-m," said Prim, "how about that night at Gloucester last summer?"

"Well, Prim, perhaps it is the exception that makes the rule, but the way that happened was that I went to the railroad station to meet a friend who was to sail with us and, after he got aboard and talked, I forgot entirely about the stove and of course it was dead next morning. Consequently, we made a late start, and I

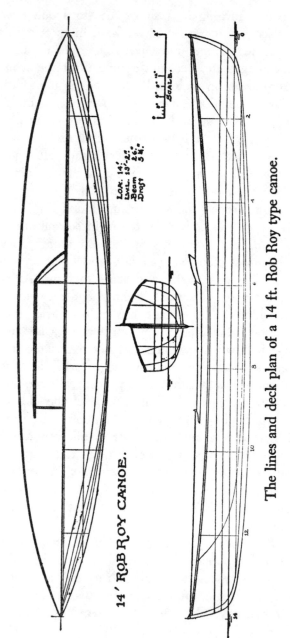

14' ROB ROY CANOE.

L.O.A. 14'
L.W.L. 13'-2½'
Beam 26"
Draft 5¼"

SCALE.

The lines and deck plan of a 14 ft. Rob Roy type canoe.

may have done some muttering before we got under way that morning."

"I was wondering," said young Briggs, "just what is the smallest and cheapest cruiser one can have."

"You can have a pretty small one, all right," said Coridon, "but just how good she would be is another question. The whole thing is a matter of taste. Some people, and good men too, like to cruise in canoes and perhaps get more pleasure than anyone else in arranging and acquiring light gear particularly for that recreation."

"I suppose," said Goddard, "about the smallest successful cruisers were the several canoes named *Rob Roy* that John MacGregor designed for himself and in which he made his famous cruises during the 1860s and 70s. I have his four books at home and if I remember right they are named, *A Thousand Miles in the Rob Roy Canoe; The Rob Roy on the Baltic; The Rob Roy on the Jordan* and *The Voyage Alone in the Yawl Rob Roy*. MacGregor was a barrister-at-law in London, England. He had been an Army officer but turned to canoeing after being disabled in a railway accident. His first Rob Roy was built, I think, in 1865. She was 15 feet long and 28 inches wide and, strange to say, these have been the favorite dimensions for double paddle canoes ever since. His second canoe was 14 feet long and 26 inches wide. The third one, that was planned to be carried over land much of the time in the rough country of the Holy Land and the River Jordan, was 14 feet long, only 24 inches wide on deck, and weighed 72 pounds including her paddle, mast, yard and sails."

"Seventy-two pounds seems very light for a decked boat, doesn't it," asked Coridon, "when you think that the usual useful dinghy of 12 feet or so weighs over 250 pounds when water-soaked?"

"Yes, that is so, but there have been some very light canoes built. Perhaps the lightest of all was the canoe *Sairy Gamp* designed by and especially built for *Nessmuk*, the great American writer on woodcraft and field sports, whose name was George Sears. The *Sairy Gamp* is in the Smithsonian Institution Watercraft Collection. She is 10 feet, 6 inches long, 26 inches wide and only weighs 22 pounds. She was lap straked over small frames closely spaced which is still the lightest construction, apparently, but it must be admitted that the *Sairy Gamp* was undecked and had no gunwale strake or other reinforcements. *Nessmuk* said she was designed for wilderness cruising where many long portages must be made, so perhaps the *Sairy Gamp* was the smallest cruiser. And that brings up the question of just what is cruising."

"Now," said Coridon, "a Maine woodsman calls it making a cruise when he takes his gun under his arm and starts out for nowhere in particular."

"To finish up with the Rob Roy canoes," Goddard said, "in developing these craft, MacGregor started with the Eskimo kayak as the basis of the design. That is the little craft that was to be propelled principally by a double paddle with the canoeist sitting very low in a small cockpit, using an apron around his waist to keep out what sea might slop upon the deck. As for model, he chose a shape which might be described as about half way between an elongated life boat and a kayak. The Rob Roys had very little freeboard amidships, and even some tumble home at their widest part where the paddle might strike the sheer strake.

"Let's get back to the definition of cruising. While I have at home three or four nautical dictionaries, I only take the small one called *Sailors' Language* with me while cruising. This little book was written by the nautical writer, Clark Russell, and it seems to contain most of the words that puzzle me in my nautical reading. Let's see what his definition of cruising is. Here it is: *Cruise. Strictly, traversing a given part of the ocean on the lookout for an enemy. But a trip in a yacht or steamer that extends over a few days is now called a cruise.* Russell wrote this little book in about 1880, but with the use of radio and aircraft, naval vessels cruise back and forth in search of an enemy rather less than formerly, so that today there are few naval vessels classed as cruisers, whereas in olden times more than half of them were used for that purpose. So, leaving the naval significance of the word one side, I would say cruising meant leisurely sailing or moving from place to place in search of pleasure, and has distinctly the opposite meaning from racing."

"But these cruising clubs!" burst out Coridon in a loud and heated voice.

"Just a minute, now," said Goddard as he called out in a change of tone: "Have you gone to sleep, Prim?"

"Yes, Father," she replied from the forward cabin which rather made the men chuckle, but Prim continued, "Well, I am in bed anyway."

"Beg your pardon. Sorry," said Coridon, "I had entirely forgotten that little Miss Prim was only a few feet away, but when I think of the type of boats that the cruising clubs have developed, and you might say *forced* on the unsuspecting public, I become roaring mad."

"Why do you dislike them so much?" asked Briggs, "for many young men like myself have had lots of exciting fun in them."

"I know," replied Coridon, "and what you say may be true, but did you ever stop to consider what the modern ocean racer costs to sail?"

"No, I don't know as I have," Briggs answered him.

"Most of the young men who go along as crew don't know or care, I guess," Coridon went on, "but the owners of these ocean racers must be fools, for they pay from $100 to $200 an hour for their sailing and have little or no real pleasure in return for it, at that, while I suppose it costs me something like fifty cents an hour to sail the *Piscator*."

"Where did you get these comparative costs?" queried Goddard.

"I'll tell you," Coridon answered him. "The average ocean racer of today, with its six or seven sizes of large jibs, costs about $40,000 or more to build. When she races, she has a double crew or two or three watches, most of whom are of considerable expense to the owner. Yes, sometimes more expensive than professional crew members. The sailmaker's bill for the season may very well be $1,000 for he will usually have to recut several sails as well as repair tears in two or three spinnakers. Now, on top of that, put the annual storing and refinishing that that class of craft requires and you will have a figure of something like $60,000 for the first year. Then, suppose he sells the yacht for her original cost, which is doubtful unless she is a consistent winner. Still his expense for the season is some $10,000. Now again, suppose he has sailed in her 100 hours—what is the cost per hour?"

"I see," Goddard said. "It does seem like $100 an hour when figured that way. Yes, and $500 an hour the first year, but many of the ocean racers are sailed more hours than that a year."

"Suppose they are," Coridon answered him. "You will find that their annual expense is greater."

Young Briggs then chimed in: "But think of how many people get pleasure out of it when the crew numbers six or eight on the ocean racer!"

"I don't know how much real pleasure the crew gets outs of it," Coridon said, "but in a race usually all but the winner get real disappointment, and in an ocean race all are subject to real discomfort, sometimes even danger. This seems a strange thing to pay $100 an hour for. Now take my little packet, the *Piscator*. She was built at Edgartown on Martha's Vineyard in 1910 and they say that she only cost $850. To be sure, I had the engine put in her which, all told, cost me about $600, but she has only one sail and that usually lasts five or six years. Her annual upkeep, hauling and storing, is not much in the yards which charge so much a foot for this service and, as I do my own painting and refinishing, her annual expense to me is only something like $300. A boat like the *Piscator* is so easy to get under way that she is sailed many more hours a year than the ones which require a large crew. It might be safe to say I sail her, or at least live aboard her, 600 hours a year. You see, she generally goes in commission in May, and is not laid up until sometime in October. Quite often, I spend 48 hours a week on her, so I figure her expense to me is about 50 cents an hour, or perhaps one two-hundredth of the cost to run an ocean racer."

"My response to that," said Goddard, "is the oft quoted saying: 'If you have to consider the cost of a yacht, you should not have one.' "

Coridon replied: "That saw might have been all right before the income tax came into being and when there were a few men who had steam yachts of several hundred tons, but there is almost no one today who can disregard expense unless he is spending his principal, as they tell me some of the owners of ocean racers are."

"Cheer up," said Goddard, "and let us return to our talk about the Rob Roy canoes for *there* is something which costs even less than 50 cents an hour to use. In fact, if you have a garage or a woodshed where you can store one; the annual expense is trifling and, as they will last forty years or so with good care, the first cost can be forgotten."

"I don't see why you call them cruisers," said Briggs, "for I should think they were nothing but canoes."

"That is just the point," Goddard replied, "for canoes have proved by the long cruises they have made that they are among the best cruisers of all. It is true enough that most young Americans do not know it at the present time, for canoe cruising has almost entirely gone out of style in this country."

"Why do you suppose that has happened?" inquired Coridon.

"I think," Goddard replied, "the young American is too lazy to paddle, or has degenerated because of the outboard motor, but if he knew that a little healthy exercise like paddling or rowing made a person feel better than anything else, he might realize what he was missing."

"Why do you say," inquired Briggs, "that this exercise makes you feel better than anything else?"

"I suppose some of the reasons for it," Goddard answered him, "are that the exercise makes one somewhat indifferent to the changes in temperature. It creates a surprising appetite, and as the paddler is usually in the best of outdoor air, and perhaps breathing a little deeper than usual, he gets much more good from it. There is also the everlasting thrill of noiseless movement, fully as captivating as in sailing. While the young man in the outboard motor boat may be going much faster, he is very uncomfortable. He is sensitive to changes in temperature, and as the noise and vibration are distressing to the nerves, the trip in the outboard motor boat only causes nervous fatigue without any of the beneficial results of light exercise. But I must say it is difficult to explain these matters to the gasoline minded youth of today, for to really get the thrill of paddling one must paddle or row until he gets his second wind."

"What do you mean by second wind in paddling?" inquired Briggs.

"Well," explained Goddard, "when one begins to exercise or develop more power, the heart and lungs, and perhaps some of our other internal parts, begin to do more work. At first, this seems uncomfortable and sometimes even distressing, but after a while, when the heart and lungs are timed or adjusted to this increase in work, a very refreshing sensation seems to permeate the body and one feels as if he could paddle or row just as easily as he could sit doing nothing. Those who paddle or row, or even ride a bicycle some distance every day, easily get their second wind, or we might say go into high gear, but to those who are not used to it, it sometimes causes distress and the average young American is not willing to make the effort necessary to get his second wind. Instead, he prefers to jump from sedentary pastimes to heavy and exciting exercises which are harmful because the heart does not have time to become adjusted to strain. Some of these people are too lazy to walk. Instead they ride to the squash court in an automobile, whereas, if they had taken a moderate outdoor exercise like paddling, their nerves would be much more at rest and they would enjoy life more, and live longer."

"Seems to me you lecture like a doctor," said Coridon.

"Perhaps so," replied Goddard, "but one of the troubles with our modern civilization is that moderate outdoor exercise is out of style, and I believe that is the cause of the increase in heart ailments."

"Now," argued Coridon, "golf is a moderate outdoor exercise, but many middle-aged men seem to drop on the golf course."

"Yes, I know," agreed Goddard, "and the reason for it is that golf is a competitive game and some of these old bucks who drop on the courses get hopping mad when some business competitor is beating them, or when they top the ball and flub their drive. If they had been men who really enjoyed nature and had taken a quiet walk or paddle, they never would have had a heart attack. I can't help thinking that the nerves and heart are closely connected and, in these worrisome times of high taxation, threatened wars, and general dishonesty and immorality, the nervous system becomes overtaxed. Perhaps too much auto driving and watching of television also exhaust the nerves, whereas a pleasant paddle down a stream through the woods and marshes would have been beneficial to the whole system."

"I thought," said Coridon, "that you were going to tell us something about MacGregor and his canoes which you call cruisers."

"Well, so I was," rejoined Goddard, "but it seems that these talks in the cabin become somewhat wandering. However, after MacGregor developed a satisfactory double paddle canoe and made a couple of long cruises or tours across Europe, he was instrumental in starting the Royal Canoe Club in 1865. Within a few years, several members of the club made quite extensive cruises in Europe, of course going from river to river by steam train, so that by 1879 canoe cruising in England and Europe had become an organized sport."

"I don't see, Goddard, how you remember all these dates and dimensions," said Coridon.

"In my younger days," Goddard replied, "my principal hobby was thinking and dreaming about cruising canoes and, although I never owned a first-class one, I did read all I could about them. At any rate, I am under the impression," he continued, "that MacGregor started most of it, for not only did he originate a very fine model of canoe for that purpose, but he worked out innumerable light gadgets to carry along in the canoe to make sleeping and cooking practical. Perhaps his experiences as a world traveler helped him in these matters. Anyway, he devised an air mattress of tubular construction, quite similar to the modern ones, but he had the tubes running crossways, instead of longitudinally, so the mattress could be rolled up into a very compact cylinder when deflated. He devised several convenient watertight bags for food and clothing, besides a folding sheet-metal stove. He worked out an apron to keep water out of the cockpit and many other ingenious gadgets. And this time I speak of was about 90 years ago."

"All this certainly is interesting," said Briggs, "but I think anyone who cruises or paddles single-handed loses a lot of fun."

"Yes, I know," replied Goddard. "Many people consider single-handed cruisers odd or queer, but if one has a high appreciation of landscape beauty, or an interest in nature, he is never bored or lonely, and to me paddling down a river or stream where the scene is always changing seems the most delightful type of cruising. There are certainly many who like to cruise alone, and it is said the Britons are particularly that way. Perhaps their natural love of nature and rural scenes is best shown in their landscape paintings and their poetry of the last few hundred years. However, for those who prefer to share their outdoor joys with a companion, the double paddle canoe is still one of the best ways, for when two canoeists paddle in company, each in his own canoe, there can be the combination of companionship with a little competition which, if the competition is not overdone, seems to make the work lighter. In the portage, the double camp, and the conviviality as the two canoeists get their evening meal before a camp fire in the lee of a shelter cloth, there seems to be a sense of companionship greater than if they had been in the same boat all day. But, best of all, after a good day's paddle, is to turn in on an air mattress stretched along the bottom of the canoe. One is much more comfortable there than in other kinds of camps, or even in some other kinds of cruising."

"Why, sir, do you say that?" queried Coridon, "for I would rather be in the cuddy of the *Piscator* than stretched out in the best canoe in the world."

"No doubt you would," agreed Goddard, "particularly when cooking in a rainstorm. And while I agree with you perfectly in the cooking part of it, still I can tell you that one can be surprisingly snug and comfortable inside a decked canoe, for not only are you entirely protected from drafts of air but you are insulated against the damp ground. Also, if a heavy rain comes up in the night you can keep perfectly dry if the cockpit cover is properly arranged. You see, in a certain way the decked canoe becomes a sleeping bag or waterproof shell which, after you get used to it, is extremely comfortable. In camping with the regular open canoe, I grant you things are quite different. In that case, you sleep on the ground and have the canoe over you as a sort of lean-to. I suppose you know the ends, bow and stern, of the regular river canoe are carried up in a pronounced sweep so that when she is on the ground bottom-side-up she will lay at about 45° to make a sort of lean-to to sleep under."

"Well, you know," said Coridon, "I never realized before why the ends of river canoes were turned up so sharp, but had always supposed it was done for looks or in imitation of the Indian canoes."

"Perhaps it was done for the latter reason," replied Goddard, "but no doubt the Indians knew the reason for it, even if not one in a thousand of the canoeists of today do. However, sleeping under the shelter of a canoe is entirely unsatisfactory. In the first place, you are on the cold, damp ground. Then, you are exposed to what seems more wind than in the open, for the drafts of air seem to draw all around you. If it comes up to rain, not only will the drip bother you but the dampness may creep underneath your mattress. While I have never heard that insects or snakes bother one sleeping on the ground, still one cannot help thinking about them when going to sleep and this gives one a very different sense of security from sleeping *inside* the canoe."

"Sir, why not sleep inside the open canoe?" asked Briggs, to which Goddard replied:

"Many have tried it, but if a rainstorm comes up in the night, no matter how well you think you have covered the canoe, a stream of water gets in somewhere and seems to work right under where you are lying, so that at times the canoe becomes a vessel to hold the water in instead of out."

"Why," asked Briggs, "do you suppose the open canoe is so popular in this country?"

"I guess," Coridon told him, "seven-eighths of them are used by young men who want to take a girl out paddling and don't intend to go far."

"I expect that is right enough," agreed Goddard, "and perhaps it is fortunate that they don't go far for they are one of the most dangerous craft we have. I suppose there are more drowning accidents from open canoes than any other type of craft, while the Rob Roy canoe, or kayak, is about the most seaworthy craft of her size known."

"Why should there be this great difference between them?" persisted Briggs.

Goddard answered: "In the first place, one sits low in the Rob Roy canoe and cannot shift or slide sideways in the narrow cockpit. In fact, in the properly arranged decked canoe he has a shaped seat, back rest, foot rest and knee brace so that he is held in place almost as securely as a man on horseback and, though he can bend at the waist, his lower parts are almost a part of the canoe. Thus, he can usually right her with the use of the paddle under the most adverse conditions.

"Many Rob Roy canoes are in model like an elongated lifeboat, almost all decked over, so they are amazingly good sea boats. In the case of the open river canoe, or what they call in England a Canadian canoe, the canoeist or paddler has to sit very high, almost up to the gunwale, otherwise he could not handle the single paddle that they use. Now, the weight of the canoeist, though well below what is called the metacentric height, is still so much above the center of lateral resistance (or underwater parts of the canoe) that any slight movement of the crew makes the canoe tip. In fact she will feel unsteady all of the time, if the canoe is light and the crew heavy. Now, if some slip is made by one of the paddlers, one or both will slide sideways and over she goes. Of course, I do not mean to say that the open canoe is dangerous for experienced canoeists who are always braced to balance a tip, or who have seats so hollowed that the paddler cannot slide sideways, for a good many long trips have been made in open canoes. However, when they are ballasted with 30 or 40 pounds of baggage in their bottom they are safer than when light.

"As for seaworthiness, there is no comparison between the open and the decked canoe. If one gets caught in an open canoe in a breeze of wind and chop of sea, he is almost helpless, for the wind resistance of the high ends will make her unmanageable with a single paddle. Of course when it is really rough, the seas will slop into her from any direction. After she has some water aboard, her crankiness is so great that the paddler can no longer put much power into his strokes. Under these same conditions, the Rob Roy canoe will go along with no inconvenience or danger and have all of her dunnage below deck perfectly dry. While of late years there have been few, if any, properly arranged Rob Roy canoes in this country, there have always been some in England, the central European countries, and in the Scandinavian countries since Mac-Gregor's time. Many of the young men of these countries spend their summer vacations in Rob Roy canoes, and apparently some delightful cruises have been made in them, particularly down the rivers and fjords of Norway in the long summer days up near the midnight sun."

"Haven't the folding kayaks taken the place of the Rob Roy canoe in Europe?" asked Briggs.

"I don't know," replied Goddard. "They certainly have become very popular and have introduced many people to the sport but, as their underwater model is not very good for long distance paddling, it is doubtful if they will ever take the place of the planked-up canoe for long distance work."

"Why do you say their underwater model is not good?" inquired Coridon.

"Now," said Goddard, "if you have a nicely shaped frame and carefully stretch the fabric over it, the kayak will look pretty good when bottom-side-up in the air. But when you put her afloat and add the weight of the paddler, then the fabric will bulge in, making the underwater shape a series of ridges where the framing comes. This waffle-like grid not only increases the wetted surface of the canoe but pushes the water that runs under the canoe in and out as it follows the natural streamlines of the vessel. It is true that the folding canoes are very light, so that when one first starts off in them they seem to go very easily, but if one paddles five or ten miles with 25 or 50 pounds of baggage aboard he will find that the nicely shaped planked canoe, although heavier, will go so much easier that it is far better. As for sleeping inside them, I should say for several reasons the folding kayak was impossible."

"You don't seem to like the folding kayaks," said Briggs.

"Yes and no," returned Goddard. "The folding kayaks have introduced many to the sport of using the double paddle; it is the only kind of craft that many poor young men can have, for many city dwellers do not have a place to store even a canoe. The folding kayak has proved to be strong enough for shooting rapids, and sometimes because they can spring or give they will stand striking boulders or smooth rocks in a stream better than a planked-up canoe, but, as they cannot very well be called 'cruisers,' why should we talk about them now?"

"Well, tell us about the cruising canoes the Scandinavians use," requested Coridon.

"I only know about them," said Goddard, "from reading and seeing photographs of them, but in Norway they call this sport *turpadling*. They use canoes about 14 feet long and 26 inches wide, framed about as we would build a light row boat. They are planked with soft, light wood about one-quarter inch thick which is riveted to the frames. Then they are canvas covered like the usual river canoe and, while this is not the lightest construction, it does stand up better than any other that can be made for the cost. The Norwegian *turpadler* usually sleeps outside his canoe—in fact, he has to, for they use canoes or kayaks with very short and small cockpits. He usually sleeps beside the canoe under a very small tent only big enough to cover a sleeping bag; the tent being an unsymmetrical pyramid held up at one end by a half-section of a paddle. These canoes usually have a fair sized hatch in the after deck which will allow the sleeping bag, tent, etc., to be stowed aft of a bulkhead or forward of the cockpit. There usually is no bulkhead forward of the cockpit but instead, before the canoe is decked over in building, a rope is rove through a sheave near the stem-head below deck. This rope is used to haul duffel bags, and gear way up in the bow or to shift their weight fore and aft for trimming purposes. Of course, the rope is made fast to the bags so that they will not turn over or jam below deck when they are hauled aft by the end of the rope used for that purpose.

"In Norway many of these small craft are built by amateurs and I imagine they get a great deal of fun out of it, especially making or getting together the lightest and most scientific camping equipment."

"How much weight of equipment do you think can be carried in a cruising double paddle canoe?" asked Briggs.

"Why I can't say just how much can be carried," replied Goddard, "but I will say it should be less than 50 pounds, and 25 pounds would be better for every pound will be noticeable in a long paddle. As far as the weight is concerned, I suppose it holds back a canoe as much as it does a bicycle. While the bicycle, of course, travels much faster, it is my opinion one can travel 10 or 20 miles about as easily in or on one as the other, and the weight will affect them somewhat in like proportion. I speak of this to illustrate the importance of keeping your equipment as light as possible. Also, in comparison with the bicycle, the position of the paddler or pedaler must be exactly right or the work will be extremely tiring. But in the canoe, if the seat, foot rest and back rest, are adjusted just right, the work will be nothing more than a comfortable exercise. On the bicycle, however, you must stick to the beaten highway which is pretty terrible today, while in the canoe you can often get into the unspoiled country quite quickly, and except perhaps for the distant view of some abandoned farmhouse you can paddle through wood lots, swamps and meadow where the only things that will disturb you are the distant aeroplanes passing overhead. Often as you pass some marsh grass or sedge, a wild duck will be sailing the placid waters with her ducklings around her, quite undisturbed by your noiseless approach.

"But it seems to be getting quite late and if we intend to make an early start in the morning, we should soon turn in. However, these talks about small cruising boats are most interesting to me and if you care to continue them I would like to have you both come to dine with me some evening next week and then I can show you my canoe and the workshop where I used to work on her winter Sundays. We can also see Nat Bishop's book, *Four Months in a Sneak Box,* and the design that a friend of mine made of a sailing dinghy for what he called beach cruising."

"This has certainly been an interesting evening for me, sir," said Briggs, "and I want to thank you for the chowder."

"As for my part," added Coridon, "you know I always have a good time when aboard the *Viator,* but what do you say if we continue our cruise in company tomorrow for I suppose we are both bound home to Manchester?"

"That suits me," replied Goddard, "but if we go back around the Cape we should make an early start."

"Tell you what," said Coridon, "I'll race you from Annisquam Lighthouse to Manchester, disregarding all buoys or aids to navigation. If it suits you, we can start at eight sharp in the morning and both use motors all the way if we want to."

Goddard, who had done some racing in his day, at once felt enthusiastic but his only reply as he cast off the *Piscator* was: "I'll be at the Lighthouse at eight."

The *Piscator* dropped down to a shallow place just off the yacht club, and as they turned in Briggs said: "I call that a very interesting evening, for I did not know before that canoes could be called cruisers. If so, there is hope for a fellow like me owning a cruiser some day."

"Yes, I had a good evening, too," agreed Coridon.

Even before Coridon finished rattling around the stove, Briggs was sound asleep for the fresh air of a first spring cruise, together with a good supper and a dry, warm, airy cabin had their natural effect.

Goddard, on the *Viator,* sat in the cockpit a few minutes to study the weather, but a cold dampness made him shiver so he moved to the companionway and stood half way up the ladder to enjoy the evening with his head above deck but his body not far from the stove. There was a half moon in the southwest with now and then a faint wisp of mares' tails floating across it and only a few stars visible, while all the lower heavens were slightly shrouded in mist. All around a quiet restfulness prevailed, for the southwest wind had died to a light night wind which smelt of the marshland to windward. Goddard mused to himself: This wind will be light tonight and perhaps tomorrow in the forenoon, but after dinner I look for a good sou'wester and the *Piscator* will do some pitching between Thatcher's and Eastern Point. We on the *Viator* may have something to do, also—so I had better turn in.

2

Getting Under Way / A Race / On Inside

Ballast and Other Things / Goddard's Workshop

The next morning Goddard was up almost with the sun. It was very pleasant dressing beside the stove which soon reacted to the opening of the drafts. While he was shaving, the water for the tea boiled and he called to Prim to ask if she wanted some, but as he received no answer he knocked at the stateroom door. Still receiving no answer he opened the door and found Prim so sound asleep that he had to shake her to arouse her. Finally she said: "What is the matter, Dad? Is it time for school?"

"Of course not, Prim. We are on board the *Viator* and going to have a race today."

"Gee!" said Prim. "I will dress quickly then."

"You better had," her father told her. "I have brought you a pitcher of warm water and you know how to open the hand basin back of the door, don't you? Breakfast will be ready about as soon as you are."

He had started the oatmeal some time before. The bacon now began to give off its early morning smell, and almost before they knew it the eggs were sizzling in the pan.

Goddard was just finishing his second cup of tea as Prim came aft all smiles and said: "It's nice to get up early after you are up."

"Yes," rejoined her father, "and we have a lot to do, for we are

38

to start a race with the *Piscator* at eight, so I would like you to clean up and stow the breakfast things while I look at the motor."

Goddard had already cleaned the frying pan by rubbing it briskly with a large piece of newspaper, which now was roaring in the stove.

Goddard now cleaned the strainer in the gas line and, after removing the spark plugs, cleaned each of them by rubbing between the points a strip of thin wood he kept for the purpose, which soon polished the points. He then felt all the battery connections and checked the oil level in the crank case.

"Now," he said, "after you have made things ship shape below you can come on deck and take off the sail stops."

The *Viator* had a nine foot pram dinghy and Goddard had put a strong flange eye on her bow transom to which a special towing rope could be secured. The tow rope was spliced into a snap shackle which could easily be attached to this flange eye. The tow rope itself was of nylon because of the spring that is natural to that material. It was of larger circumference than her regular painter and about 100 feet long. After attaching the tow rope, he coiled down the painter in the bow of the pram, put the sponge in the dory bailer, and jammed the bailer in a certain place under the forward thwart. He next took the oars and, one after the other, tucked their handles or grips under the forward thwart and slid them forward enough so that the blade could be sprung down under the after thwart. He then slid the oars outboard as far as they would go so that if one were to board the dinghy hurriedly in a seaway the oars would be out of the way. Goddard next jammed the oarlocks between the planking and seat stringers and said to himself: I guess nothing will get loose or bang now even if we slam into a head sea all day.

After boarding the *Viator*, he hauled the tow rope in quite short so that if there were any backing and filling in breaking out the anchor the tow rope could not get caught in the propeller.

Then he went forward and hauled the anchor rode in until it was nearly up and down. The *Viator* did not have an anchor winch, for Goddard thought that a winch on a boat of this size was more in the way than it was useful, but in its place he used a three-part tackle like a long watch tackle. The standing end of this tackle was hooked into a strong flange eye out at the rail, just inside the mizzen chain plates. He then fleeted the tackle along the deck until its forward or running end was up to the mooring cleat. Goddard always had this tackle ready to use if the anchor broke out hard when he was single-handed. He attached the running end of the tackle to the anchor rode with a tapered whip spliced into the block. The whip was secured to the anchor rode with three or four half-hitches in the usual way that a watch tackle is secured to any rope or shroud, for with this arrangement he could slide the hitch along if he wanted to take a fresh nip farther along on the rode. Goddard had always planned to purchase a metal gripe for this purpose like the ones used on racing yachts to attach a tackle to the main sheet, but as this breaking out tackle was so rarely used and as the tapered whip was so useful when the tackle was used for other purposes, he continued with the half-hitch arrangement.

Next, he hoisted the mizzen and trimmed it quite flat with the sheet and, after starting the motor and seeing that it ran smoothly in the idling speed, he steamed or went ahead slowly until the anchor seemed as if it were broken out. Then he put the clutch in neutral and went forward to haul up the anchor while the mizzen, meanwhile, kept the *Viator* head to the wind. This time the anchor came up easily, for there had not been much wind during the night to make it bury deeply. After hauling in the rode so that the stock of the anchor was nearly up to the bow chocks, he went aft to the tiller and put in the clutch to go ahead. As she gathered way, he slacked out the towing rope so that the dinghy was some 40 feet astern.

By this time, Prim was on deck and had removed the stops from the main and fore sails, and had come aft again.

Goddard said to her: "You see how we are heading by the compass now?"

"Yes, Daddy," she replied.

"Well, you keep her steady that way while I secure the anchor."

He then went forward and lifted the anchor over the rail, unstocked it, and secured it in the chocks by a stout lashing which went through a flange eye on deck. Goddard only carried one anchor on deck but he liked to have it so securely lashed in place that if one used it as a foot brace when working on the fore deck it would not move.

While they were steaming slowly to windward they came in sight of the *Piscator* where she lay at anchor off the yacht club, and as there was no signs of life aboard her Miss Prim said: "I think they will be late at the start." Goddard replied: "I doubt it, for the *Piscator* can hoist anchor and sail in about a minute and a half."

This soon proved to be so for, after a little smoke and steam showed up from the exhaust under her stern, her crew was seen hoisting the anchor, which they did from the cockpit. When the anchor warp was secured, they grabbed the halyards and, grasping both the peak and throat halyards together, the sail was run up in a few seconds.

"You see now what I told you?" said Goddard to Prim. "A cat boat can be gotten under way very quickly when her crew knows how to do it."

In the meantime, Goddard was coiling down the anchor warp. When he had stopped it up with four or five stops, he picked up the whole warp and swung it over the skylight in the middle of the cabin house so that the skylight was encircled by the warp. He then passed a turn or two of the stops around the handrails which ran along the cabin top and figured to himself that the warp would now stay put even if they took green water on deck.

He then sang out to Prim to bring her up in the wind while he hoisted sail. The mainsail went up very rapidly for it was hoisted with a single-part wire halyard that was tailed out with manila. However, at the juncture of the wire and manila there was a snatch block so that when the sail was nearly up, the block came down to about four feet above deck. Goddard then took a turn with the manila under the horn of the main halyard cleat and carried a bight of the halyard up and into the throat of the snatch block. He had thus quickly changed the halyard from a single purchase to a three-part tackle. As it is only the last few inches in the hoist of a leg-of-mutton sail that requires power, he could do this last hauling with comparative ease. This arrangement also has the advantage in that the amount of loose halyard to be coiled down is less than with any other arrangement. This is so because several feet of the halyard is used in making the three-part tackle. The hoisting of the mainsail took much less time than it takes to describe it.

The fore staysail (or jib, as some people call it) was hoisted with a two-part manila halyard which Goddard ran up quickly hand over hand. He preferred this long tackle for the jib halyard as he occasionally used this halyard to hoist the heavy anchor over the rail and for other odd hoisting jobs, including running a man up in the boatswain chair.

When all sail was set, he called to Prim ordering her to bear off until the course was nearly NNW, or, as he explained, "between the red and black buoys you will see in that direction."

At that time the *Piscator* ranged up alongside and Coridon hailed, saying: "I know we are both a little early for the start, but as we are nearly abreast of each other let's start here and now."

"That suits me," agreed Goddard, as he reached down to open the throttle.

They were soon off the beacon west of Annisquam and they both passed this mark very close for the water is good close to this day mark, but even by this time the *Piscator* had drawn well ahead as she was a faster boat than *Viator* when under motor alone. Although they were now nearly dead before the wind, the boom of both boats swung inboard, for apparently the wind velocity was less than their speed through the water, which was a little over five miles per hour.

Prim said: "Gee, Dad, it has come dead calm and I don't think this will be much of a race."

"Well," answered her father, "the race isn't over yet. Last night, as I was looking at the moon, the sky was partially flecked with small clouds of the type that make what the sailors call a mackerel sky. Over to the westward, you can see those long stringy clouds which are called mares' tails. The sailor's proverb for this sky condition is 'Mackerel sky and mares' tails make tall ships carry low sails.' In other words, I expect a good breeze before the day is over. Now, Prim, do you think you can remember this proverb?"

"Yes, I think I can," she said, and repeated it correctly, but she then inquired about the meaning of the words in the proverb "make tall ships carry low sails." Her father explained that in the sailor's language "tall ships" meant large or lofty vessels and when the square riggers of the past took in sail they took in the upper ones first so that in a strong breeze only the lowest sails were used.

By this time the *Piscator* had drawn nearly a mile ahead and Miss Prim thought their case was hopeless, but occasionally now the main boom of the *Viator* would swing out in a businesslike way which shook the water out of the main sheet as it tightened. By the time they were off Halibut Point and had shifted course to wind abeam, the *Viator* heeled perceptibly and the engine made a slightly different sound as the sails began to draw. Although it was still early in the day, the southwest wind was becoming fresher in each puff of wind that came off the land, so in the close reach across Sandy Bay the *Viator* seemed to make a slight gain. After rounding Straitsmouth Point, the *Piscator* could head up toward Thatcher's Island and, although it was evident the *Piscator* planned to go inside Thatcher's, the *Viator* stood outside with the sheet slightly started, hoping that the weather-going tide outside the island would make up for this longer course. As the *Viator* went well on that point of sailing and seemed to have better wind offshore, it appeared as if she were doing well.

After the *Piscator* tacked inshore, or toward the westward for some time, she bore almost abeam of the *Viator* and Miss Prim was again quite enthusiastic, but her father said to her: "The next time we both tack ship she will bear nearly ahead of us, for she is really far to windward of us now."

By this time, the *Viator* had rounded Thatcher's and with all sails unusually close-hauled stood well up to the windward, for with her liberal draft and the motor going she was a very close-winded vessel. The wind now had some weight to it and, as the *Viator* lay down to it, the reef points tapped a merry tune on the sails which could occasionally be heard over the sound of the motor, which the wind seemed to carry to leeward.

After standing on the tack for a while, Goddard said he wanted to tack inshore to see what effect the tide was making on their progress. After coming around, Miss Prim said: "I don't see, Dad, how you can tell about the tide." So he explained: "When the wind is so steady that we can keep a true compass course for some time, you can tell by ranges or sights on shore whether we are being carried to windward or losing ground. Now, if you come amidships and sight by the weather side of the mizzen and main masts you will see ahead a white house on the shore. Note that we are heading West one-quarter South. After about five minutes, I will bring her exactly on this compass bearing again and we will see what comes in range by the masts."

When this was done, it was quite evident that they were moving to windward, and Goddard continued: "Knowing the effect of the tide is not only important in racing but in cruising. It is often useful to tell if you are being carried to windward or leeward, particularly in rounding a rocky point or tacking through a narrow channel. When there is a sea running it is difficult to hold a steady compass course, but with practice it becomes almost an instinct to check the effects of tides on your course. The sailor likes all the tides which range from what he calls a lee bow tide to a weather stern tide, and detests those from ahead to abaft the weather beam. When racing in light weather, a lee bow tide can have a very powerful effect. It seems to make the yacht that has the tide on her lee bow go faster for it presses her up against the wind and her course to windward is higher than she heads, while the yacht on the other tack will go slower and be carried off bodily to leeward. I have known some old time racers who were quite happy if they had a lee bow tide when standing toward the finish ·mark in light weather. In our case, we have a true weather-going tide and I fear it will build up quite a sea if the wind keeps increasing, so before the next tack offshore you had better go below and put on your oilskins and then bring mine up."

In the meantime, the whole horizon had taken on a sort of hazy look and Goddard remarked that he had expected they would have a smoky southwester before the day was over. While it was only about half-past eleven, he thought it would be well to have lunch over with before the spray started to fly, so, after they had come about and stood toward the South, he turned the helm over to Prim and went below to make some sardine and potted him sandwiches which they took turns eating; one standing in the companion way while the other was steering. Goddard washed his sandwiches down with a thermos of coffee while Prim, with a bottle of ginger ale in one hand and a bar of sweet chocolate in the other, looked the picture of contentment for she had a real sailor's stomach which seemed never to be affected by motion.

The *Piscator*, which was still well to weather, was making the shallow passage inside of Milk Island. As she carried rather a large sail and Coridon realized the wind was increasing, he took advantage of this spot to run dead to windward under power while a reef was tucked in her sail, for as he said to Briggs: "The old girl steers hard and lays over on her curved sides when driven too hard close-hauled. She seems to wallow and plunge instead of working to windward, so I think we will do better with a couple of reefs in."

While Briggs steered, Coridon dropped the sail and tucked in a reef very quickly. This was possible because the *Piscator* had a strong topping lift and Coridon tied the main sheet block to one side of the traveler with a sail stop while he took the end of a rope through a flange eye at one side of the stern and secured it to the boom so that the boom no longer thrashed around. The *Piscator* carried her reef clew outhauls all rove which is quite customary in catboats; and as she had reef points instead of reef lace lines, the reef was put in within a few minutes which is only possible as the result of practice. So what with the motor taking them dead to windward, they had not lost much by the time the sail was up and drawing again.

While Coridon was aware that there was a fair tide offshore, he believed by close tacking inshore the *Piscator* would do best for head seas really slowed down a full, wide boat like *Piscator*. At first, Coridon thought he had overdone it by putting in two reefs but the sea and wind were rapidly increasing so that the *Piscator* acted more like a bucking bronco than a respectable old Cape Cod girl. Every time she bucked into it, she took almost solid water over the weather bow and before long the bilge water began to slosh so noticeably under the cockpit floor that Briggs thought they had sprung a leak. But she had a built-in pump, which emptied into the centerboard case, and after that had been manned awhile most of the water was put back where it belonged.

It was a hard thrash to windward, all right, but in the few miles from Thatcher's to Eastern Point the *Viator* took the lead. Her comparatively sharp bow sliced through the seas easily and, thanks to her liberal draft, she carried full sail quite easily although it was blowing some 25 miles an hour. However, things were quite lively aboard the *Viator* just the same. She was heeled down to nearly 45 degrees and occasionally stuck her bow under when considerable green water ran aft along the weather coaming. Goddard took part of the mizzen halyard and tied the end around Miss Prim's waist. She seemed to object to this and protested: "Oh, Dad, I'm not a sissy!" Although it was not easy to talk in the wind and spray that was flying, he told Prim the reason he wanted her secured on board was because if he had to go forward, he did not want to have her to worry about. That satisfied her. She said: "I'm having lots of fun. You wait till I tell Mother that it was so rough I had to be tied in the cockpit."

It was a long close reach from Eastern Point to Manchester and both boats carried the spray well up into their sails but the sea began to be less noticeable as they approached the shelter of Baker's Island and, although the *Piscator* was fully a half-mile astern, she seemed to be holding her own. Miss Prim thought they had won the race easily, but Goddard, with his good seamanship, had such a dislike of a lee shore in a wind and sea that he went way out around Whale Rock. He fully expected the *Piscator* would take the shorter passage close outside House Island, and thought the *Viator* would still have a good lead. But the *Piscator* went way inside House Island through a rather shallow and rocky channel used only by lobstermen, so that after the *Viator* had run nearly a half mile on her northeast course toward Manchester Harbor, the *Piscator* was running nearly abreast of her, but inside several rocks which are in that region. When they got to the very harbor's mouth, Goddard did not want to rush up the harbor before the wind with the motor at full speed so he lowered the staysail and slowed down the motor. Then the *Piscator* passed him and rounded up to her mooring a few seconds ahead, which caused merry shouts from her crew. These in turn were answered by a hail from the *Viator* inviting them aboard.

They were all glad to remove oilskins and wet clothes and, in anticipation of liquid refreshments, it did not take the crew of the *Piscator* many seconds to don dry sweaters and shorts, so that even before Goddard was half dressed they were alongside in their dinghy. In the meantime, Miss Prim was in the forward stateroom making a complete change and a few minutes later came aft looking as dry as a bone, for she had kept her hair tucked well up under her sou'wester when the spray was flying.

"Come below out of the wind," invited Goddard, and as they settled on the transom seats each side of the cabin table he took advantage of this respite to mix an eggnogg for Prim. After putting a heaping tablespoonful of malted milk in a large tumbler, he mixed some evaporated milk and water in a cocktail shaker, about half and half. Some of this he added, very little at a time, to the malted milk in the tumbler, working it with a spoon until he had produced a smooth mixture about the consistency of heavy cream. He now beat an egg in a cup with a fork and, pouring these ingredients into the cocktail shaker together with a heaping teaspoon of brown sugar, he shook them up very rapidly so that as it was poured into a tumbler it appeared a very rich mixture. Then, handing Prim a pilot cracker, he said: "I hope these will stay your stomach 'til supper."

They now all sat contentedly enjoying their refreshments when

Prim remarked: "We would have beaten you, anyway, if we had more wind at the start."

"Well," said Goddard, "maybe so, but, Prim, you used the word 'if' and I can tell you all boat races and yacht races are full of 'ifs' when you get to talk them over. That is one of the things that makes them so much fun. But the real thing that counts is to be ahead at the finish. If we had been ahead then we would have

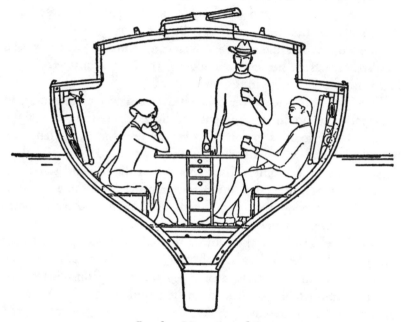

In the *Viator's* cabin.

won, but as it was I have had the most fun of any day for years. I think trying out different types of boats is ever so much more fun than racing one-design craft together, and when it's done the way we have—when the shallow boat can take advantage of her virtues—I think it is most enlightening. Certainly there is an added thrill in cutting corners, going inside rocks, and so forth, that is almost entirely taken out of present day racing. In the days of pirates and smugglers, to be able to creep along inshore of obstructions to navigation was the exciting part of those important life-and-death races. I am afraid, though," he continued, "that if the yacht clubs gave some races around islands or rocky points without regard to the buoys there would be numbers of expensive groundings for the hot-headed youth of today knows much more about changing rule-cheating sails than he does about local piloting."

"Howsomever that may be," said Coridon, "I have ten times as much fun in these informal brushes than in any yacht race, for in the first place you are rid of any frowning regatta committee, or sea lawyers with books full of all the changes in the Vanderbilt Rules. I want to have fun when I go sailing and not be a sadist thinking of luffing, fouls, collisions and disqualification."

"You are going good now," said Goddard, "and better have another cup."

When he got up to get it for Coridon, Miss Prim swung her feet up on the transom where her father had been sitting and before he returned her eyes were closed. As Goddard sat on the edge of the transom he said to her: "Are you sure you are quite comfortable?"—but she was sound asleep.

"I guess Miss Prim swallowed a lot of good southwest wind this afternoon," he commented, "and feels about as I did at her age when I went cruising with my father. The first trip of the season always knocked me out and I used to fall asleep wherever I was, on deck or below. But Prim has had a hard, long drive to windward and I am not at all surprised the sandman has got her."

"I suppose we will disturb her if we talk loudly," whispered Coridon. To which Goddard responded with a smile: "I guess not, for she will have her nap out and wake quite refreshed in spite of noise or motion." He took a light blanket from the pipe berth back of the transom seat and laid it over her, remarking that she would be all right now for an hour or so and prophesied they would have a hard time to rouse her for supper.

Goddard then asked Briggs what he thought of the day's sail.

"Well, sir," Briggs responded, "I had the most fun I have had for a long time and had no idea before that racing and cruising could be combined with so much excitement. To tell you the truth, I was so absorbed and thrilled at watching Coridon tacking the *Piscator* inside islands and between rocks that the hours almost seemed like minutes. I wonder why the cruising clubs do not foster some such kind of racing which combines piloting and seamanship instead of racing freaks that cannot be used for cruising, and sending them over courses one never would take in cruising."

"Some such things have been done," Goddard told him, "for 'way back before World War I there was a yacht club in England that gave the season's championship to the yacht of any size or shape that sailed the most times in the season from the club anchorage to or around a certain lightship that was about 20 miles away. The clubhouse was some distance up a river that had many shoals and, as the end of the season approached and the score between the leading yachts became close, the competition was very keen. It happened that I knew one of the men who went on these, what you might call, 'cruising races.' He told me that at the last of the season some of the competitors tried to make the lap of the course twice in a weekend, and that accomplishing it in foggy or foul weather, or at night, was a test of piloting and seamanship that developed real sailors. You understand they could start at any time, or anchor on the course. They could disregard buoys and aids to navigation. He said tacking up the river with a head tide at night was the most fun of all, for working back eddies behind sand bars required the most exact knowledge of the river. They did their sounding with a pole about two and a half fathoms long, believing this arrangement gave quicker and more accurate results than a sounding lead. You will say this sort of racing or sailing would much favor a shallow vessel, but as the lightship they rounded was in open water the weatherly qualities of a moderately deep boat also had its advantage.

"Well, it seems that we have rather strayed from the subject of cruising, but at the present time it is a strange thing how few yachts or boats we have that are suitable for cruising. It seems that the members of the cruising organizations either want a tub loaded with salt and loose cast iron, or a racing freak with six sizes of lapping jibs, and all the types of sensible cruisers which range between these two extremes are nearly disregarded."

To this Briggs spoke up: "Perhaps the present trends in cruising can be blamed on those who set the styles in that recreation."

Coridon answered: "That is very likely the case, but I would like to inquire of Goddard what are his objections to inside iron ballast and salting down a cruising boat."

Goddard replied: "As for the loose inside iron ballast, it is impossible to keep the bilge clean and sweet. Even if one were contented to cruise with some red pea soup swashing around underfoot, this sort of ballast should be taken out when the boat is laid up in the winter, for it brings an unnatural strain on the frames and planking. Some people lay the iron ballast on the ground alongside the yacht over winter so the rain will wash it off. Some even paint it all, one piece at a time, with red lead or other less porous paint, but however you look at it, it is a mess. While I admit it is possible to stow iron ballast so it will not shift on a cruising boat, still if you ever strike bottom in a ground swell the boat with much inside ballast is bound to be strained, and leak. I remember very well going through Canapitsit Channel between Cuttyhawk and Nashawena Island in Buzzard's Bay many years ago. We were on a heavily built vessel with all inside ballast. She only touched bottom slightly, or rubbed over a smooth ledge which is there. This grounding hardly caused a perceptible quiver on deck but apparently the garboards were started, for she at once began to leak. This was a great revelation to me who had often fetched up all-standing on rock in racing yachts which had no resulting leaks, and I had also heard of cases of outside ballasted yachts pounding for hours on a ledge so hard that the crews had to leave the yacht. But when they were floated off with a rising tide, they were perfectly tight. This Canapitsit experience made me swear I would never have an inside ballasted boat, even if some people think their motion is easier. But I can tell you some precautions to take with iron ballast if you must use it. The first is: it should be all cast iron for that rusts least. Second: it should all be in pieces of over ten pounts weight, for smaller pieces have much more surface for the weight and will thus rust more quickly. Steel boiler punchings and other waste steel junk are often used as ballast when set in cement, but somehow or other during the summer the water soaks through this semi-porous mess so that when it freezes in the winter, cracking will occur. In some ways, a boat with cemented bilges is best if kept afloat all winter for then she will not shrink up and let water run down between the planking and the cement which often starts the garboards after two or three freezings. Perhaps, after all, if you have room for them the old-fashioned round beach cobblestones, as used in the Block Island boats, are best, but they are prone to shift some unless the lower planking has much deadrise."

"Now that's interesting," said Coridon, "but certainly you do not object to a few pigs of lead in the bilge."

"No," answered Goddard, "for a few pieces of lead are often necessary for trimming purposes and they will not stain the bilge water. However, I should say seven-eighths of the ballast should be outside if you expect the yacht to stay tight after a grounding, or to have a long, useful life. In fact, I will go so far as to say I do not know of a boat or yacht with much inside ballast which has lasted very long unless she has been periodically rebuilt, but we have many yachts over fifty years old with outside ballast."

"Well, tell us now what you think about salting down," requested Coridon.

So Goddard continued: "I believe there is no scientific evidence that a strong solution of salt will preserve wood, but on the other hand there is much evidence that strong crude salt discolors, weakens and even breaks down the fibers of wood. I have seen a Gloucester fisherman being repaired, and in all the bays that were salted down the wood was either rotted away or so cracked, charred, and burnt by the strong salt that it had little strength left. Of course, salt is nearly the worst thing for all metal fastenings, either bronze or iron, and so probably only a trunnel-fastened vessel can stand it for long. Although the average life of Gloucester schooners was never very long, there may be a reason that salt was desirable in a vessel that carried a cargo of fish, but I see no earthly reason for a yacht being salted down. Certainly, salting down makes the yacht forever after unfit to live in."

"Why do you say that?" inquired Coridon.

"Because," Goddard answered, "the vessel will always be unnaturally damp. In warm weather, much of the interior will give off a disagreeable odor as if the woodwork, blankets, clothes and everything were mildewing and rotting—which they probably are. Furthermore, if the yacht is thoroughly salted down, her weight will be very much increased so that her ballast will have to be reduced."

"I don't doubt that all that is very true," pursued Coridon, "but why do you suppose in old times they drilled holes in stem heads and other big timbers and packed them with salt? Why do you suppose they had salt boxes and salt stops in places that were apt to rot?"

"I believe," replied Goddard, "that they did not know any better and simply thought that if salt preserved meat and fish it would preserve wood, but in most cases the salt boxes and salt stops actually caused rot for they often prevented a free circulation of air around the frames between the planking and sheathing. If they had poured kerosene into holes drilled in the stem head and other places, they would have preserved the wood, for kerosene is definitely known to kill the bacteria that causes rot and it does not seem to have any chemical action that breaks down or burns the wood as salt does. But after all is said and done, the best way to preserve a wooden yacht is to have a free circulation of air around all of its interior parts. Where there is not a free circulation of air you will often find rot, and this is particularly so on yachts where the cabin floor or cabin sole runs 'way out to the planking. On yachts or boats so constructed, the planking is usually soft just below this line."

"What do you think about painting all of the interior parts?" inquired Briggs.

"Well," Goddard mused, "that is a great question. Old George Lawley in his quaint way used to say 'Wood has to breathe and should not be painted on both sides,' while N. G. Herreshoff was

very particular to have bilges well painted-out and have butt blocks
set in white lead. In fact, he tried to have all of the surfaces of
every piece of wood either painted or varnished. The yachts built
by these men have outlasted all others in America and the reasons
for it probably are that they were built of well-seasoned woods and
had a free circulation of air around all parts. Personally, I believe
the paint does no harm, and if I were having a boat built I would
have all interior parts painted during construction with a mixture
of kerosene and raw linseed oil. The kerosene is very penetrating
and kills the bacteria which may be in the wood, while the linseed
oil has a tendency to seal up the surface of the wood so that it will
not shrink and swell so much. After this, if the bilge is painted-
out with a mixture of white lead, linseed oil and turpentine, colored to taste with ochre or burnt sienna, you will have a bilge that
can be kept clean. On a straight sail boat, the bilge water will be
odorless and transparent. On the power boat or auxiliary, the
painted bilge is far better to wipe clean of oil."

"I agree with you in these matters," replied Coridon, "but
tell us how your dinghy towed today."

"I only looked at her a couple of times," replied Goddard.
"Once I saw her jump clean out of the water, for it was quite
rough and choppy off Eastern Point, but I knew from experience
she would tow dry in any sort of a headwind for most light tenders
like her that have a quick turn-up to the planking aft will stand
up on end, hold back on the tow rope, and keep free from water."

Coridon added: "Perhaps you noticed we carried our tender
right in the cockpit. We even hauled her aboard last night, so if
the tide was against the wind she would not disturb us. In rough
going I always try to carry her aboard and that is one of the advantages of our large cockpit."

"I should say so," replied Goddard, "but how do you get her
aboard easily?"

"I don't say we get her aboard easily," Coridon answered him,
"but, in the first place, she is a very light tender. My first move
is to haul the boom well up with the topping lift and swing it to

one side where it is held with a tie around the sail gaff and boom. The tie is secured to one of the halyard cleats on the after face of the cabin bulkhead. I have an old piece of canvas that is laid over the *Piscator's* rail and coaming. When alone, I have a hard time of it as the dinghy comes up rather diagonally, but when there are two of us standing out with our knees against the cockpit coaming she comes up between us quite easily. After she is up, balanced on the coaming, one at a time we step down on the cockpit floor and swing the dinghy around 'til she faces nearly fore and aft. Then, with a man at each end, we lift her toward the foreward end of the cockpit where she is lashed down partly over the engine box. It seems that a maneuver of this kind becomes easy with practice."

"I should think," said Goddard, "that it would be difficult to haul or launch the dinghy in that manner if under way."

"Yes, it would be," agreed Coridon, "and I do not intend to launch her when under way except in an emergency, and in that case it is to be expected that both the dinghy and the coaming will be scratched. However, I do not haul the dinghy aboard more than about once a year. It just so happened that I hauled her aboard last night with the idea that the *Piscator* would sail faster, otherwise I might not have a dinghy now. I am surprised," continued Coridon looking around, "that everything is so neat and shipshape in the *Viator* cabin, for I saw you well heeled down some of the time, and you haven't had time to pick things up."

"It *is* a hard thing to secure everything," replied Goddard, "but there are some pretty good arrangements aboard the *Viator* if I do say so. The best of them are the folding pipe berths back of these transom seats, for they make folding receptacles about six feet by two feet that can contain a surprising assortment of things that will never get loose or damaged in the roughest going. I try to have my guests or crew keep all of their personal things in their pipe berths and not scattered around. You see, besides their bedding and clothes, they can perfectly well keep duffel bags, cameras, books, guns, etc., there. I would open this berth back of me if

Prim were not sound asleep on the transom under it, but I think you can see how quickly the pipe berths can be let down by untying the lashing at the top, and if you both care to stand up, Briggs can let that one on your side down. I can tell you, beforehand, that you will find some life jackets there besides the brass fog horn, some flares, a Very pistol, a roll of charts and a small case of first aid medicinal things. You see, I try to remember where everything is so that if it is wanted in a hurry you can always put your hand on it."

Briggs let down the berth and they saw all the things just mentioned lying on the life jackets at the bottom.

"You see," continued Goddard, "everything can be gotten at or found when the berth is opened way up. But if, for instance, you only wanted a sweater you could reach it without opening the berth much. Sometimes things can be kept near the ends, such as the light blanket that I threw over Prim, which, though perfectly safe, can be gotten at without opening the berth."

"Next in convenience to the pipe berth," Goddard went on, "are these four long, narrow drawers in the central section of the table. They can be drawn from either end with the table leaves opened or swung down, and they hold a miscellaneous lot of things besides the table silver. Then, perhaps you have noticed that we have a very deep sink. Well, we almost never use it for washing purposes. Instead, when the going gets hubbly, this is the general receptacle for the hot water kettle, the ketchup bottle, the jam jar, the pickle jar, besides almost anything else that does not have a regular rack. All these things are generally jammed in place with the addition of the tea mop, or some other flexible object. Yes, the deep sink is a useful thing, for if a jar of jam or a ketchup bottle gets loose and breaks you have a real mess to clean up, but when things are in the sink, if an accident occurs, it is easily remedied. Of course, we have tight racks for china and glassware and a food storage compartment with a strong button to keep the door closed, even if the weight of all its contents comes against it.

"By the way, some of the most awkward things to stow on a small yacht are suitcases and traveling bags. On the *Viator* we have a place for these in the forward stateroom just forward of the main mast, between the built-in berths. You know, many people stow them under the cockpit floor but if, as is usual in a boat of this size, the compass is under a glass in the cockpit floor the handbags will very much affect the compass for they invariably have some iron in their framework under the leather covering, and while the compass can be corrected for permanent iron work or the engine, I never allow movable iron things near it when I am using it to steer by."

"Well," said Coridon, "everything may be ship shape on the *Viator* but it isn't on the *Piscator,* for the last time I looked in the cuddy almost everything that is movable had sought its level and that seems to be the cabin sole, so I must go back and get straightened out. I suppose a short, wide boat like the *Piscator* jumps and pitches more than you do when driven hard in a sea."

"I have no doubt that is true," replied Goddard, "and I think those people who say wide, shallow boats have the easiest motion are mistaken, for certainly when you drive a vessel into a head sea she goes the smoothest and easiest if she is long and narrow. But we will talk about the effect of model on seaworthiness another time, for I must get to work straightening out things on the deck of the *Viator*, and I have to get Prim home tonight, otherwise her mother will have a fit as she will want to prink her up for school tomorrow."

As Coridon and Briggs started back in the dinghy, Goddard called to them, saying: "Now remember, we expect both of you for supper next Thursday night, and come early because I want to show you my workshop. After things were made ship shape on deck, Goddard went below and woke Prim, telling her to put on her shore-going shoes as they were going to have supper at some restaurant on the way home. Prim was much surprised that it was beginning to get dark and became hungry at once when told it was near seven o'clock. But she was not thoroughly awake until they got half way ashore in the dinghy, when she suddenly said: "Dad, I had lots of fun today."

On the next Thursday evening, at about quarter of six, Coridon's car drove into the gravel driveway of Goddard's place in the country. Miss Prim ran out to welcome him and Briggs, his companion. Her father also came out to invite them in, saying: "I am glad you came early for now we can have a look at the workshop before dark."

"I knew Pa would take you there first thing," said Prim, "for he thinks more of his workshop than all the rest of the place, flower gardens and all."

"Well, Prim," said her father, "you like the workshop pretty well yourself, and Mother is busy in the kitchen, so we will all go out there. Perhaps among other things Coridon and Briggs will like to see the bird house you are building."

So, after walking through the library, they came to a door that entered directly into the workshop where Goddard explained that when he had the workshop built he was determined to have a dry, heated room that he could step into without going out-of-doors, since he knew he would only be able to use it on winter nights and Sundays.

"This shop is 25 feet long," he explained, "and 12 1/2 feet wide, and I know you will think that longer than necessary. But as for the length—sometimes I make or refinish a spar here so that the bench along the north side runs the whole length. The windows back of the bench, as you see, are quite close together and as the shop runs nearly east and west I have a lot of north light to work by."

"Is north light best for working?" inquired Briggs.

"Yes, decidedly so," replied Goddard. "It casts less shadow and is never so bright that the iris of the eye has to close down as it would on the south side of the shop if you happened to get in the direct sunlight. You can read the graduations of a rule, or see imperfections in your work much better and you will find that it is ever so much less tiring to work with a north light. While the dif-

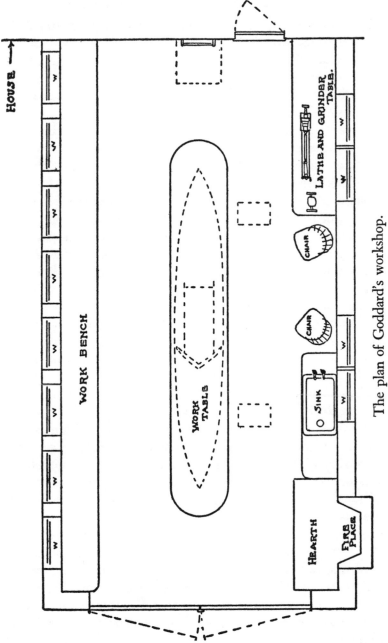

The plan of Goddard's workshop.

ference may not seem so great to eyes the age of yours and Prim's, still even young people can do much the best work with a north light. See the bird house Prim is making? Don't you think that is a good example of the help of a north light?"

"I think it is pretty good, all right," said Coridon, "but I think she had some other help than the north light."

"Maybe so," replied Goddard, "but anyway Miss Prim did all the painting and I must say it is pretty good."

"I'll bet she got more paint on her hands and clothes than the bird house," teased Coridon.

"No, that is not so," countered her father. "You see, her mother rigs her out in some sort of overalls when she comes out here to work, and we lay newspapers on the bench, as you see. She has a piece of cheesecloth which she wipes the brush handles and her hands on and, altogether, is a very neat worker, I am glad to say. After some training in the workshop, I hope she will help me in painting the cabin of the *Viator*."

"I hope to, Dad, and I think it will be lots of fun, particularly on cold days in the springtime. If we have a fire in the stove and a warm lunch, we won't care then how much it rains and blows outside, will we?"

Briggs then asked: "Why do you have a fireplace in a workshop like this?" and Goddard told him:

"We don't often use it for heat, but a fireplace is almost a necessity if you do much planing or wood turning for you can sweep the shavings right into it. While one of the old fashioned airtight stoves that has a lifting top will serve the purpose, still the shavings must all be picked up with a dustpan, but with a fireplace, whose hearth is at floor level, the shavings, sawdust and chips sweep right in. On account of the shop being attached to the house I am very scared of fire, so we keep the floor and benches free of shavings. The brick hearth is also useful if we use the blow torch to melt lead or anneal bronze. You see, there is also an iron sink near the fireplace, with running water, for not only is this good for fire protection but a sink in a workshop is most useful, and the bigger it is the better.

"If I only did woodwork it might be dispensed with, but if you have nice tools and want to keep them from rusting you must wash your hands before handling them."

"I didn't know that," said Coridon. "I must admit most of your tools look like new, but I can see many of them are almost antiques."

"Some of them *are* antiques," returned Goddard, "and were owned by my father before me. As I have been picking up my tools one at a time during the last 40 years you can guess many are 30 or more years old. Some people's hands rust tools and other's don't, but the best way of all is to wash your hands before handling them. Also, I often make things of metal that was purchased at a junk yard, and they all need washing. Sometimes I overhaul small motors, or parts of them, and then the large iron sink comes in handy. Always, when I do work on anything that has been near salt water I wash it off thoroughly first."

"I see you have a fancy tool chest under the bench there," said Coridon, and Goddard explained that he had bought that from the widow of a boat builder he used to know, and he thought quite a lot of it. But he went on to say that, while a tool chest is indispensable if one travels about much, it is not very handy in a shop for it is easier to keep tools and other things in drawers. He pulled out a large drawer that contained about twenty planes of various sizes.

"Goodness!" said Briggs, "I never knew there were so many kinds of planes. Do you use them all?"

"Why, yes," Goddard told him, "but some like that bull-nosed rabbet plane in the corner are only used occasionally but, when required, are very useful. You see most of the planes are of wood, and I find that after you have learned to set the blade properly they work better than metal planes."

"Why do you suppose that is so?" Coridon asked.

"That is a question," Goddard said, "that I admit I can't answer, but it may possibly be that the wood plane affords such a comfortable grip that one can push harder on it without discomfort. It may be that wood planes use a much thicker blade, and while a thick blade takes longer to sharpen, it seems to work much better."

"I notice that you have no power tools," remarked Briggs. "Most of my friends who have workshops have band saws, circular saws, buzz planers, thickness planers, and molding machines."

"I have no doubt of it," replied Goddard, "but in my case the hand tools do well enough, and outside of the lathe over there, and a hand electric drill, I get along without all the rest and thus save myself much room and cost. Most of the power tools also make a lot of dust and dirt, and they often take more time to set up or adjust and sharpen than the whole job would take with a hand tool. You will say, young man, 'How about the work?' and I will answer you that the exercise of using most of the hand tools is very beneficial, particularly light planing and sawing, so by the use of hand tools one can combine healthy exercise with pleasure, and at the same time be producing something that is useful and attractive. No doubt you know that it is extremely difficult to make anything that is attractive or artistic with power tools.

"I have noticed that, too," put in Coridon, "and why do you suppose that is so?"

"I suppose," answered Goddard, "that anything which has circular saw marks or buzz planer marks all over it simply looks cheap, while the marks left by the hand plane give the looks of craftsmanship. Also, if the object is to have an oil polish, it is easier to build up this kind of surface right on the wood as left by a sharp plane. A sandpapered surface, or even a scraped surface is very inferior to that left by a very sharp plane."

Goddard continued: "You see this long table down the middle of the room? Well, it is 18 feet long and intended to build canoes or small boats on. The top of the table is level and straight, just 29 1/2 inches above the floor. I have built two or three double-paddle canoes on it and found it most useful for that purpose. You know, when a boat builder is to build a dinghy or row boat he usually sets her up on the floor, but that necessitates much of his time on his knees and, while these men are used to that sort of thing, it isn't very pleasant for most of us who are over fifty. Besides, it really calls for overalls that are awkward and uncomfortable. But when a canoe is set up on a table of this height, the work at once becomes very comfortable. What I am getting at, is that a table of this height is convenient to plane on. I used to do the planing of planks on the long bench, which is 35 inches high, like most benches, but you can certainly plane easier on a table 29 1/2 inches high. It is the general custom to have the top of the vise right at the height of a man's elbow, believing that one can file straighter and evener at this height, but I prefer a vise one or two inches lower than this because the work itself is generally held above the vise."

"I see," said Coridon, "that you have a lathe over in the corner. This is something I have always wanted to have, but never got around to it."

"I guess you've missed something, then," Goddard told him, "for I am quite sure that lathe has given me more enjoyment than anything I ever had including my various boats and canoes."

"I am surprised to hear you say that," answered Coridon.

"Well, I tell you," Goddard said. "You see, I use the lathe almost entirely to make pieces or parts of boats, but as the lathe is right at hand, only a step out of my library, I can use it all during the long winter. I do not know whether it has paid for itself as an asset to cruising, but it certainly has given me much pleasure and satisfaction to be able to make special gadgets that are used on boats, besides repairing and refinishing parts. You see, if I have a new idea for a pulley block, a cleat, or a hinge, I first turn the wooden pattern on the lathe. Then, after it is cast, it is machined, turned, drilled, tapped, etc., on the lathe. This particular lathe is a very versatile one and, besides turning, it can mill, saw, slot and grind. Some people call it the lathe of a thousand and one jobs."

"What type of lathe is it?" inquired Briggs.

"It is a precision bench lathe."

"How does it differ from a small engine lathe?" pursued Briggs.

"With an engine lathe, the slide rest is permanently attached to the ways or bed of the lathe, and if one were only to turn long cylinder-shaped pieces, or to cut threads on rods, it would be the best arrangement. But when one is to do wood turning, drilling, tapping, etc., the slide rest is very much in the way, so that where a great variety of work is to be done the bench lathe which has a quickly detachable slide rest is much better than an engine lathe. One of the greatest advantages of all, for the amateur without much money to spare, is that the headstock bed, hand steady rest, tail stock and other small accessories can be bought for about $200. After you have mastered the use of these parts in wood turning, then from time to time you can purchase the other parts, one at a time, and the expense will seem trifling, whereas an engine lathe of like capacity and quality would cost in the neighborhood of $700 for first cost."

"Where was your lathe made?" queried Coridon.

"Not far from here," replied Goddard, "for it was made by the Hjorth Lathe and Tool Company of Woburn, Massachusetts."

"I thought lathes and things like that were mostly made in the Middle West," said Briggs, and Goddard told him: "It is true many of them are today but the development of the precision bench lathe in America took place to a great extent just west of Boston where Waltham has been a great clock and watch manufacturing city for some 100 years, and some of the best small lathes are still built in this district. It is true that lathe makers around Boston advertise very little, but that may be why they are the best value for the money. In other words, they put their effort into making a good lathe instead of talking about it. But I must hurry and show you the loft over the workshop for we shall soon be called in to supper. Prim, you run up the ladder and open the door at the west end of the loft so we can see something."

Goddard had a trap door in the ceiling over the workshop with a ladder on the east wall, and as they climbed up the ladder he explained that a shop without a good storage place for lumber was a poor thing, and that a shop which did not have a loft over it was hard to heat in the winter and uncomfortably hot in summer.

As they entered the loft all were impressed with the pleasant odor of cedar and pine. Briggs burst out: "Oh, look at the canoe!"

Coridon said: "I should think you would be afraid a craft like that would dry up, shrink, and crank in such a warm, dry place."

"Yes, well, that might be true, but she is a canvas covered canoe —much the same construction as a regular open river canoe," Goddard explained. "If you look in the cockpit you will see she is planked up of rather narrow planks so the shrinkage of each plank is not enough to open the seams one-sixteenth of an inch. You see, in canvas covering a canoe, it is customary to stretch the canvas dry, which is quite different from canvas covering the deck on a yacht where the canvas should be laid in white lead or other semi-flexible bedding. So the shrinkage on this canoe is of no consequence. If she were put overboard now, she would not leak a drop."

"Where did you get her?" inquired Briggs.

When Goddard said: "She was built right below here on the long table you saw there." Coridon exclaimed: "By jiminy, you've got a great place here and I envy you. I don't know as I have ever coveted anything before as much as I do this workshop, and I am mightily tempted to acquire one myself. Tell me, are there any other things that are essential in a shop of this kind?"

Goddard answered: "Yes. In the first place, you should have a good door in the end of the shop (mine is a double garage door about ten feet wide), for it is very discouraging if you build something in a shop which you can't take out. Also, if you have a storage loft like this, there should be some small traps or hatches in the floor for it is a great convenience to be able to pass planks below in the winter time without going outdoors. You see, there are two small traps in this floor, each about eight feet in from the ends of the building. This one I use for sliding planks up into the loft when the outside door is open, and the one over there I use in sliding planks down into the shop; in which case the planks sometimes project into the house through the library door during the process of sliding them down, and that is not unpleasant in the winter time. In this way, I can pass planks or spars up or down that are about 17 feet long without going outside. Another important thing in a workshop is to have it arranged so the temperature does not vary much. Otherwise tools—and particularly a lathe or other large metal piece—will sweat and rust. Perhaps you noticed there are long hot water pipes under the bench on the north side, and while I do not like a warm shop to work in, preferring it to stay between 50° and 70°, of course I can't help the higher temperatures of summer. But these come so gradually that they seldom cause sweating in a dry building like this workshop."

By this time, the men were going down the ladder to the shop when they heard a dinner bell being rung in a determined manner, but as they passed through the shop Goddard paused to say: "There is another important requisite for a shop and that is that the walls and ceiling be sheathed with wood and not plastered, for you will want to put up shelves in various places, change light fixtures, and arrange hanging places for tools. Also, at times, you may want to nail or screw temporary braces to the wall to hold the work, such as holding a bent keel in place over the molds.

"Another thing that may not be essential, but certainly is convenient, is to have a couple of comfortable chairs in the sunlight of the south windows. When you are building a boat of any kind there will always be one or two of the neighbors who will want to tell you how to do it, and I find if there are a couple of comfortable chairs out of the way it is much better to have them smoke themselves into semi-consciousness than have them in the way, leaning up against the work bench. I have trained myself to entirely disregard their conversation and they do not bother me at all. I simply say every few seconds, 'Yes.' 'Is that so?' or 'You don't say so!' In this way, they have the satisfaction of being great oracles while all the time I am quite undisturbed."

Just then Prim came running in and told her father that her mother said everything would be cold if they didn't hurry up, so they went into Mrs. Goddard's small parlor, a pleasant room that looked out on the flower beds with a background of rhododendrons which were in bloom. Mrs. Goddard looked as fresh as if she had not seen the inside of a kitchen for years, and after being introduced to Briggs they all felt at home, for Coridon was an old friend of the family. Goddard then said: "I have grown tired of the cocktails that everybody drinks nowadays. Also, I am proud to say, Mrs. Goddard's cooking doesn't need any artificial appetizer."

"You had better be careful what you say," she replied, "for you know Mr. Coridon is a good cook."

After Goddard passed some relishes on a plate, Coridon took a cracker with some sort of spread on it, and, after taking a bit of the relish, he remarked: "M-m-m; just what is this anyway?"

"Well it isn't much," said Mrs. Goddard.

"Maybe not," Coridon pursued, "but I would like to know how to make something like that myself."

So she explained: "I take some tasty Roquefort and mix it with some cream cheese."

"Why do you mix them?" interrupted Coridon.

"Simply so the cheese mixture will stick together and spread. I put a little of this cheese mixture on each Triscuit and then add a drop of Worcestershire Sauce on top. That is all there is to it."

"Well, Ma, when do we eat?" asked Prim, which rather provoked Mrs. Goddard, but of one accord they all walked into the dining room which was what Mrs. Goddard had desired, so as she sat down with a smile she explained rather apologetically: "I haven't given you any soup because we will have a rather hearty dish that Goddard requested me to make, for it is his favorite cruising dish."

Mrs. Goddard had one of the neighbor's daughters in to help for the evening and, as they sat down, the girl brought in a steaming tureen which, when the cover was lifted, gave off an odor that seemed to hold everyone in pleasant expectancy. This entree, which appeared like a stew, was served in soup plates and taken with soup spoons. After Miss Prim was served, Coridon lost no time in bringing his spoon into action, and at the first mouthful exclaimed: "This is the best thing I have thrown my lip over for years. Now tell me, just what is it?"

"It's a lentil stew," said Goddard, "and you better get my wife to tell you how to make it, for it is a wonderful thing to take cruising as it will keep for two or three days in normal weather without ice and, like some chowders, gets even better with a little aging."

Said Coridon: "I don't think it would last two or three days if I was near it. But, Mrs. Goddard, do tell me how you concocted this marvelous lentil stew. I hope it is not confined to Lent or too sacred for the *Piscator*."

"No," she replied, "it is simply made of lentils with a few other things."

"What are lentils?" inquired Briggs. "I don't think I ever heard of them before."

Mrs. Goddard continued: "Lentils belong to the legume family and are related to beans and peas. They have never been popular in this country because they take four or more hours to cook, but for centuries lentils have been one of the staple foods of the agricultural workers of Europe. With a pressure cooker they can be prepared in half an hour and, as they are cheap and nourishing, they make a very economical food. You asked me, Mr. Coridon, how I cooked this lentil stew. Suppose five servings and a little over are wanted, as tonight. I take a four quart pressure cooker (use the Flexseal which is all of stainless steel) and fill it one-third full of water. While it is on the stove coming to a boil you add a full teaspoon of salt. After it is boiling, slowly pour in a cup and a half of lentils. In this stew I also put about a quarter of a cup of wild rice; then two good sized onions quartered; then as many beet greens as usually come on a bunch of beets, or about half a potful. Of course, I only use the green part of the leaves. Then one beet cut up; then one pound of pork tenderloin. A pound of either lamb or beef kidneys may be substituted."

"Yes," broke in Goddard, "she usually succeeds in varying these lentil stews so that we never get tired of them."

"If I want to thicken the stew," went on Mrs. Goddard, "or make it about the consistency we have tonight, I add a little (say, a quarter of a cup) of Pablum, and these are all the ingredients. After that, I simply let it cook under pressure for half an hour. When we are cruising, we keep the lentil stew right in the pressure cooker and reheat it that way. Perhaps it is the reheating that makes it keep so long, and perhaps it is because the original cooking is done under high temperature and pressure for half an hour. However, it is a peculiarity of most of the legumes that they keep well after cooking. In cruising, we can get three midday meals from it without cooking, and they are much more easily digested meals than beans."

Mrs. Goddard served pumpernickel with the lentil stew and remarked that this also was a favorite cruising bread, as it kept better than other breads. She also served a green salad and, as it was made of things that had been growing in her garden an hour before, it was very pleasant. For dessert, she had another dish that is suitable for cruising, for its ingredients will keep well before being used. This dessert Goddard had jokingly named *Pomme de la Pomme*. It was made by first placing a disk of canned pineapple in a saucer, and covering it with another disk of a russet apple cut crossways as the pineapple had been and, like the pineapple, its core had been removed by a circular cutter. On top of this she had placed a small piece of cream cheese, then poured some of the pineapple juice over the top and added a teaspoon of sweet vermouth. This seemed to bring out the flavor and bouquet of the two apples. Triscuits were served with the dessert, so that, much to Miss Prim's delight, the meal had commenced and finished with Triscuits, which Mrs. Goddard remarked were also very good to take along cruising for they kept very well before the package was opened, but after that, as Mr. Coridon would say, they don't last very long if Prim is around, for it seems that most people who were brought up on shredded wheat when young have an unnatural craving for Triscuits.

As they passed into the parlor, Briggs said to Mrs. Goddard: "If that is the kind of meal one can have when cruising, I certainly will take up cruising."

Coridon knew that Miss Prim was studying the piano, so as

they sat down in the parlor he said: "Come now, Miss Prim, you have promised to play me a tune. What do you say?"

Miss Prim, being under the age of bashfulness, was delighted, for she could really play well. It so happened that her father had given her a book of chanteys the Christmas before, so she had had time to practice them. First she played *Shenandoah* and several others, but by the time she got to *Blow the Man Down*, Goddard's bass, together with Coridon's and Briggs' tenors, had come out strong while the last of Mrs. Goddard's soprano carried on the refrain when the others gasped for breath in the high spots.

Unfortunately, at this point Mrs. Goddard noticed the passing of time and said: "Prim, it is nine o'clock." Her father added; "Yes, Prim, it looks like your watch below."

"Oh, now, Pa," said Prim, "Mr. Coridon hasn't been here for a long time. Won't you let me play one more?" So Miss Prim gave them *Santy Anna,* and shipped off after giving her parents a kiss.

When Prim was out of hearing, Coridon said: "That is the most attractive youngster I know."

Mrs. Goddard, pleased, said: "I am glad you think so, but sometimes I think you men are spoiling her."

"Well," replied Coridon, "I think she is letter-perfect, even if you don't, and part of her good nature and alertness probably comes from her training in cruising."

As Mrs. Goddard picked up her knitting, she said: "Sometimes I wish she would be a little less boisterous." Then Goddard, who did not like to hear any criticism of Prim, said: "If you men will come in to the library, I will show you MacGregor's and Bishop's books about their cruises in small craft."

While he showed them the books, he remarked: "Of course, MacGregor's cruises were the most spectacular as they were the earliest and in the smaller craft; also, no doubt, in the most perilous waters. But, on the whole, I think Bishop's book, *Four Months in a Sneak-Box*, the most interesting to read and it is not hard to pick this book up in second hand book stores.

"I remember reading this book the first time when I was quite

young, and I certainly enjoyed it. I have since read it three or
four times, and several times have been tempted to build a sneak-
box but, as you grow older, you are apt to want a boat that can
take two or three people comfortably when you are sailing. Bishop
made this cruise in 1875 and 1876, and it is interesting that after
his previous experiences in the paper canoe *Maria Theresa* he
chose a planked-up, wooden boat for this trip. His sneak-box was
named *Centennial Republic* and was built on the shores of
Barnegat Bay by a man who specialized in these craft. Strange
to say, the bare hull cost only $25, but Bishop says she came to
about $75 when completely fitted out. I suppose a similar boat
today would cost at least $500. Bishop also says that the sneak
box builders of that time got from $1.50 to $2 a day, which is
nearly what a good boat builder today gets per hour. There is no
doubt that the sneak-box is about the best of all very small
cruisers: she is quite well decked over and so is adapted for sleeping inside. The model is the development of several generations
of experience in the shallow, choppy waters of that region.

"These sneak-boxes are very good sailers and, on account of
the flaring sides all around, are not as wet as you would suppose
for a boat of such small freeboard. This is particularly so when
they heel a little in sailing, then the windward side keeps the
spray down quite well. In rowing to windward in a sea and wind,
a triangular weather cloth is rigged just ahead of the rower and,
as this cloth or apron comes up to the shoulders, he can be very
snug in cold weather. Nevertheless, Bishop must have been a
hardy man for he started this cruise at the headwaters of the
Ohio River in the first part of December. The first day or so he
was bothered by floating ice, and he often had to stand up and
pole his way through the ice pack. He slept aboard many nights
with the temperature way below freezing but, as he proceeded
downstream, the weather became warmer until one morning
he heard the cry of the Carolina parakeet in the trees. After
descending the Mississippi to New Orleans, he crossed Lake
Ponchartrain and from there skirted the Gulf of Mexico to Cedar
Keys, thus completing a cruise of some 2600 miles. Nathaniel H.

Bishop was certainly a great man and, like John MacGregor, had been instrumental in forming The American Canoe Association in 1880 and, if I remember right, was the first Commodore of the Association."

"Perhaps at our next meeting we can talk about canoe yawls and beach cruisers," suggested Coridon, "but I am afraid we must be getting along as I do not like driving at night."

After Coridon and Briggs had thanked Mrs. Goddard for the cruising supper and said good night, they started on home. When they came to a clear stretch of the road, Coridon said to Briggs: "I call that a pleasant evening, and you see it is possible to have a nice talk about cruising without having your mind confused by liquor. Why some people today confuse cruising with drunkenness and singing lewd songs I don't know."

"I suppose," answered Briggs, "it is the example set by members of the cruising clubs."

"Yes, I suppose that is it," replied Coridon, "for they seem to only favor rowdyism and racing freaks. It is about 25 years ago now since I have attended one of their rendezvous, for I soon found out they knew and cared nothing about cruisers and cruising. It certainly is time that someone started a *cruising* cruising club."

3

Life Saving Practice / Furling Sail

A Beach Cruiser / The Rozinante

On the next Saturday Goddard took his daughter Prim and another girl of her age for a sail on the *Viator*. School had closed a few days before so the girls were full of pleasant expectancy for their summer vacation and ready for anything within propriety that would make excitement. Goddard knew from experience that plain sailing soon becomes boring to young people, so during the past summer he had worked out a game which seemed to occupy the young ones while it taught one of the most important things in all seamanship.

This game consisted of throwing a life ring over the side, at the same time calling in a loud voice "Man overboard!" The girls took turns at the helm while Goddard with a stop watch timed the number of seconds which elapsed from the throwing of the life ring to the time when it was caught by one of them with the boat hook. He used a round, painted life ring with the yacht's name on it which was always carried loose on the floor at the after end of the cockpit. While it was out of the way here, being right under the tiller it was always ready for fun or emergency.

When they first started this game, Goddard explained to the girls that the best maneuver was to jibe over at once as this is the only way that the boat can be brought back to a point to leeward of her previous course. He explained that they should be far enough to leeward so that as they shot up in the wind the boat or yacht would come to a standstill just as she was abreast the life ring.

He further explained that, if the yacht were running before the wind when the man went overboard, then it made little difference whether the yacht jibed or came about for, after coming around, she would have to take a short tack in either case to bring her directly to leeward of the man or life ring. He also showed them how the *Viator* could be quickly lay to by flattening the mizzen sheet and casting loose the other sheets and explained how the yacht under that condition would move sideways with little motion either ahead or astern so that if the swimmer were on the leeward beam she would sag down to him. In a wind and sea, this is the best way to approach and pick up an object that may take some time to secure. But he also warned them that, while light things like a hat or hatch cover would move to leeward faster than the yacht, a swimmer would not.

At first, the girls were not very expert at judging the distance to shoot for the life ring, and either overshot or lost headway before reaching it. At times, it took them 20 minutes or so to hook the life ring, for after missing it they had to jibe over once more to bring the yacht in the proper shooting position again. After a little practice in this competitive game, the girls could pick the life ring up in about 15 seconds if the wind and sea were moderate. Both girls were good swimmers and scared of nothing, so that, after they had become real skillful at picking up the life preserver, when they had on their bathing suits he would let one take turns at jumping overboard while the other brought the *Viator* up alongside of the swimmer.

He told the girls many things about ways to get aboard and had them practice them all, as he said if a yacht has a bowsprit and bobstay there is a way to climb up there, but you should not attempt it if the yacht has much way on or is pitching. If you are thrown a rope, he told them, and it is long enough, you should take a turn around your body under the arms and make a quick hitch if you can. If you can't do this, then hold the two parts of the rope together very firmly with the hands as you hang onto the rope nearly at arm's length. Do not let go of the rope until you are sure you are aboard or you will slip overboard again. He showed them how a loop could quickly be made in a rope by taking a turn around the main or mizzen rigging and hanging the bight overboard to act as a stirrup for the swimmer to put his foot in when climbing aboard. The reason this loop or stirrup should be at the rigging or chain plates is that the shrouds are a great help as hand holds when climbing up over the side.

Goddard also mentioned that, as a last resort, sometimes the man overboard can catch the painter or tow rope of the tender if it is being towed. If he knows how, he can then climb into the tender over her stern even if there is some wind and sea or if the yacht and tender are forging ahead slowly. However, it is usually best, after grabbing the painter, to approach the yacht hand over hand along the tow rope. Should the yacht have an outboard rudder like the *Viator* with a fancy curve to it at the waterline, then you can easily climb aboard. He also told the girls that most old-time sailing vessels hung two ropes from the after quarters that were called drag ropes. These were made up with Turk's heads sewed on them about 18 inches apart, so that anyone who fell overboard could grab these ropes.

"That reminds me of a funny accident that happened to me once," Goddard mused, "and I will tell it to you because it has to do with trying to climb aboard after falling over. Several years ago, another man and myself chartered a power boat for the summer."

"What!" exclaimed the girls. "You chartered a power boat?"

"Well," he answered, "we wanted to see just how bad it was cruising in that sort of craft. But, anyway, early one Sunday morning while we were at anchor, my friend decided to go ashore in the dinghy for some supplies. While he was away, I thought that was a good time to patch or paint up some places where the bill of the anchor had scratched the bows. While I was busy reaching over the side doing this, I saw a couple of bare spots much farther down so I tucked one toe under the spare anchor and leaned 'way over the side. But just as I reached the lowest spot, the anchor lifted or moved so that I made as pretty a dive as you could wish."

This made both of the girls laugh immoderately, but just then Goddard threw the life ring and shouted: "Man overboard!" Prim, however, swung the helm hard up almost before the life ring was abreast of the transom, so it was very quickly pulled up.

Then the girls asked him to continue with the story, and Prim remarked: "I bet you were furious when you went overboard with the paint brush."

"No," he said, "the thing struck me as so funny that I came up laughing and still had hold of the paint brush. However, what I am about to tell you was no laughing matter, for the launch was so high-sided that I could not get aboard again. After I had thrown the paint brush on deck, I tried to climb up the anchor warp and, though I got up as far as the bow chocks a couple of times, I finally slipped back exhausted. Then I tried climbing up over the stern with no better success because her rudder was well under the stern and afforded no foothold. Although there were several yachts anchored close to me, it was early Sunday morning and no one was on deck. I was ashamed to call for help, but luckily there was a Friendship sloop anchored near by, so I swam to her and easily climbed aboard, for her freeboard was low abreast the cockpit. While I was sitting there waiting for my shipmate to return with the dinghy, I swore to myself that I never again would have a boat or yacht that a swimmer could not climb aboard, and so on the *Viator* there are bronze footholds or steps on each side of the rudder, one about two feet down and the other one foot below the water. They are shaped like very wide staples and cause little resistance when sailing. After climbing on these two steps it is an easy matter to put one foot on the fancy part of the rudder and then hoist yourself over the stern."

"Gee, Pa, I want to try it now," said Prim, but Goddard thought the water was too cold off there at that time of year. Prim's friend was named Veronica, and both the girls said they had brought their bathing suits in hope of a swim and did not mind cold water, so Goddard said: "All right, but you must undress and dress in the forepeak as usual and rub yourselves perfectly dry with bath towels, for I will not have salt in the cabin if I can help it."

About two minutes after the girls had gone down the fore hatch with their bathing suits and towels, they reappeared on deck dressed for swimming. They seemed a little hesitant, now, about taking the dip, so Goddard said: "I will come up in the wind and stop, then when I throw the life ring we will see who gets it first."

When he threw the ring, both girls dove at once, but Prim, being the most practiced at the game, grabbed it first and as she knew how to stick her arm through the hole and swim with the ring against her cheek they started for the stern of the *Viator* as quickly as they could, for the water was really cold. Veronica reached the stern first and climbed aboard without difficulty, but Prim was in such a hurry to get out of the cold water that she let go of the life ring to climb out. However, Goddard had the boathook handy and hooked it before it got out of reach astern. He told the girls to go down in the forepeak and have a good rubdown for they were both shivering and chattering. As they went below, their skins were as white as a couple of salt cod, but after they had dressed and come aft they were as pink as two smoked salmon. Veronica was a pretty blond and looked particularly healthy with all her color.

Prim's father said to her: "You look like a real primrose now." She asked her father if she could go in the cabin yet and he said, "No, for even if you have had a good rubdown, your feet and legs still seem to be wet. But," he continued, "if there is anything you want I will be glad to get it for you."

The girls, who had been whispering together, said: "We want some sweet chocolate," so Prim took the helm and her father went below.

After giving them the chocolate, he said to Prim: "If you

keep the helm a few minutes I will tie the bathing suits and towels up to dry." So he went forward with a piece of reef line and tied a half hitch around each of the wet garments, one after the other, about a foot apart. Then he reached up to about seven feet above the deck and made a clove hitch on the shroud with one end of the reef line, and tied the other end below the turnbuckle. Thus, the bathing suits and towels could get a good airing without going overboard.

After he had gone aft and taken the helm, the girls spread a steamer rug, brought from below, in a sunny spot on the cockpit floor. As they sat munching their chocolate, Prim said: "Pa, I feel fine."

Goddard didn't make any reply to this remark but he thought to himself, as he settled back at the helm, This is one of those moments to be remembered. Here we are all perfectly contented and happy; this is the sort of thing that more than makes up for the work and expense of the *Viator*. I suppose the secret of it is to have everyone comfortable, well fed, out in the fresh air, and free from all worries. Perhaps there is nothing better than a small auxiliary to accomplish this.

As he looked around, he saw some classes of racing sailboats over to the southwest and thought to himself, I suppose seven-eighths of the people on those craft are uncomfortable and miserable. He then spied one of those nickel-plated sport fishermen with three decks and no bottom, and he chuckled to himself as he thought what people would do to show off even if they made fools of themselves. Yes, he said to himself, I suppose our friends on the *Piscator* will haul in ten times as many fish in a season as that flying float-stage manned with a lot of cowboys and would-be actresses. But I suppose everyone must try to have fun in his own way.

The *Viator* was standing back toward Manchester in a light westerly wind and, as she slipped noiselessly along, the only motion that was perceptible was a slow rising and falling caused by the easterly ground swell. This gave the nerves such a pleasant sensation that everyone was in delicious, silent relaxation. Goddard thought the girls might be bored, so he said: "There are some other things about going overboard that I want to speak of, and the first one is the propeller. A propeller is a very dangerous contrivance: it might be compared to a three-bladed sword being rapidly revolved, so the first thing to think about in falling overboard is the propeller. If you can, you should spring away from the side of the boat as you fall and always draw your feet up, as the afterpart of the vessel passes you. If you are at the helm when someone goes overboard, try to swing the helm so that the stern will swing away from the swimmer and the propeller will clear him. Of course, this cannot be done on a fast power boat, but it usually can be done on a quick-turning auxiliary. Always, as you approach a swimmer to pick him up, throw the ignition off so the engine will really stop. It is not enough to throw out the clutch because most clutches drag enough to revolve the propeller slowly. So, first and last, think of the propeller for it is a very dangerous thing. It is far better to take a few more minutes to pick someone up than wound them with the propeller. With a power boat, it is usually best to lay athwart the wind, a short distance to windward of the swimmer, and drift down on him with the engines stopped. Most power boats will want to lay side-to-the-wind, anyway, so they can be held in this position with the engines stopped. The side-to position also brings the swimmer in the slick of the lee, which is important if he is not a good swimmer.

"When anyone goes overboard, it is best to cast a life ring as soon as possible so that it will fall near him and he will not have an exhausting swim to get it. The white, hard rings, such as the one we use in our games, are far the best because they can be seen from some distance. This is not only important for the swimmer, but more so for the man at the helm of the rescuing yacht for there is no sensation more heart-breaking than to lose sight of a man overboard. When you throw a hard ring buoy, be careful not to hit the swimmer on the head for it may stun him. Several good swimmers have been drowned because of going overboard in a stunned condition: that is, they have hit their heads against the rail or something when going over. So it is best to throw the buoy ten on more feet away from him. At any rate, having the ring to cling to gives the swimmer confidence at once, and while this is very important, it also makes it much easier to pick him up.

"Sometimes a swimmer in his panic tries to follow you as you circle around. Then he will not be in the position you had maneuvered to shoot for. But when he lies quietly holding the ring, a good skipper can stop his vessel just as the swimmer is beside the chain plates. If it is rough, he can swing so that the swimmer will be to leeward as the vessel heels before gathering way, and thus the swimmer can be hauled aboard easily. The weather side of the yacht would have been a nearly impossible place because of its height and because of the seas breaking there. Sometime, when we are in warm water, I want you girls to practice swimming with the round life buoy for there are several positions you can use it in, although just hanging on to it will keep you up.

"No doubt you have heard people say you should take off your clothes if you fall overboard, and while that may be right if you must swim far or fast, it definitely is not best if you are to hang on to a buoy, or only have to swim a short distance to the buoy. For it is a fact that the air in your clothes will tend to support you for a few minutes. While it is desirable to throw off heavy shoes or rubber boots, you will find you can swim pretty well for a short distance with them on, and it is generally best to pick up the life buoy first and then leisurely remove your shoes rather than to get into a panic removing them before being supported by the buoy. As for your clothes; if the water is cold, the more you have on the better for they certainly conserve body heat. If one must stay submerged a long time in cold water, long heavy woolen underclothes are the only things that will keep you alive.

"But now, girls, while I have lectured you about what to do if you are overboard, I must tell you most emphatically that the best thing of all is *not* to fall overboard. It is a common saying that a good sailor has one hand for the ship and one hand for himself, and this means that he always has hold of something and can't be thrown overboard. While it is true that when a sailor has locked his legs around a bowsprit or yard, he uses his two hands for the ship, still a good sailor does not get thrown overboard unless something he has hold of gives way. When you see a young man walking forward with his hands in his pockets you may be sure he is no sailor. No doubt, you have heard people speak of the rolling gait of a sailor. Well, this peculiarity in walk comes from the sailor balancing himself on each foot before he takes the next step. When on board ship, he generally stands in a rather crouching position, somewhat like a boxer in the ring. Then, if the vessel makes a sudden move or lurch he can step backward or in any other direction without losing his balance. While the swinging gait of the sailor is very bad for walking fast or far, you will find it hard to knock him off his feet whether he is ashore or afloat. When a real sailorman goes forward, he usually runs one hand along the rail cap, hand rail, or life line. He will do this through habit even if the vessel is at anchor or in a calm. This is the sort of man who is a constant joy to the skipper or man at the helm, for he knows that this sailor will get to his destination quickly and come back safely. Few people realize it today, but there is hardly a ruder thing that a person can do on shipboard than be forward in an unstable condition, for this keeps the skipper or man at the helm on tenterhooks. Let him eat with his knife, or be ungrammatical, and he will show no greater lack of manners than to be forward with a poor footing or without a hand on something."

By this time the *Viator* was reaching up the channel to Manchester. As the wind was light, Goddard decided to carry all sail up to the mooring, so he told the girls to go forward to gaff the mooring buoy with the boat hook. When they went forward this time, they were both crouched down and had hold of the grab rail on the deck house as they went along. Goddard smiled at this but said to himself that if all youngsters were as anxious to learn as these girls, we would have a lot of good sailors.

After the mooring can was aboard and the pickup rope made

fast, they lowered sail; Prim taking the fore staysail, Goddard the mainsail, and Veronica the mizzen, so that all sail came in at once. While this would not have been noticed by the novice, there was a professional aboard a yacht near by and he was pleased to see things handled smartly as they used to be.

Prim was a little out of breath with her hurrying around with the mooring rope and fore staysail, but she noticed the *Piscator* and said to her father: "Pa, Mr. Coridon and Briggs are aboard the *Piscator*."

"So they are," said her father as he straightened up and waved to them. He called across to them and invited them aboard, saying to Briggs: "I have brought down some things to show you if you are still interested in small cruisers."

They were getting ready to furl sail on the *Viator* when Coridon and Briggs arrived. They were just in time to hear Goddard say to Prim: "You must wipe your hands on the mop or something else, for I won't have you handling the sails if your hands are salty or dirty from the mooring line."

"We'll help you with the furling," offered Coridon, but Goddard replied with thanks and said he was teaching the girls to furl.

"Now, girls," he said, "I think we will go sailing tomorrow so we won't bother with the sail covers tonight, and in that case we'll furl the sails in quite a different way than we would have for sail covers."

At this, Briggs, who had been watching the girls with sort of a weather eye (for he was not much older than them) said: "I didn't know there were different ways to furl."

"Oh, yes," answered Goddard, "and this time we will make a rolling furl, as Coridon does on the *Piscator*, for that is the best furl for shedding water if the sail covers are not used." He and the girls pushed all of the mainsail over to the starboard side of the boom where it lay in the lazyjacks. "Now, girls," he went on, "stick the sail stops and use the shortest ones aft." The girls passed the sail stops between the boom and the foot rope so they were evenly spaced and hung down on the deckhouse. Goddard said to them: "On large yachts the sail stops are usually stuck through before the sail is lowered away for the weight of the sail makes it hard to do this later."

Briggs broke in, saying: "I have always seen the stops put on after the sail is furled when they are passed around boom and all."

To this Goddard answered, "No doubt, that is the usual way it is done, but this way holds the sail in a tight roll above the boom instead of forcing it down around the boom as the other way does. Also, after the second turn of the sail stop is taken (which goes around boom and all) the sail will stay above the boom and not fall down one side or the other."

"Why should that be?" inquired Coridon.

"It is something like this," continued Goddard. "You see, the foot of the sail is fastened to the boom and can't move sideways. Now, if the first turn of the stop holds the sail in a roll above the boom, then, after the second turn is made (which goes around boom and all), the sail must stay above unless the stop slips on both the sail and boom, which it is not apt to do."

In the meantime, Goddard was going along the leach pulling the sail aft so that it was free of puckers, and removing the battens as he went. "Now, girls, you roll the sail up as best you can, always tumbling it toward the boom until you come to the part near the foot, while I work in from the clew putting in the last tuck." As Goddard moved forward, the sail was changing into a long, smooth cornucopia, and as he tied the stops as he went along it stayed that way. The work progressed rapidly and all the while the men were carrying on general conversation. Goddard remarked that it was much easier to put a good furl in a gaff sail than a leg-of-mutton sail.

"Why is that?" asked Briggs, but Coridon answered the question by saying: "You see, in a sail cut like the *Piscator's*, the hoist or luff of the sail is the same length as the gaff, so a great deal of the sail can be rolled up. But on a leg-of-mutton sail where all of the luff is fastened to the mast, then the furl must be half roll and half twist, but I am anxious to see how Goddard proceeds when he gets near the mast."

When Goddard got there, he took quite a wide piece of the foot of the sail, and making a fold in it that started at the tack carried the folded part over the bunt of the sail so that the furled sail carried its smooth cornucopia shape up to within two feet of the mast. He then pulled some slack in the halyard and swung the headboard down over the folds of the luff, and, passing a stop around the shackle and then around the gooseneck, he drew the headboard down so that it would shed water at the luff. The stop that he used here was a very long one so that the ends of it were taken up and around the bunt of the sail, holding it all snugly in. Whereupon, Coridon remarked: "Pretty good!"

Goddard then turned to the girls: "You see what you can do to the mizzen, while I furl the fore staysail."

After this was done, they all sat down in the cockpit when Prim suggested: "Pa, this is a beautiful afternoon and I wish I could stay down and sleep aboard the *Viator*."

"Prim," her father answered, "so do I, but your mother expects us home, and how about Veronica?"

"Why, Pa, she was going to visit with some friends, anyway, so that won't make any difference."

"Yes," he replied, "that might be so, but how about supper and breakfast?"

"I'll do the cooking and cleaning up, Pa, if I can stay down."

So Goddard said: "I tell you now; if you take the dinghy and row up to the town float, then walk up to the boardinghouse where we eat sometimes you can telephone your mother to get her permission to stay down. If she approves, then you can stop at the store on your way back and buy something for supper and breakfast. By the way, what do you think you can cook? Could you make a mushroom omelet?"

"No, Pa, I can't turn an omelet the way you can, but I can make scrambled eggs with mushrooms in them."

"All right," he replied, "and now get a pencil and paper to make a list of what is wanted."

While the girls were below, Goddard said to Coridon: "If all goes well, I think the girls will have fun and be occupied while we can talk about cruisers and cruising."

When the girls returned on deck, he went on: "Number one; bread, and if you can, get some of that Portuguese bread from Gloucester. Number two; one dozen eggs. Number three; half a pound of mushrooms. Number four; half a pound of butter. Number five; if there are any good looking ripe strawberries, get a box. Number six; half a pint of cream and a quart of milk."

After this was written down, the girls got in the dinghy. But, just as they pushed off, her father added: "Now, Prim, when you are talking to your mother, don't just say we are going to stay down, but be sure to ask her permission. Tell her Mr. Coridon and Briggs are here and I want to talk with them about cruisers and cruising." He then gave her some money and told her to count the pennies carefully the way he had to.

After they had pulled away, Briggs remarked: "Those girls are having the time of their life."

"Well, what are you going to show us?" inquired Coridon.

"First," said Goddard, "I'll try to show you some hospitality." He went below and came up with tumblers and a choice of liquid refreshments. After their thirst was slaked, he said, pointing to a roll of blueprints: "Perhaps you remember that I spoke about a beach cruiser that a friend of mine designed. Well, I found the drawings the other night and have them here.

"The man who drew those up had considerable experience with dinghies and small craft. He was much impressed with Bishop's sneak-box, the *Centennial Republic*, and first made a reconstruction of her from the dimensions and other data in the book, *Four Months in a Sneak-Box*. First I will show you that drawing."

So Goddard unrolled it and laid it on the cockpit floor, holding the corners down with four small lead weights which had wooden bottoms and which he normally used to hold charts flat in various

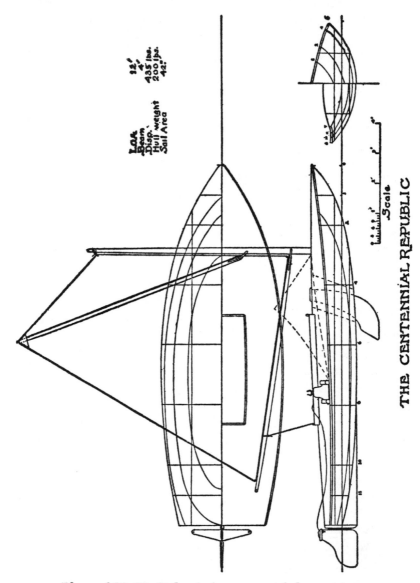

Plans of N. H. Bishop's famous sneak box cruiser.

positions. He continued: "A sneak-box has some remarkable qualities. It can get along with much less freeboard than boats of the usual dinghy model because of having flared sides all the way around, and because it is much decked over. In a head sea, these boats are remarkably dry because the flat bow throws the spray down. This is particularly so when they are heeled so the weather side rises a little, while the usual dinghy with a plumb bow is very wet when heeled because her bow then becomes shaped like a plow which scoops the waves up in your lap."

Coridon and Briggs were both much surprised at the low freeboard of the *Centennial Republic* but Goddard explained that the sneak-box was originally developed for duck shooting and it was made as low as possible so it would not be noticed by the ducks. Briggs laughed at the small, low sail plan. Coridon said: "I should not think that that cute little dagger-board would hold her on the wind."

"Low sail plans," Goddard answered, "used to be customary on small craft and the spritsail has the advantage that all the spars can be nearly the same length. The low, wide sail is just as good as a high, narrow one when running to leeward, and I imagine the sneak-box was usually rowed to windward so that the small dagger-board would be sufficient for most cases. Also the small, curved dagger-board allowed the centerboard case to be 'way forward out of the way. The *Centennial Republic* had a very small cockpit—only 44 inches long and 18 inches wide. She had a wooden hatch or cockpit cover that was carried on the after deck and that could be quickly put in place in case of rain or while the crew slept. The weather cloth, or apron, which protected the rower, went from the mast hole to the folding rowlock sockets. On the drawing, she is shown at a displacement of 435 pounds but, as her hull weighed 200 pounds, she could not have carried more than 55 pounds of equipment if the crew weighed 180 pounds. What I am getting at is that my friend started to develop a beach cruiser from a sneak-box."

"What do you mean by a beach cruiser?" inquired Briggs.

"It means a boat to cruise along the beaches in shallow water,"

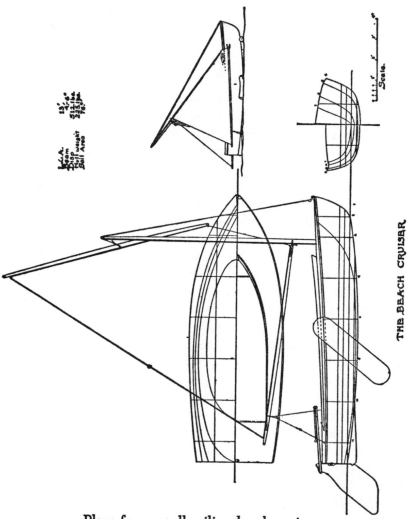

Plans for a small sailing beach cruiser.

Goddard replied, "a boat to sleep aboard when hauled out on the beach, and I can tell you that this is an interesting and risky sort of cruising. It takes skill and experience to sail close to the shore if it is a rocky region and there is a sea running, but you can visit many unfrequented places in a beach cruiser. Of course, there are sheltered waters in rivers and marshes where there is no danger. A beach cruiser emphatically does not mean a boat to hang around bathing beaches, or anything of that sort, but rather a boat for a naturalist who wants to study shore birds and animals. It is the best sort of craft for the poor man who has an urge for cruising. Even Conor O'Brien, whom most of us think of as a deep water man, wrote a chapter in his book, *On Going to Sea in Yachts*, that was called 'The Beach Cruiser'."

Goddard then unfolded the other blueprint that he had brought out and said, "This is the beach cruiser my friend developed. She is 13 feet long and 4 feet, 6 inches wide. She only draws 5 inches of water with a displacement of 512 pounds. He thought the hull would only weigh 225 pounds, so there would be some 280 pounds for crew and equipment. Of course, this boat could take two persons with only a couple of inches increase in draft. The principal features of this craft are that the mainsail is shaped to be used as a tent, as is shown on the drawing. In that case, the mast acts as a ridge pole, as you see, with the boom and yard holding the sail stretched along the gunwales where it can be tied down easily. When the mast acts as a ridge pole, the foot is on deck against the cockpit coaming forward and the after end is supported by two 7 foot oars that are lashed together near the handles. The handles act as a crotch to support the ridge pole. The blades of the oars are at the after end of the cockpit. There is a grommet sewed on the leach of the sail at a certain point where the halyard is attached when the sail is used as a tent, and this stretches the sail along the ridge pole."

"Well, now, that is quite ingenious," remarked Coridon, "but I should think the sail would have puckered or sagged down forward on account of the curve of the sides of the boat."

"Yes," responded Goddard, "but, you see, he planned to put

sand bags on the deck forward which, if they were placed right, would take up the slack in the sail."

"What would happen," inquired Briggs, "if the wind shifted so it came from aft after the tent was rigged?"

"If you were asleep," Goddard replied, "it might be a nuisance, but the little vessel can be so easily swung around on her flat bottom that you can always keep her head to the wind. You see, she doesn't have any centerboard slot to get jammed with sand and pebbles."

"That is all pretty good," chimed in Coridon, "but, just the same, I wouldn't care to be under that tent in a thunder squall."

To this, Goddard remarked: "No tent is very pleasant in a thunder squall, but if the boat were properly chocked up on the beach and kept head to the wind, everything should be safe. Although this tent would have considerable drip in a hard rain, it is only intended for the usual summer night and certainly would keep the dew or light showers off the sleeper.

"The other feature of the design is the use of leeboards, instead of a centerboard, which allows a comfortable place to sleep. You see, she is quite flat bottomed so that an air mattress as much as 40 inches wide could be used, and that is wide enough for two people. Altogether the little craft combines some of the good features of the sneak-box with much more room. While the *Centennial Republic* was definitely a single-hander, this boat could accommodate two at night and three or more in the daytime, particularly if some of them were children. So, all told, she is a pretty good cruiser for her cost."

"I'm surprised he didn't use a swinging rudder for shallow water sailing," said Coridon.

Goddard answered: "My friend thought an oar was best to steer with in shallow water, so he planned to unhang the rudder and steer with an oar in a rowlock socket aft. This, certainly, is a good arrangement, for then he can scull when he wants to."

"How do you suppose he planned to build her?" inquired Briggs.

"He had considered two ways. The first method, and perhaps the better, was to build her like a river canoe or the way the Old Town Canoe Company often builds quite good-size outboard motor boats. That is to use flat frames closely spaced and square seamed planking, canvas covered. The other method was to have her double-diagonally planked with the two layers of planking glued together and covered with a thin coat of Fiberglas. He believed that with the latter method, frames could be done away with almost entirely although, of course, the boat would have to be built on a mold, or trap. If there were few frames, she would be easy to clean and paint inside. With both these methods of construction he had planned to use no keel, the way a river canoe is built but, of course, the stem would have to extend aft some way as it does on the usual canvas covered canoe."

Coridon then asked if Goddard thought a boat as wide as that would stay in shape without floor timbers or regular framing, to which Goddard replied that the modern glues are quite wonderful and, as long as the seams can't start, the boat would have to hold the shape her planks were in when glued up. "Of course the panel of this boat's deck would stiffen her enormously," Goddard added, "and prevent her from twisting when under sail. Naturally, this sort of craft would have to have special framing around the mast to take the strain of sailing."

"That might all be so," said Coridon, "but wouldn't such a flat bottom spring up and down if built without floor timbers?"

"Yes, I think the bottom would spring up and down in places," agreed Goddard, "and so it does in the usual canvas covered canoe, but it will come back to shape when the strain is removed. And, unless the boat is improperly laid up in the winter, the springing in and out of the bottom should be of no consequence. In fact, it is sometimes desirable to have the bottom spring up rather than being stove in."

"I must admit," said Coridon, "that is a good boat for the purpose: she is light enough to haul up on the beach with a couple of those Airollers. She would be a fair sailer and a good sea boat,

if handled properly. The cost of hauling, storing and transport-
ing such a craft should be very little. What do you think she
would weigh?"

"The man who drew her up thought the stripped hull would
weigh less than 250 pounds."

The next morning Goddard woke early and went forward in
bare feet to take down the riding light, and then took the stops
off the mainsail to let the standing rain water run off. Everything on deck looked bleached and well washed, but as he dried
off the bright work with a chamois it soon regained its natural
hue. He had opened the drafts of the stove when he first got up
and now quietly put on some green coal and refilled the tea
kettle. He was just hauling the dinghy alongside to bail her out
when he got a hail from Coridon, but Goddard, by putting his
finger to his lips and pointing below made Coridon understand
that Miss Prim was still asleep and her father did not want her
disturbed. So Coridon came over in the *Piscator's* dinghy and,
speaking in a half whisper, said, "We met the owner of that
canoe-yawl last night: he came in while we were having supper
at the lunch room, and as most people sit at the bar there we were
soon in conversation. He seemed a very agreeable cuss and before
we finished supper I talked him into inviting us over to look at
his craft this morning."

"Well," said Goddard, "I don't like to horn in on a single-
handed cruiser like that."

"Oh, it's all right," replied Coridon, "for we told him about
you and he is anxious to talk with you."

"All right, then, but what time are we supposed to go over?"

"He told us about nine."

"Well, I'll be ready," replied Goddard, "if I can get Prim up
and fed by then."

After Coridon rowed away, Goddard knocked on the stateroom
door and asked Prim how she felt. She replied: "Just fine,"
whereupon her father said he would like her to get up because
they were to visit another cruiser. "O.K., Dad, you start breakfast

and I will be with you before it is ready." And she continued, "Hand me some water in the tin pitcher, will you?" "Do you want it hot or cold?" he asked. She answered, with a merry laugh, "Neither, just warm." When he handed her the water he also gave her a glass of orange juice and perhaps this retarded her some, but she was as good as her word and was sitting at the table taking her cereal before the bacon and eggs were ready, for some of the modern girls can dress quickly if they want to. The only thing is to make them want to.

Everything was straightened out by 8:30, but by quarter to nine Prim, true to her sex, decided she must change her dress and arrange her hair differently. This would have made Goddard cross a few days before, but now he patiently sat on the *Viator's* stern holding the dinghy in place with his feet while Coridon and Briggs bobbed in their dinghy a few yards astern. Finally the Chelsea clock struck two bells and Prim bounced into the dinghy and said: "I want to row, Pa."

"No," said her father, "you are too prinked up for rowing."

The boat they went to visit was anchored about a quarter mile east of them and near the place where the Coast Guard life boat had its launching ways. The north wind was still quite fresh, and as the two dinghies rowed in company it was an exhilarating short pull. Unfortunately, quite a little spray flew and Miss Prim was kept busy shaking the drops off her clothes, saying, "Now, I wish I hadn't changed my dress."

"You women will never learn," quoth her father.

As they neared the craft they were to visit they saw her name was the *Rozinante*, and although the *Rozinante* was a narrow double ender painted white, her dinghy was a black pram of liberal beam, named *Sancho Panza.*

Coridon, who arrived first, boarded the *Rozinante* to make the introductions when the *Viator's* tender came alongside, but before Goddard unshipped the port oar and took out the oarlock the owner of the *Rozinante* said: "Won't you come aboard, sir? It will be a great honor to have a visit from the crew of the *Viator.*"

Goddard held the dinghy while his daughter boarded, where-upon Coridon said, "This is Miss Goddard, Mr. Weldon," and after Goddard made the painter fast and had turned around he continued, "I would like to introduce Mr. Goddard, the owner of the *Viator*, to Mr. Weldon, the owner of the *Rozinante*."

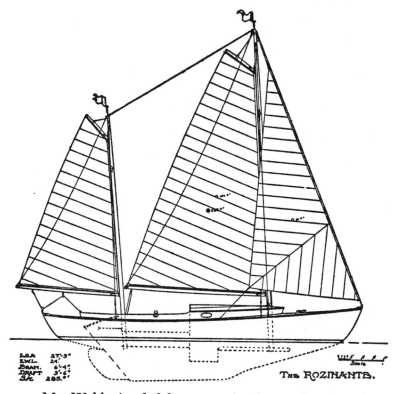

Mr. Weldon's whaleboat type, ketch rigged cruiser.

"This is a small ship, sir," Weldon said, "but the cockpit is large enough to seat us all comfortably, I hope." The *Rozinante* had an open cockpit about eight feet long and, like many other open cockpits, it was comfortable because the cockpit coaming supported the back way up to the shoulder blades. The wind was still blowing briskly from the north, and as they sat in the

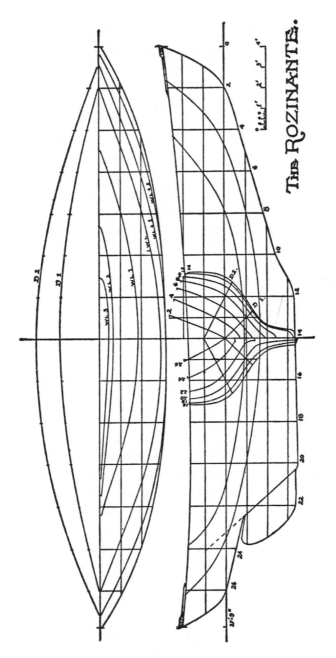

The lines drawings of *Rozinante*.

lee of the deckhouse with the morning sun pouring in on them it seemed a perfect place for a gam.

In the first pause in the conversation, Miss Prim inquired the meaning of the names *Rozinante* and *Sancho Panza.* Weldon explained; "Rozinante was the name of Don Quixote's steed. She was a long, thin animal but every time the Don mounted her he had remarkable adventures. Perhaps seven-eighths, of the romance of these adventures took place in Quixote's mind, for he was a great reader of romance who rather looked down on the times in which he lived. Like Don Quixote, every time I venture out on this Rozinante I meet with great adventure and romance. Perhaps, also, seven-eighths of it takes place in my mind, but each point that I round opens up new vistas with all sorts of possibilities. Each rock or shoal which I clear has its adventures for me, for I am a very timorous sailor. As for my tender, she is named after Don Quixote's squire, or companion, who followed him faithfully in his exploits and often saved him from disaster at the last moment. Sancho Panza was a short, stout individual of a dark complexion, and so is the dinghy."

Goddard was the only other one who had read Don Quixote, so much of this explanation went over the heads of the *Rozinante's* visitors, just as much of the wit in Cervantes' book goes over the heads of the average modern reader.

Goddard remarked; "I think *Rozinante* is a splendid name for a boat whose owner has an appreciation of romance, for I am sorry to say romance is a rare thing today and some people even laugh at it, whereas it used to be the incentive that carried one through fog, calm and tempest. It even seemed to make one enjoy the hardships which occur in cruising. But the modern cruiser has to have a vessel so cluttered up with mechanical gadgets and electrical devices that the cabin no longer is fit to live in and the boat has to be served by a mechanic, whereas a sailorman in the old days could take care of everything if he had a spark of romance in him. I suppose most modern cruisers are so unromantic in looks that all romance is killed as you board them. It is a strange thing that some of the modern merchant ships, particularly the motor ships, have very impressive and romantic looks —looks that fill a sailorman with admiration and respect when he sees them, for they seem to be modeled to perform their duties in the most efficient way. But these modern pleasure cruisers, particularly the motor boats, seem to be planned to be a receptacle for the insane and perverted, whereas fifty or sixty years ago the yacht was the most beautiful thing afloat."

Coridon broke in here to say: "I don't understand this business about romance."

"What!" exclaimed Goddard in surprise, "and you the greatest romanticist of them all with your Cape Cod cat?"

"What has the *Piscator* got to do with it?" inquired Coridon.

Goddard answered: "She is one of the last survivors of one of our most romantic types."

Miss Prim then spoke up: "Pa, just what do you mean by a boat or object being romantic?"

"Why, Prim," he replied, "when a thing is out of the usual and pleasing to contemplate it is romantic. When an object is nicely proportioned and has retained some well-proven ancient quality, it is romantic looking. I suppose to a sailor a romantic vessel is one that looks like a good sea boat, one which has a good sheer and nicely proportioned ends: in short, a vessel that he falls in love with at first sight, as we all did when we saw the *Rozinante*."

Briggs, who had been quiet all this time, then said: "Sir, if pleasant to contemplate means romantic, then I agree the *Rozinante* is most romantic and I wish we could get Mr. Weldon to tell us about her for I certainly have fallen in love with her."

They all joined in this entreaty, so Mr. Weldon began: "As a general rule, I do not like to talk about myself but, because the *Rozinante* was designed for my particular requirements, I must tell you something about my life. I am an engineering designer by profession, and work at a giant electric works. During my working hours, my mind is so constantly on new, complicated electrical and mechanical devices that at times I get disgusted with modern life and long for the simplicities of nature. I considered a log cabin in the Maine woods, but experience had taught me that while that sort of life is pleasant in the spring and fall, it is too hot and stupid in the summer. Besides, I would probably have to travel a hundred miles or so to get to a restful place but, as my principal object was to get away from mechanical things and rest the mind, the long ride by automobile made that scheme impractical. So, instead, I decided to have a small cruising boat that was entirely free from mechanical things and electrical gadgets. After searching for a boat several years and finding nothing worth considering, I went to Old Fussbudgit, the yacht designer. I went to him because he was one of the few left who could design a boat which was a good sailer and still had romance in her looks."

"I thought he was an old crank," remarked Coridon.

"I can imagine he would be," said Weldon, "if someone asked for impractical things in the design, but my requirements were so simple that he was very enthusiastic about the work."

"Just what did you ask for?" inquired Goddard.

"I told him I wanted a boat I could have peace and freedom in. I also requested that she be small enough for light ground tackle, and small enough to row reasonably well. I requested that there be no other iron on the little vessel than was necessary for the stove, frying pan, anchors, and the rigging. I wanted her to be a good sailer, a good sea boat, and, although I intended to go single-handed most of the time, I wanted her to sleep two comfortably when required. He came back with a design that was much longer than I had anticipated and, as you see, the *Rozinante* is a long, narrow, double-ender, but she certainly sails well, rows easily, and is a good sea boat. As for the length, the designer said it was necessary if I wanted the sails inboard with a short-masted ketch rig. He also said a long cockpit was necessary in rowing, if the oarsman sometimes stood facing forward and pushed on the oar and sometimes stood aft, pulling the oar. He said length alone does not affect the cost of a boat as much as most people think; rather, it is the general size and weight of the craft that really makes the difference, and that simplicity is the best way to reduce cost."

All this time, Briggs had been sitting on the edge of the cockpit seat listening with rapt attention, for the *Rozinante* seemed to him the type of craft he would prefer to all others. He asked Weldon to tell them more about rowing a boat of that size and if he never missed having a motor. Weldon answered; "I won't say I never miss having a motor but I will say 99 per cent of the time I am thankful to be without it. When there is any wind the *Rozinante* can take care of herself; when it is calm, the white ash breeze (as they used to call it) does very well in taking me by dangers in case a tide is setting me toward them."

"Can you row far or against a head tide?" inquired Coridon.

"My philosophy is never to buck a head tide whether ashore or afloat. Instead, I wait until conditions are more favorable. It is said time and tide wait for no man, but I prefer to wait for the tide and make it work for me instead of against me. Sometimes, I get up early in the morning and get a jump on the tide, or as they used to say 'save a tide.' As for the question of how far I can row the *Rozinante*, all I can say is as far as I have ever wanted to, for along our coast north of Cape Cod it seldom stays dead calm for long. South of the Cape, away to the head of Long Island Sound, they have higher wind velocities and much longer calms. As for the rowing, there are four requisites to success. First, you must have an easily driven boat. Second, you must use a long oar or sweep. Third, you must stand up to the work. Fourth, you must have a way of steering unless you have a companion who can do it. The *Rozinante* with a beam of less than six feet at the waterline rows easily. Her oar is more than ten feet long; her row locks are three feet above the cockpit floor. As for the steering, when I am alone I lash a stick or extra sail batten on the tiller so that it extends beyond the mizzen mast. This holds the tiller to one side just about the right amount to keep the *Rozinante* on her course. If she swings against the oar, I row harder. If she swings with the oar I row easier. Mr. Goddard can tell you that many old time boats of this size were rowed in light weather and that the rower usually stood facing forward with the tiller between his legs and moved sideways to steer the boat. If one is not used to rowing a heavy or sizable boat he may become discouraged at first but, if he patiently lets the boat gain headway, she can often be propelled with little effort and slip along nearly as easily as a Venetian gondola. I believe I can keep up a speed of a mile-and-a-half an hour for several miles at a time and can perhaps row the *Rozinante* half-a-mile at the rate of two miles an hour without much discomfort."

"Then you are quite contented without an engine?" asked Coridon.

"Yes," said Weldon, "very much so, and some of the reasons I dislike an engine on a boat of this size are:

The cost of engine and installation,

The cost of fuel and repairs,

The drag of the propeller,

The weight of the engine,

The space required by the engine, tank and exhaust line,

The smell and dirt,

The compass deviation it causes.

But I dislike an engine most because it takes the romance out of sailing."

"I admit," said Coridon, "it isn't too much fun when the motor is going, but why do you object to it when it is stopped?"

"I don't like a motor either running or stopped because the principal reason I go sailing and cruising is to get away from just such things. You see, I look on sailing as sort of a game where I pit my wits against the elements. With me, it is a sort of solitary competition which at times is as absorbing as a yacht race. I try to outwit the wind and tide by forecasting their actions and placing the *Rozinante* in a position where the winds and tide will favor her."

"Are your forecasts always right?" inquired Goddard, to which Weldon answered: "No, sir, and if they were the game would be no fun. It might amuse you to know that I do not use tide tables or give any regard to weather bureau forecasts. I prefer to do everything in the old fashioned way. That is, I look at the shore or the tide marks on spiles before leaving port to tell if the tide is coming or going. After I am outside I depend on the way lobster pot buoys are pointing to tell the direction and force of the flow. As for the wind and weather, I depend on the looks of the clouds and the state of the barometer, principally, but also by one hundred and one other indications which have been known to seamen for centuries. So, you see if I had a motor or radio, a direction finder, a depth recorder or any of the other modern aids to navigation, it would spoil the game I am playing and kill the romance that I get out of cruising. As I told you before, the *Rozinante* was designed for peace and freedom, but I must tell you I do not recommend my type of sailing to fools, as they should have all the artificial aids they can afford. Nevertheless, it is a great mistake for them to think these gadgets can take the place of a knowledge of seamanship."

Miss Prim then spoke up and said: "Sir, do you ever get caught in squalls by disregarding the weather forecasts?"

"I do not think the forecasts often give warning of squalls because squalls seem to be local affairs. As to the *Rozinante* being caught in squalls, that is a rather amusing story for I tried hard to be out in one for several years and never could quite arrange it. You see, I wanted to find out how she would act in a squall when laying-to under the mizzen. I went out in the bay several times when a squall was building up, but somehow or other the squall went to the north or south of us, or petered out. Once it hailed hard, and once the thunder and lightning were heavy without much wind. So, although many people have been caught in squalls when not prepared, I was trying to catch a squall when I was prepared."

Coridon then remarked: "Laying-to in a craft like this is all right if you have sea room, but what would you do if you were near a lee shore?"

"I don't expect to be caught on a lee shore in a squall because summer squalls give pretty good warning. The northwest squalls, which are the most common, usually can be seen building up for an hour or two, or show thunderheads which can be seen from many miles off. The north or northeast squall usually comes out of murky weather and is not always easy to see as it approaches. The southerly squall, which is rare off our coast, comes out of a very black sky, so I never let the *Rozinante* get in restricted waters when the sky indicates the likelihood of a squall. Of course, if there is a nearby harbor or cove I will make for that shelter in time so that the anchor will be down long before the squall strikes. But your question was: 'What would I do if caught on a lee shore in a squall?' And I will answer it by saying that, on a small boat like this, I carry the anchor in the cockpit all secured to the warp which leads outside the shrouds to the bow chocks and comes aft to the coil in the cockpit. In this way I can cast the anchor instantly from the cockpit without going forward. I usually do not carry the anchor stocked for, as this can be done quickly, it is of no consequence. The *Rozinante* has downhauls on her jib and mainsail and, as her halyards lead to the cockpit, sail can be taken in and the anchor let go very quickly, all from the cockpit. I must also mention that, with skillful handling, an outside ballasted boat like the *Rozinante* can carry all sail through an extremely strong squall. I have seen this done many times in racing yachts, but it takes a cool, capable skipper to do it without hurting the sails. The way it is done is to have the sheets trimmed about as you would for a close reach, but be headed up into the wind so only the leach of the sails is full. This is where the skillful helmsmanship comes in, for the boat must be kept so the leach never flaps and she must be kept going fast enough so she will mind the helm instantly. This, of course, is called luffing through a squall and a thing that is only proper to do on an able boat with good crew and strong gear. So you see, Mr. Coridon, if the *Rozinante* was caught on a lee shore in a squall, the two alternatives would be to take in sail and anchor suddenly, or to luff through the squall which I probably would do under the mainsail alone. I believe I could carry her by all danger unless we had to tack ship before the wind had let up some."

"Why would you use the mainsail instead of the jib and mizzen?" inquired Briggs.

"Because a jib or fore staysail is a poor sail to luff with; its leading edge is only supported by the stay and it will get shaking so violently that it may carry away something or even strain the mast. As the luff of the mainsail is attached to the mast it will not shake much; in fact, the forward part of the sail will belly to windward while the after part stays full without much hard shaking in between."

Briggs said: "Thank you, sir," when Miss Prim piped up with the question: "Weren't you afraid of being struck by lightning when laying out in the *Rozinante* waiting for thunder storms?"

"Yes and no," replied Weldon. "Before a thunder storm, I am as nervous as a cat and when I was a child was scared of thunder storms, but now I do not dread them much after the rain has started to fall, for I realize the film of water over the rigging and hull will carry off a discharge of lightning better than any complicated lightning conductor. So, in a thunder storm, when it starts to rain I give a sigh of relief. It is strange how few straight sailboats are struck, and perhaps a small sailboat is good to be in during a thunder storm if safely anchored."

Coridon, who had been looking the *Rozinante's* rigging over with a critical eye, then asked: "Why does the *Rozinante* have short gaffs instead of the usual leg-of-mutton sails?"

"There are several reasons for it. First, I wanted short masts to cut wind resistance when laying at anchor. With this rig, both masts are about three and one-half feet shorter than they would have been with leg-of-mutton sails of the same area. With the two masts, the reduction in exposed length is seven feet, which is something on a boat as small as this. Second, the designer thought that with such shallow draft (only three feet six inches) it would be well to keep the center of sail area low. Third, we thought a high, narrow, gaff sail, if properly proportioned and properly rigged, would be just as fast as a slightly taller leg-of-mutton sail, and after using it I am under the impression it *is* faster."

"Why do you suppose that could be?" inquired Briggs.

"That's a rather involved question to answer in a few words but, in short, the last few feet of the usual leg-of-mutton sail is too narrow (compared to the diameter of the mast that is in front of it) to have much drive, so it seems only to cause wind resistance, whereas the head of these sails is more like the end of an aeroplane wing."

Goddard then inquired about the weight aloft, if the gaffs swung to leeward, and if two halyards to a sail were a nuisance. Weldon said that the short gaffs were very light and if the total weight is a few pounds more, that weight is lower down. "As for the gaffs swinging to leeward," he went on, "all I can say is that the upper part of the sail does not luff or flap before the lower part. The two halyards are no inconvenience in hoisting the sail for they are held together in the hands like one rope until the sail is up. Then, by hauling on one at a time you not only can make adjustments which will help the set of the sail but, best of all, the two combined halyards give such lifting power that on sails the size of the *Rozinante's* there is no need of jigs or winches. Although I have to sway up hard on the throat halyards, the two single-parted halyards run so easily that the sail can always be lowered or taken in easily. I hope, sir, this has answered your question."

"Now to get back to the subject of the short masts," Weldon continued. "There are two or three highway bridges in places I might want to cruise which have a clearance that allowed the shorter masts to pass, but would not pass the longer spar that a leg-of-mutton sail would require. The truck on the top of the *Rozinante's* main mast is just 27 feet, 9 inches above the water line. This is easy to remember because it also is just the overall length of the *Rozinante*."

"I am surprised to hear that," said Goddard, "for most modern boats and yachts require a mast much longer than they are."

Briggs then asked if he could look in the cabin for he certainly was much interested in the *Rozinante*. Weldon replied: "Yes, certainly; go in and look around all you want." As the *Rozinante* had her cabin doors unhung and stowed in the racks under the cockpit seats, those who were in the cockpit could see her whole cabin plainly.

However, Weldon thought he would make some remarks on the layout: "The double berth that runs from side to side may seem to take up a lot of room, but I find it very useful to sprawl out on. Of course, it is quite triangular, being 60 inches wide aft and only 20 inches forward."

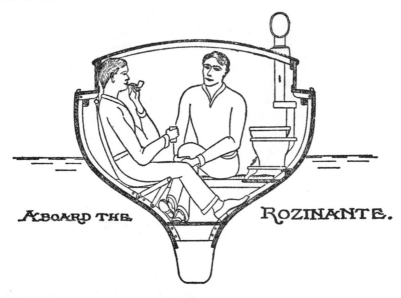

ABOARD THE ROZINANTE.

"That's all right," said Goddard. "But how about the mast that comes down near the foot of the berths?"

"Well, a man's feet may be a foot long but the size of one's legs at the shin is not much and the mast actually seems to do more good than harm, for when two people sleep on that berth they each have to keep their feet where they belong."

"How about the drip around the mast hole?" inquired Coridon. Weldon replied that with a proper mast coat put on every year there is no drip there. Mr. Goddard agreed to this and Weldon went on: "The berth is supported by ropes that run from one side of the boat to the other, much as the ropes were arranged on old-fashioned beds before springs came into use, only here there is an arrangement for tightening or loosening the ropes easily. This rope support for the mattress is particularly good, for when the space under the mattress is used to store small things like canned goods you simply roll the mattress back, pass your hand between the ropes and reach what you want.

"When I had the *Rozinante* built, I was determined to have a comfortable place in her to sit and read. You know in most small craft you either sit upright as in steering, or else lie down, but I wanted a comfortable intermediate position where I could sit and relax for hours at a time. Not only do I get a great deal of pleasure out of reading but, besides, if I am anchored in some quiet cove I find I can do constructive thinking better in a small cabin than where there are other distractions. So, that is the reason for the built-in adjustable easy chair you see in the after starboard side of the cabin. After some experimenting we adopted a canvas seat and back such as a folding deck chair has, but the side of the ship supports the frame, as you see. This arrangement can be removed easily for painting and cleaning. Right across the ship from my easy chair is the galley with a coal-burning stove."

"Isn't this a pretty small craft for a coal-burning stove?" asked Coridon.

"Yes," replied Weldon, "but it is a pretty small stove. It is a recent model made by the Marine Manufacturing Company, New Brunswick, N. J., who make the Shipmate stoves and is called the Skippy Stove. Although it is a very small stove with an oval top 19 inches by 14 inches, it has a larger fire box than some stoves that have an oven. It will keep a fire easily overnight and its top is big enough for a frying pan and a teakettle, or a pressure cooker can take the place of the frying pan."

"Isn't such a small cabin hot with a coal-burning stove?" asked Goddard.

"Yes and no," said Weldon, "the stove is going now but with the cabin doors off you see it is not hot in there. Rather it is dry, comfortable and airy, but I can tell you I was glad of the stove last night for it was just right below with one cabin door hung. Of course in warm weather we use the Sterno canned heaters set in a frame which is placed down in the stove when one or both stove covers are off. That makes a particularly good arrangement for the Sterno cannot then be tipped over, and if it did tip, the fuel which has become liquid would only fall or drip into the fire box."

Goddard then broke into the conversation: "I believe you really have achieved simplicity and comfort beyond anything that I have ever seen in a small cabin. But tell us about these cockpit seats. Aren't they too low for steering?"

"Yes," replied Weldon, "and they are purposely made that way, for you will see that the helmsman's seat at the after end of the cockpit is three inches higher, thus the helmsman can look over the heads of the passengers while the low seats keep the passengers dry when the spray is flying. Also when the *Rozinante* is heeled, one can see over the deck house from the low seats, and when sailing single-handed I often sit there for the better protection from wind and spray."

"Do you think an open cockpit is entirely safe on a boat like this?" inquired Goddard.

"Yes, sir, certainly. When you consider that the lifeboats of a ship are entirely open and will go through almost any sea, then a boat like this that is almost three-quarters decked over would seem nearly free from the danger of swamping."

"That may be so," said Coridon, "but the usual lifeboat either has no sail or a very small one and therefore is not apt to get knocked down in a squall."

"Well, the *Rozinante* has never taken in water to leeward and I never expect she will take in more than a few bucketsful at a time, which is of no consequence. The self-bailing cockpit is a comparatively new thing in small craft; even the racing sailing canoes did not have them until about 1895, but while there is excuse for a self-bailing cockpit on racing craft, all other small boats have gotten along without them for centuries."

"What's your objection to a self-bailing cockpit?" inquired Goddard.

"I have no objection to them on yachts of over thirty feet waterline for then the helmsman must sit up high to see over the bow, and on a boat of that size the space under the cockpit can be used for storage. Also, the space will be enough so one can get in there for painting, repairs, etc. But on small craft a watertight or self-bailing cockpit is uncomfortable and it keeps you up in the wind and spray. It is very expensive to build, and adds considerably to the weight, while the space under it is practically all waste. To be sure, an open cockpit takes in water in a rainstorm, but that can be obviated by having a tent or weather cloth over the boom which comes down over the cockpit coaming each side. However, it is my opinion that getting rain in the cockpit and pumping it out tends to keep the bilges clean and sweet, and there is no doubt that boats which are pretty well open deteriorate less than those that are more enclosed."

Goddard said: "The more I think about it, the more I can see you have a thoroughly efficient craft, and I believe your theory of being propelled by sail and oar only is very sensible."

"Well, sir," Weldon replied, "you know the wind is about the only thing that is free these days for they haven't yet thought of a scheme for taxing it. Even the annual tax on the *Rozinante* is so small that it can hardly buy a vote. Also, if worse comes to worst and the country is no longer fit for a lover of freedom to live in, the *Rozinante*, the *Sancho Panza* and I can all sail down to some isle in the Caribbean and live happily ever after. As I have mentioned before, the *Rozinante* was designed for peace and freedom and I well remember the first night I spent on her. It was a drizzly, cool evening in May as I came to anchor for the first time, but after I had lit the coal-burning stove, my peace and freedom commenced and I have been enjoying it most every spring, summer and fall weekend ever since."

All this time, Coridon had been looking at the seas breaking across the mouth of the harbor. When there was a pause in the conversation he said to Goddard: "I think I will leave the *Piscator* here until next weekend and take Briggs into Boston by bus in the morning."

Goddard answered: "I think you would be wise not to take the

Piscator through the combers, but as we are starting for home right after lunch we would be glad to take you and Briggs along with us." Before Coridon could accept this invitation, Weldon spoke up, "If the *Viator* is going out through the combers, it is a challenge to the knight errant spirit of *Rozinante* and myself, so I believe we will follow you out and, as I can just as well go to Manchester as other ports, I would be pleased to take Mr. Coridon along."

Briggs was a little disappointed at not being asked too but a sail on the *Viator* with Miss Prim aboard also had its charms for him.

It was half past ten when they broke up their visit aboard the *Rozinante*. Goddard said he wanted to have an early lunch and start back before one, to which all agreed. Coridon said to Weldon: "I would like to haul my tender aboard the *Piscator* so would be obliged if you would shoot alongside when you get ready and I will jump aboard." "Certainly," agreed Weldon.

As the two tenders were rowing up harbor side by side, Coridon said: "How will it be if we help you on the *Viator* with your two anchors and, in return, you send your tender over to get Briggs?" "O. K." replied Goddard.

After the large anchor was up and stowed below, Coridon and Briggs left the *Viator* and rowed alongside the *Piscator* where Briggs went aboard, but Coridon rowed over to the yacht club and very wisely had a talk with the steward, whom he knew. He said to him: "I expect to leave the *Piscator* here until next weekend and if anybody calls up to inquire about me or my crew, Briggs, you can tell them that we have sailed to Manchester on the *Viator* and *Rozinante*. But if any waterside characters inquire about us you can tell them that I have only gone away temporarily and may show up any minute. If I come back to spend the night on the *Piscator*, I will get you to take me aboard, so if you see anybody tampering around her you will know it is not I." Coridon then gave the steward a couple of dollars and said there would be something more due him if the *Piscator* was all safe when he returned.

The steward said: "I wish everyone would tell us what they expected to do when they leave a boat here, for when their friends begin to call up on the telephone and inquire if they are drowned, have committed suicide, or only gone crazy it is hard to tell what to say. You can be sure I will keep a good eye on the *Piscator*."

When Coridon returned to the *Piscator*, he and Briggs hauled the tender into the cockpit and secured everything to be safe for a week. Among other things, he reparceled the anchor warp and took a small part out of the magneto so no one could start the engine in his absence. The *Piscator's* only ignition was through an impulse magneto, and with a part of the magneto missing the engine could not be started.

After they packed their bags and straightened out the cabin they had a simple lunch which Coridon had been preparing over the last of the heat in the stove. It was a can of beef stew but, as often happens in leaving ship, they tried to finish off the leftovers so that they were well fed by the time Miss Prim came over in the dinghy for Briggs. Briggs wore his shore-going hat and jacket on the way over but on arriving aboard the *Viator*, Goddard took him below and assigned him the port berth as a place to stow his bag and other gear. Goddard and Prim had had their lunch and straightened out the cabin, so when Briggs appeared on deck in jersey and sou'wester they were ready to start.

It was still blowing a fresh breeze but the wind had shifted into the N.N.E. and showed signs of showers though there was sunlight coming through the broken clouds. The *Rozinante's* mizzen had been set for some time, and now that the *Viator* hoisted her mainsail the main on the *Rozinante* went up almost simultaneously, and, though Weldon was single-handed, he got his anchor up and was filled away before Briggs and Miss Prim could break out the *Viator's* anchor. However, the *Viator* under motor and main sail was making good speed toward the harbor entrance before the *Rozinante* had picked up Coridon.

Coridon was still a pretty spry man and did not wear glasses, so as the *Rozinante* luffed alongside the *Piscator* he jumped over with a handbag in one hand as he grasped the *Rozinante's* main shrouds with the other.

After he had stowed his bag below he said: "What do you say, do you want the jib on her?"

"Yes," replied Weldon, "for the *Rozinante* ought to run the gauntlet in style." So the jib was hoisted and sheeted home. This made the *Rozinante* heel considerably more than Coridon was used to on the *Piscator* and, to tell the truth, he was quite apprehensive about going through the combers with an open cockpit.

The tide was almost low as the two boats approached the jetties, and straight out ahead of them the seas were breaking heavily, but Goddard knew the channel and took a bend to the east-southeast as they cleared some rocks on the south side, and he could see that the seas were not breaking much in mid-channel. However, as the rocks were awash and close on their lee the whole scene certainly was startling. Miss Prim felt rather scared for she thought things looked much worse than when they ran in the night before and thought it strange that her father did not make her put on a life line, but instead he told her to stand in the companionway ready to pull the slide over. He also told her that head seas were never as dangerous as following seas. Goddard told Briggs to take hold of the backstay tackle where it led to the cockpit, and if a sea broke over he should hold on with both hands. He told them that he would brace himself against the mizzen mast. Just as they cleared the north jetty, a good sized comber came along, but it broke so heavily over the shallow water to windward that by the time it struck the *Viator* it had little life and, as Goddard had slowed the engine the *Viator* had time to climb up its side. However, the *Viator* took a deep roll and a corkscrew as she was thrown bodily sideways. While nothing but spray and spindrift went across the deck, Miss Prim who was in the hatchway heard the roar of the sea as it passed under them, and it was certainly quite different from noises she had heard before. The waves out here were some distance apart and all between their crests the water was covered with long streaks of soapy foam. After the first comber the others seemed fun, and the *Viator* only had to pass through about three before she was in open water and they could turn around and look at the *Rozinante*.

If Briggs and Miss Prim had felt a little squeamish with the strange motion of the *Viator*, they now had something to look at that took all their attention, for as the *Rozinante* came out under a full press of sail she certainly was a thrilling sight. She had the wind abeam, but as the combers came along Weldon first luffed her up to meet them, then at the last moment, just as the crest was near her now, he swung hard off so instead of the wave striking the bow, the wave, the *Rozinante* and all lifted and went leeward together. Of course she heeled some as the crest leapt up beside her, and each time they could see Coridon duck below the coaming.

It is a pretty sight to see a nimble sailboat work her way out of harbor when it is rough. Each wave as it comes along appears to overpower her, but as she climbs up and passes the crest she is as nimble as a ballet dancer. As she sweeps down the valleys between, one would think her no mere man-made thing but some enlarged petrel which should call forth or twitter at the thrill of motion. So the *Rozinante* looked to the crew of the *Viator*, and glancing back at the high land in front of the Coast Guard station they saw several people had gathered to witness the spectacle. Both boats now stood out close-hauled toward the E.N.E. but the *Viator*, with her motor going, pointed the highest while the *Rozinante* footed well but seemed to make leeway in the head seas.

Coridon said to Weldon: "It looks to me like long and short tacks from here to Manchester," but Weldon replied, "The barometer has been falling slightly since morning and I expect the wind will swing the right way this time and soon be from the east."

Giving the helm to Coridon, he went below to tap the barometer, but the seas were so large that the motion of *Rozinante* made the barometer very unsteady, and after making an aggregate setting he came aft again and took the tiller saying: "I think we will stand offshore until the wind heads us off to the east, and then when we tack we can make Manchester in one hitch. There was a good wholesale breeze blowing at the time, and Coridon asked Weldon if he thought there was danger of the weather changing to a southeast storm during their run up. Weldon answered that he did think the wind would veer to the east and then the southeast during the afternoon but he did not expect it to blow hard because the barometer was falling very gradually.

As they stood offshore, the visibility was impaired by rain in places although streaks of distant blue could be seen below patches of light-colored clouds, so the effect was similar to the edge of the Gulf Stream where the sea changes from blue to the brownish green of colder water. The light was kind to the eyes and seemed like dawn, but the occasional shafts of light which pierced the clouds showed the sun was past the zenith. The seas were long and gradual offshore with only occasionally a foaming crest, but as the wind veered toward the east the waves in places built up pyramids of dancing water. The *Viator* had tacked toward the northwest some time ago and now she and the land were shrouded in the westerly murk. The *Rozinante* was now forced off to the east so Weldon called "Ready about!" and after some slatting they took up a northerly course. There was still spray flying, but as Coridon settled down behind *Rozinante's* deck house and high coaming he stretched out with his feet to leeward and lit his pipe in comfort, for the wind and spray went right over his head. He remarked: "I now understand the comfort of a deep, open cockpit and believe you have one of the finest little ships ever built."

There were few boats or ships in sight that day, but in a temporary clearing they saw a freighter off the weather bow a mile or two away. She was bound to the eastward and, as the cross seas met her wake, a trail of white water marked her path. Far to leeward the lightship and Boston pilot boat could be seen, when well to the northwest the *Viator* appeared. "She has the lead," exclaimed Coridon, "and is doing well."

"So it would appear," replied Weldon, "but we will see. I am holding a little to weather of my course but believe the wind will now let us ease the sheets a hair."

The *Rozinante* had a comparatively large jib, and as the sheet was lifted, it pulled like a harpooned dolphin. Before, the *Rozinante's* motion had been short and labored, but now she seemed to find her pace and without much rolling or pitching appeared to lift and fall with the waves as she reached ahead. The old sea was from ahead while the making new sea was more abeam. While this twisting combination did not seem to slow the *Rozinante*, the *Viator*, being close-hauled and under power, labored hard as she pitched into the confused waves.

A smother of rain now shut out the *Viator* but, as it cleared, the wind had shifted to the southeast and began to blow fairly briskly. They were now running wind-on-the-quarter so they could carry all sail, even if the wind should increase. Coridon remarked that it certainly was a pleasant sensation to be making port as a southeaster came on. "Yes," agreed Weldon, "and we can't make it any too soon to please me." The rain now let up, as it often does for a while as the wind veers to the southeast, and they saw the *Viator* two or three miles to the westward but running a parallel course. Coridon knew the *Viator* was headed inside some of the ledges southeast of Bakers Island, which would shorten the course, so he persuaded Weldon to swing more off the wind and remarked that they should see Half Way Rock soon.

"I see it already," replied Weldon, so Coridon continued: "All we have to do is to pass a quarter-mile or so the east of Half Way Rock and continue that course until we see the beacon on the rocks called the Middle Breakers which we must leave close to starboard, but I will warn you beforehand that we will pass between places where the seas will be breaking."

"That's all right," responded Weldon, "if you are sure there is good water there."

Coridon replied: "I am as sure of it as I am of death and taxes."

Aboard the *Viator* they were surprised that *Rozinante* under sail alone was overhauling them so Goddard dove into the fore peak and came out with a storm jib which he and Briggs soon had drawing. But before they passed Half Way Rock, the *Rozinante* was rapidly leaving them behind for there were few boats of her size that could best the *Rozinante* running wind-on-the-quarter in strong wind and sea. Coridon was fascinated at the way she slipped along without yawing or trying to run her bow under. As a wave lifted her stern and they scudded to the northward, Coridon remarked: "This is like a Nantucket sleigh ride."

"That's right!" agreed Weldon. "The only difference is that they had a whale pulling them and we have a whale of a breeze pushing us. After all, the *Rozinante* is a whaleboat with a keel and snug rig and why shouldn't we push her?" They passed Half Way Rock some five hours out of Scituate so their average speed was about five knots, which was good considering that they were close-hauled some of the time. Now that they were wind-on-the-quarter, they were going seven knots or more and it took nerve to head in to a place where there was broken water on all sides and a southeast gale behind them, but the beacon could be easily seen now and beside it a narrow strip of water free of breakers. Almost before they knew it, they were through and in the somewhat smoother water beyond. Their course was now a little west of north until they passed House Island and rounded up in the smooth water of the lee, when Weldon said; "If you will take the helm I will stock the anchor and take in the jib."

Coridon replied; "There will be no need of the anchor, for we can pick up the *Piscator's* mooring buoy and I will take in the jib if you like." "O.K.," Weldon replied and Coridon went forward as Weldon pulled the downhaul. Coridon called aft: "The buoy is well in the northeast part of the harbor and if you round astern of that black yawl you will about fetch it."

They just about had things snugged down and the tender partly bailed out when the *Viator* shot for her mooring close aboard.

While Briggs and Miss Prim were lowering the mainsail, Goddard called over to congratulate the crew of the *Rozinante* and invite them aboard.

Briggs called aft: "Sir, do you want me to take the storm jib off the stay?"

"No," replied Goddard, "for if it rains this evening that will wash the salt out of it which I want before it is stowed away."

As the *Rozinante's* tender came alongside, Coridon said with elation: "Weldon has invited me to stay aboard the *Rozinante* tonight which I should very much like to do if we can find accommodations for Briggs ashore, otherwise I will have to drive home this evening and I hate the roads Sunday night."

"Well, come below and we will talk it over after we have our oilskins off," said Goddard. "I feel more comfortable when I am wet inside than out."

The men had settled back on the transom seats in the pleasant relaxation that comes from a day's sail when they heard rain falling on the deck, so Goddard stood up and closed the skylight over the table. Then he said: "You know today's sail was one of the best ones I have had for a long while. To me a sail of over four hours is apt to be tiring unless you have relief at the helm, but today Briggs and Prim did most of the steering so I stood in the companionway and enjoyed myself. Some people like bright sun all day but to me that is exhausting, while the delicate tones and shades we saw on the way up give a truer picture of the sea, and although there was spray flying most of the time the never ending rows of greenish gray seas with an occasional white cap were marvelous. It was a great satisfaction to be headed for a safe harbor before a southeaster strikes, and perhaps that added zest to the sail. But, best of all, to have shipmates aboard who are enjoying it gives the most satisfaction. I have done my share of single-handed sailing and now prefer to share my pleasures with others."

"I think the *Viator* is nearly perfect for your purpose," said Weldon, "and think it perfectly remarkable that you have so much accommodation on such short length."

Goddard replied: "We may not be much longer than the *Rozinante* but we are quite a little wider, and perhaps two feet deeper, and according to the law of cubes an increase in all three dimensions makes a whale of a difference. I suppose our displacement is twice that of the *Rozinante,* and because of our high freeboard and long cabin house perhaps the usable space below decks is between two and a half and three times as much as yours. I believe there would be a like difference in the cost of the two boats if they were built at the same time and place. As for speed," Goddard went on, "you made a good demonstration this afternoon that the *Rozinante* can be driven faster than the *Viator* in spite of the difference in size."

"Well, but you did not have your regular jib and mizzen set," Weldon remarked, "and in a strong breeze they would have pulled more than a good sized engine."

"I quite agree with you," said Goddard, "but I doubt if we could have held you the last part of the race if we had had full sail and the motor too, for you know it is pretty hard to drive a full boat like the *Viator* over six knots."

"That may be so," replied Weldon, "but I believe you could best us under sail alone either on or off the wind in light weather. I also think you could best us close hauled in heavy weather. So, in other words, the only time the *Rozinante* can hold the *Viator* is running in strong breezes when her speed is over six knots."

"I think you are right, young man," Goddard agreed, "and now, if you like, I'll show you around below deck." He took Weldon in the stateroom and said: "You must excuse us if everything is not in order, for Prim has been changing her clothes back and forth.

"Forward of this watertight bulkhead is a small fore peak where I keep everything that is messy or salty. The stateroom is only six feet long but because the berths are on an angle there is plenty of room. While I do not like built-in berths in a main cabin where they would take up too much room, they are excusable in a stateroom. The stateroom is very small but by a certain arrangement of doors the toilet room can be made a part of the stateroom to be used, you might say, as a dressing room. As you see, when the stateroom door is swung back it conceals the water closet and the two rooms together give sufficient space. There is a folding basin on the back of that door which of course is now over the water closet but when the stateroom door is closed the hand basin is right amidships."

"How do you drain the hand basin?" inquired Weldon.

Goddard chuckled as he replied; "In the way that doesn't require any plumbing. You simply lift the hand basin out of its frame and empty it in the water closet."

Goddard then closed the stateroom door and showed how the frame which held the hand basin opened and closed. Weldon remarked that that beat anything he had ever seen for simplicity, but he did wonder what was the object of the three mirrors on the forward side of the after door.

"I'll tell you," said Goddard. "The ladies not only like to look at their faces in the mirror but also like to see around their waists and how their skirts hang. They seem as anxious to have everything set right, as I am with a new suit of sails. Now if you step into the stateroom and look at the mirrors you will see your head in the upper one, your waist in the middle one, and your legs in the lower one. Then, if you move closer to the mirrors, the angle of your sight will show you parts of your body you missed before. Of course one long mirror would do the same thing, but if the mirror were in one piece it would have to be thick and heavy, but these three little mirrors are not apt to be broken."

Weldon acknowledged, "That is very clever but, thank God we don't need any mirrors on the *Rozinante*."

"That may be so, young man," Goddard told him, "but if I can do anything to please the ladies I will do it, for they seem to get more out of cruising than men do. They have a very high appreciation of scenery and get more pleasure than most of us men do out of visiting new places. If the ladies were given the respect, comfort, and privacy they used to have in cruising there would be as many of them in the game as there were before some of the cruising clubs tried to change cruising into racing, and rendezvous of rowdyism. Cruising will never enjoy the refinement and decorum that it once had until it is again safe to take wives, mothers and daughters along."

Goddard continued with a chuckle, "I don't know as you should call them ladies, but these reckless tomboys that are the result of the late war are a disgrace to their sex, for even if they have good morals few will believe it, and the owners of the craft that take them along are doing a great deal to degrade yachting in the eyes of the public. However, when wives, mothers and daughters are taken along in cruising the result is just the opposite and the whole game is refined."

Just then the dinghy was heard alongside, and as Goddard moved aft, he hurriedly said: "All of the *Viator's* other arrangements below deck you can see for yourself." It was still blowing from the southeast with a drizzle, but as the bundles were passed aboard there was merriment in the cockpit for they were trying to pass things below as quickly as possible, and jokes were bantered back and forth as Briggs took the dinghy astern. Goddard who had stayed below called up the companionway: "What are we to do with all this damp truck?" but Coridon said softly, "Don't get excited before the squall strikes for it may all blow over and amount to nothing."

"Well, I hope so," grumbled Goddard, and as soon as Coridon was below he explained, "This big bundle is nothing but the Sunday paper which you can all look at while Prim and I are getting supper; and this," he continued, "is a bag of charcoal briquets." "What are those for?" demanded Goddard, but Coridon just said, "Wait and see," and continued, "This sizable package contained the ingredients of a salad, while this package encloses five rather nice steaks I found ashore, and the other package contains the dessert that Prim picked out."

"What is it, Prim?" her father asked.

"It's ice cream and macaroons, Pa, couldn't you guess?"

Goddard replied: "No, I couldn't guess, for you like all desserts, but haven't you just had an ice cream soda?" "Yes, sure," she answered, "but what of it?"

After the oilskins were off, Briggs and Weldon sat looking at the Sunday paper while Goddard cleaned the ashes out of the stove which he could do very neatly. He looked up suddenly and said: "Are you sure you are not wet, Prim?"

"Yes," she replied, "only my neck and feet, and as soon as I wipe my neck with a towel I will be O.K. for I do not mind wet feet when I am barefooted."

Coridon urged, "Hurry up, Prim, for we must get these salads made before the stove gets hot." After the salads were made Coridon rubbed both sides of the steaks with a little mustard and told Prim to make up some appetizers by putting some anchovies between Triscuits. By this time the charcoal was burning brightly for it will make a quick fire.

Coridon used real butter in the pan and just as it smoked in a certain way he put on the steaks. Although there was quite a lot of smoke in the cabin the appetizers had gone around just before so that the smoke seemed to take on a very appetizing aroma. Coridon told Prim to hand him the plates one at a time so he could put the steaks beside the salads, and almost before you knew it they were all so occupied with their supper that no other sound but the knife and fork was heard. It was nearly seven o'clock by that time and getting dark so Coridon lit the lamps in the galley and over the cabin table. He had a paper napkin in his hand as he took off the lamp chimney and said to himself: A good chef may absorb food with his fingers, but never kerosene. After the plates were removed the ice cream was served in soup plates as the *Viator* did not boast a double set of dishes.

Conversation now sprang up again and Weldon said: "Sir, how is it that some boats or yachts are what sailors used to call 'happy ships,' while others are vessels to contain boredom, misery, jealousy and even hatred? Do you think there is some mystic reason for it, like the keel being laid on a Friday, or a black cat crossing the ways at the launching?"

Goddard had his pipe going good and had settled back in his favorite position when he answered: "There are so many complications to cruising that it has always been a marvel to me that any cruise turned out well. In the first place there are few people who know how to take care of themselves on a small boat without causing annoyance to others, and right here I must say there are a great many people who shouldn't go cruising. They are too sensitive, too selfish, too conceited, too egotistical, too irritable to get along with anyone. When you are cooped up on a small boat with them for hours or days at a time they will nearly drive you crazy so that you also will act like a beast. Just why there have not been more murders on small craft I do not know, but I do know any easily irritated person can spoil a whole cruise. There are also some impossible combinations, and the worst one is a crew of three."

"Do you think three is a mystical number, like 13 or 23?" inquired Weldon.

"No," replied Goddard, "I don't take too much stock in mystical numbers, but it is quite well known in the schools and colleges that three room-mates do not get along well while two or four seem to be much better. The reason for it is that when three people are kept in close contact two will invariably team up against the third and overpower him in arguments, and annoy him with ridicule until his predicament is unbearable. Of course there are exceptions to this rule as there are to most rules, and sometimes where there is a difference in age or sex the condition is not so bad. For instance, where two young men cruise with an older man they may get along well if the two youngsters have respect for the third party. I even find in my little family of three that it often turns out that two are pitted against one, and although I am aware of the danger and think Mrs. G. is one of the best-natured souls in the world, it often happens that when Mrs. G. gets after either Prim or me we stand up for each other so that Mrs. G's feelings are a little hurt."

"Don't the two females ever gang up against the male?" inquired Weldon.

"Well, very seldom," replied Goddard, "unless it is something about the way I am dressed or the color of my necktie."

"But don't the parents ever team up against the child?" pursued Briggs.

"No, almost never, but I can't say what will happen when Prim gets a little older. In the meantime, we go cruising with two or four and think the *Viator* can be called a happy ship."

4

Mrs. Goddard Comes Aboard / The Rozinante's

Ditty Box / On Binoculars / Anchors and

Anchoring

Goddard took his vacation in August and because he had cruised the Maine Coast so thoroughly, he decided to go south of Cape Cod this time. Also, he was to take along Mrs. Goddard and the two girls. Mrs. Goddard liked Nantucket and Martha's Vineyard and the warmer water south of the Cape was pleasant for the girls who were at the age to enjoy swimming.

While it is true that there are places north of the Cape where the water is occasionally warm, still if there is an offshore or westerly wind, the warmer surface water is blown to sea and the cold lower stratas of water rise and replace it. So, north of Cape Cod there are great variations in water temperatures while south of the Cape the water remains pleasantly warm day after day. Some people think all the water north of Cape Cod is affected by the Labrador Current. However that may be, the water there is surprisingly cold with an offshore breeze, and while this cold water is not pleasant for swimming it has the advantage that the cabin of a small boat is kept cool at night; in fact a coal-burning stove is pleasant much of the time. Cruising north and south of the Cape is quite different, and it is fortunate that this pleasant variation can be acquired by a run through the Cape Cod Canal.

You would think the cabin of a small yacht would be damp in the cold water north of the Cape, particularly if there were fog off the Maine coast, but the occasional use of the coal stove keeps things dry and snug, while in cruising south of the Cape the whole cabin and one's clothes are often damp and soggy. This difference in dampness is more pronounced after August, when the northern fogs are driven away by the prevailing offshore breezes of late summer, so that in late summer and fall the Maine coast is a delightful cruising ground.

But to get back to the *Viator* . . . Mrs. Goddard liked to spend one night aboard before starting a cruise so she would have time to stow everything away in a shipshape manner. This time it was quite a job because all four of them had a lot of baggage and clothes, not to mention the hampers of food she had brought along. As they went out in the club launch, there was quite a cargo and for a while the *Viator* was a queer sight with all this baggage on deck.

Goddard had an easy job that afternoon for all he had to do was to hand below the various articles as they were called for, and several times he said to himself: Thank God it is not raining! Mrs. Goddard had packed most of the clothes in laundry boxes which were to be folded up and used for stove fuel later and, as all of the food was in grocery bags and cartons, the only luggage was the bag belonging to Veronica, and that was soon stowed before the mast in the stateroom where Prim and Veronica were to sleep.

Mrs. Goddard had learned the art of stowing clothes between the mattresses and berth bottoms, as the sailorman keeps his shore-going trousers. This takes some time to do for each article must be folded perfectly smooth and flat, but when properly done the clothes thus stored receive a continuous pressing and appear extremely fresh even after a long cruise. Each of the girls had several wash dresses, for Mrs. Goddard was determined to have them look neat when they went ashore.

As the two girls held the mattress rolled back, she carefully spread the clothes on the canvas berth bottom with layers of tissue paper between each article. This was done so neatly that the girls were surprised to find, after the mattresses were in place again, that no lumps could be felt. Mrs. Goddard told them the berths might be even more comfortable with the slight additional thickness. This they found to be so late in the cruise, for as each dress was worn or soiled, Mrs. Goddard bundled it up and mailed it home. Most of the clothes that could be rolled had an elastic snapped around them so they were compactly stored in the transom lockers.

After Mrs. Goddard had finished the stateroom, the only girls' gear that could be seen were their sweaters and sport coats which were folded on the shelves back of the berths. Even their pajamas were out of sight, folded under the pillows. As Mrs. Goddard worked aft, she kept the girls very busy handing her the various articles, and she kept saying to them: "Now remember where I put everything so you can get it at once if I send you for it." In about half an hour everything was below deck and even Goddard marveled at where so much gear could be stowed on the *Viator*, but perhaps Mrs. Goddard knew all of the below-deck cubby holes, lockers and crannies even better than he did.

The bottled goods had all had their paper labels removed by soaking in water and were now stowed in the bilge. The canned goods and other things which could stand a slight wetting were placed in a part of the transom lockers where the bilge water had been known to swash up, but the *Viator* had good sized food lockers right opposite the galley stove and here the most perishable foods were stored.

Mrs. Goddard had a long, hard job, however, to get everything to suit her. So, while she and the girls were busy below deck, Goddard took the dinghy and rowed over to the *Rozinante* which was anchored down the harbor. He had noticed that there were a couple of boys aboard. When he was alongside, Weldon came out of the cabin and asked him aboard, saying: "I've got my two nephews and we are going for a week's cruise."

After Goddard was aboard, Weldon introduced the boys as "My oldest nephew Jim; he's fifteen years old. The other boy is his brother, Dan, and I don't remember how old he is but he is quite a sailor."

At this, Dan spoke up and said: "Sir, I will be fourteen next winter."

So Goddard remarked: "Well, he is a large, strong looking boy."

"Yes," agreed Weldon, "and both of them can whittle pretty well, I am glad to say."

"It would look so," said Goddard, "by the amount of shavings there are in the cockpit."

"Yes," said Weldon, "we all like whittling out models, so first I lay an old piece of canvas on the cockpit floor and we all go to it. Whenever I can I pick up some nice whittling pieces of wood —cedar, soft pine or white wood—and as we have two or three baby planes and an oil stone we do pretty well. You know, the principal secret of the thing is good whittling knives properly sharpened, and we have three or four of them besides our jack knives."

"You must have something," rejoined Goddard, "for you have made some really nicely shaped models."

"I think so," agreed Weldon, "and the boys made most of them. They are getting a remarkably accurate idea of shape. When we visit Gloucester and other seaports the boys not only have fun looking at the models of the fishing vessels, but when we go shopping they are always on the lookout for models in shop windows. Perhaps you remember there used to be some fair schooner models in the old time beer saloon windows, but today a well shaped model is a rarity.

"However, I think the boys, and particularly Dan, get most of their fun from towing the models. We sometimes have three or four astern at a time. You see, we have a great variety of shapes; some are like heavy displacement sail boats which we tow when it is almost calm and we are going less than one mile an hour. Then we have several power boat models which run well when we are going four or five knots; and last of all we have a three-point hydroplane that will stand greater speeds than we ever get to. She is named the *Slo-Mo-Shun*, but her motions are anything but slow in the waves she encounters behind the *Rozinante*. Some of the best models we have are shaped like destroyers for that still seems to be the best shape for rough weather. All our models are very small so the waves they encounter are terrific."

"I think you are having lots of fun," said Goddard. "To sit in this deep, comfortable cockpit out of the wind but in the sun is a great treat. I can't imagine a pleasanter place to work. But tell us how you cut the sheers of the models, and how you rough out the deck lines."

Weldon said that he usually blocked out half-a-dozen models at a time when they were held in a vise and the first cuts were made with a drawknife. After the decks and profiles were smoothed up, a good penciled center line was put all around the block. All this work was done at home with the model held in the vise. Weldon then sent Jim into the cabin to bring out some of the blocks which were suitable for various types of craft. One block was about three feet long and only two-and-three-quarter inches wide, while another was only eight inches long and about three inches wide. Several much smaller blocks were just for whittling.

Weldon continued: "We have a ditty box aboard with several useful tools in it. I will have Jim bring it out to show you." The box was of wood with a sliding top and the corners and the edges had been rounded off so it was nice to handle. The box was only about 14 inches long by eight inches wide and six inches deep, but it contained several small tools that were cadmium plated to prevent them from rusting. Many of the tools or gadgets were of hard wood. One of them was shaped like the common bench stop which a jeweler uses in filing and sawing small objects, and looked like the accompanying illustration. This could be put on the cockpit seats or any other flat place and would hold things that were being planed, chiseled or sawn. Weldon then took all the tools out of the box and at the bottom there was a rather large maple carpenter's clamp taken apart so that it used up little space in the box. When it was put together it was quite a sizable affair.

"This," he said, "we use as a vise when it is fastened in place with this bronze bolt." He showed how the clamp could be fastened to the threshold of the companionway or secured to the cockpit coaming in several places.

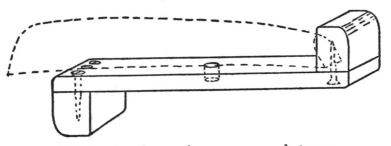

Wooden bench stop for use on a cockpit seat.

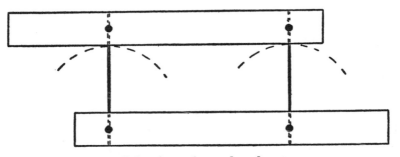

Parallel rulers of wood and string.

"You see," he went one, "we are pretty well equipped for scrimshaw work, and that keeps all hands happy just as it used to do in old times on the whaling ships. I think it is natural for boys to work on something of their own, or of their own creation, but now-a-days there are few things boys can do that are entirely their own ideas. You see all the kits for making model aeroplanes, etc. have been worked out by someone else. This gives the boys the habit of depending on someone else for shapes and proportions, while this type of work, whittling shapes, gives them artistic training and they certainly seem to enjoy it. No, sir, we don't need any radio or Sunday papers on the *Rozinante*, for everyone is busy with dreams of the shapes he is to whittle out."

While Goddard was looking over the tools in the ditty box, he spied several things that he did not recognize. He asked: "What in the world are those two sticks held together with strings?"

"Those," explained Weldon, "are my parallel rules." He stepped into the cabin and brought out a chart to show how they were used. This was similar to the usual usage of parallel rules but you had to hold the two rules apart so that both the strings were always tight.

Goddard said: "That beats anything of the kind I ever saw, because you can throw those parallel rules around or even step on them without hurting them. But tell me how you got the string through the rules and adjusted them evenly."

Weldon answered: "First, I plane up two hardwood strips which are about 12 inches long by one-quarter-inch by three-quarters-of-an-inch. Then I pick out a drill that is slightly larger than the string I am to use (and I use a high grade string like the line used on a fishing reel, about 1/16 inch diameter). Next, I drill holes across the sticks about an inch-and-a-half in from the ends, as you see, and then drill a slightly larger hole through the sticks so that it intersects the first holes drilled. Then, I take two pieces of line about 18 inches long and thread them through the first holes drilled so that the two sticks are strung, so to say. Then, I draw two parallel lines on a paper about five inches apart and put the rules on these lines and hold them in place with weights. Now, I pull the strings so they are straight and hold them so with weights. When everything is in position, I squeeze some Duco cement down the holes that cross the strings. If the Duco shrinks up much in an hour, I force some more down the holes and then, after it has set for 12 hours or more, I remove the weights and the parallel rules will be finished after I have cut the loose ends of the strings and scraped off the superfluous Duco cement."

"I think that is wonderful," admired Goddard, "and I will make a couple of them in different sizes when I get home. But tell me, do you think these parallel rules are accurate when the strings are nearly parallel with the rules, as when the rules are near the closed position of the usual parallel rule?"

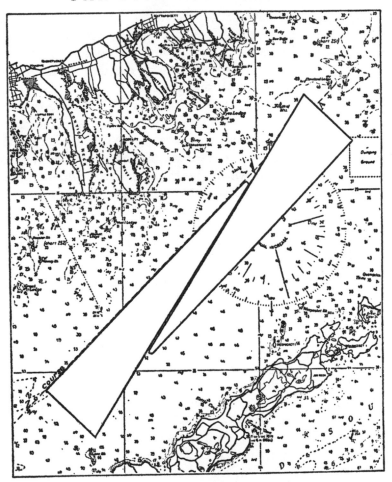

Elongated wooden triangles for taking off courses.

"No," answered Weldon, "when I am to take off a course which is close to the compass rose I use these elongated wood triangles." He took them out of the ditty box and handed them to Goddard.

When Goddard handed them back, Weldon continued: "These triangles are better than any parallel rule for many locations on the chart, and I know some sailors who use a couple of draftsman's scales when laying off courses."

Goddard said: "I have known men who could stretch a string over the course and then by eye make a close approximation of the compass bearing that was parallel and I often do it myself on short courses that are not close to dangers, but the two roses, one inside the other, make it confusing at times."

Jim then spoke up and asked his uncle why there were the different graduations on each rose. Weldon told him that the outer rose pointed toward the true North that is used for celestial navigation and surveying on shore, and the true north and south poles were the points around which the earth revolved. But the inner rose represented the direction that the magnetic compass pointed in different parts of the world, or even on different parts of the chart. "You see, it is necessary to have these two compass roses because large ships navigate from observations of the sun as the earth revolves around the poles, but we on the small craft that navigate by compass must have the inner or magnetic compass rose (pointing to the Magnetic Pole) to take our courses by."

Dan then inquired why the compass did not point toward true north, and his uncle answered: "It does point toward true north in four distant regions of the world, and there are two curved lines nearly from pole to pole with no variation between the two compasses. One of these "lines of no variation" goes across the eastern part of South America, then close by the West Indies, and then strikes North America near Cape Hatteras and passes through the Great Lakes and continues up into Hudson Bay. This is a part of the world where the variation changes rapidly as you move from east to west. In the western part of Hudson Bay the compass may have ten degrees easterly variation while in the eastern part of the Bay there may be as much as sixty degrees westerly variation. As we in New England are comparatively near this region of rapid change in variation, you will find a slight difference of variation on each chart along our coast and even a change in the various roses on the same chart. Does that answer your question, Dan?"

"Only partly," replied Dan, "for I asked why the compass did not point to true north."

"Well," said his uncle, "that is a question that can't be answered in a few words because apparently there are several forces acting on the magnetism of the earth. In the first place, it is supposed that the earth revolving around its axis becomes somewhat of a dynamo with the positive at the north end. But there are other powerful attractions and one of them is the force that pulls the earth on its annual cruise around the sun. These forces are enough to cause the Magnetic Pole to be in a different place from the true north, but it is supposed that the curved lines of equal magnetic variation are caused by the effect of temperature, trade winds, ocean currents, and the varying conductivity of the earth in different regions where the earth's crust may be thicker or contain minerals such as aluminum, iron, etc., which are better conductors than dry sand, for instance. Some people in the past have thought there were big deposits of iron in places which made a local attraction, but you, no doubt, will study these things if you take astronomy in college. If I can't tell you just *why* the magnetic compass points in different directions in different places, I can tell you definitely that it *does*."

Dan, with his sharp eye, had been looking at the compass rose on the chart and spoke up: "What does this mean, uncle, where it says Annual Increase 5 and a mark like some people use for feet?"

"Well, Dan," his uncle said, "on the chart that mark means minutes and minutes are a very small part of a degree. And the words Annual Increase mean that the amount of compass variation in that particular region at this time is increasing at the rate of five minutes a year and in some other parts of the world it is decreasing, while in some places it often stays constant for a few years. The city of Paris, France, was a location where early records of change in variations were kept. In about 1660 the needle pointed toward true north there, but before that it had an easterly variation. From that time to soon after 1800 the compass had westerly variation there, when it amounted to some 22 degrees, but since then the needle has been steadily swinging back toward the true north. So you can see, one of the reasons you should use new charts is because they have the latest corrections in variations; but as a matter of fact the annual change in New England is small at the present time."

Weldon then turned to Goddard and said: "I want to apologize for taking up so much of your time but I like to answer the boys' questions thoroughly when I can. It is said: 'Fools can ask questions wise men cannot answer' but as the boys are not fools and I am not a wise man we seem to get along pretty well. At times, answering the questions is somewhat involved and it is hard to say who enjoys it most, the boys or I."

Goddard remarked: "I think you are doing a good job of it now, but after the boys get a few years more on them it might not be so easy. I'd also like to ask some more questions about the things in the ditty box," and Goddard picked up a ruler about a foot long that had paper scales pasted on both sides of it. "What is this?" he asked.

"That is my straight edge that I use to draw pencil lines on a chart to represent courses between places. At times I also lay it along the side of the parallel rules to make them extend to the compass rose when the rules do not quite reach it. The scales on the two sides represent distance on the sizes of charts I use most, which scale 1/80,000 and 1/20,000. At the same time that I lay off a course, I can also measure the distances without using dividers. On a small boat, in wind and rain, that is a great convenience."

Goddard replied, "That's a fine gadget and I am going to make one for the *Viator*, with your permission. But tell me how you made the scales and fastened them to the straight edge."

Weldon explained: "You know I am used to drafting and have to do some of it in my work, so making the scales was quite a simple matter. The proportion, or size of the scale, was taken right from the chart, and although there is a slight variation in the nautical mile scale on different charts, the difference is not great enough to affect the short courses we sail in small craft. It is well to mark the graduations with India or semi-waterproof ink on some firm, fine-grained paper like a thick bond paper, or any good drawing paper. To fasten the scales to the straight edge, first lay the paper scale upside-down on some newspaper, then give it a good coat of white shellac. It is well if the paper scale is pinned in place during this process and you can do that by stretching the paper tight and pinning the ends down on the newspaper. This is so the shellac will go to the very edges of the scale. The paper that the scale is drawn on, of course, should be left several inches longer than the scale and these ends should not be shellacked but left dry to pick the scale up and turn it over. Now place the paper scale on the straight edge with the shellacked side down and the dry, graduated side up and adjust it in place by holding the dry ends. Rub your hand or a dry cloth along the scale and it will stick smoothly in place. However, if you had put the shellac on the straight edge and laid the dry paper on it, you would be in trouble because when the dry paper absorbed the shellac it would swell and buckle up in places and generally be a mess."

Goddard then inquired if wetting the paper scale with shellac did not swell or elongate the scale, and Weldon answered: "Yes, it does; something like a sixteenth-of-an-inch to the foot but it seems to shrink back nearly to size as the shellac dries." He continued: "After both scales have dried in place and you have trimmed up the edges of the paper to match the straight edge, then give the whole thing a coat of rather thin transparent varnish and you have something that can stand a little spray and rain."

Goddard remarked that it was strange that such things were not more available, for it seemed every small cruiser could use one. Weldon said: "There are almost no simple navigating gadgets made because the books about navigation are mostly for large craft and the writers of these books delight in complicated methods to impress the reader with their mathematical ability. In small craft, if you are single-handed in the wind and rain, you must sometimes get results quickly without paper or pencil."

Weldon then brushed the shavings off the cockpit seat beside him and spread out a folded chart. "Now, for instance, suppose I want to know the course from this buoy to that one, and I can tell by the lobster pots that there is a three-quarter-mile tide flowing diagonally across the theoretical course. First, I lay the scale across the theoretical course and get the distance, which you see is nearly six miles. Then, using round numbers, I estimate my speed which we will say is 3 mph, so it will take me two hours to cross over. The tide, during this time, will have flowed a mile and a half, so I take the scale and point it in the direction the tide is flowing and make a pencil dot one-and-one-half miles up-stream from my destination. Then I lay the straight edge between my departure and the pencil dot on the chart and at once get the correct course and distance, which in this case you see is nearer seven miles than six. If you had done this problem in the usual way you would have had to make three pencil lines on the chart and step all three off with the dividers to get your distances. In doing this —holding the chart, dividers and a pencil to mark the last step of the dividers—you would wish you had three hands. With this graduated straight edge you can take your reading at once, while holding the chart and straight edge down with one hand and steering with the other. I say: 'Who needs dividers?' when the chart is blowing or rustling around. They never come out even at the end of the course, so you have to reset them to get your last fraction of a mile."

Goddard then asked Weldon what he thought was the best length for such a chart scale and he replied: "My ditty box is only 14 inches long, so my scale is limited to that length. On the 80,000th scale it will measure about 16 miles, while on the 20,000th scale only a little less than four miles. But as I seldom lay off long courses on the 20,000th scale chart, this length has been convenient for me. However, I do think a 16 or 18 inch straight edge would be better for a larger boat. Of course, harbor charts are made to many scales. Some are 5,000ths, 10,000ths and 30,000ths, but I find I use the 20 and 80 thousand scales most."

Goddard inquired if Weldon thought any of the manufacturers of scales would make these special scales, and Weldon answered: "I think Theo. Altender & Sons of Spring Garden Street in Philadelphia would make them quickly and well in normal times, if you told them exactly what you wanted. For instance, if you said you wanted a rule about an inch wide and three-sixteenths-inch or less thick by about 17 inches long, divided for about 16 inches with a scale similar to the scale on an 80,000th chart, and divided on the other side to the scale on a 20,000th chart, I think there would be no difficulty. Of course the scale should have straight up and down edges to be used for a straightedge as this one is. Naturally, any special rule costs more than those made by the hundreds or thousands, but certainly this combination straight edge and chart scale is worth a sum. It is likely that if the armed forces knew how useful this scale would be to harbor tugs, mine sweepers and patrol boats they would have them made by the thousands, and then they would be cheap enough."

Goddard then asked Weldon how he estimated the speed of the tide by lobster pot buoys and Weldon told him: "I look at the sort of waves or fuss the buoy is making and try to compare it in my mind with how the buoy would look if towed a half-mile, three-quarters of a mile, or one mile per hour, etc., and in that way think I can make a close estimate. It is worthwhile, if you haven't done it, to pick up a lost buoy and tow it astern with a weight on the tow line to make the buoy take its natural angle in the water. Fortunately, it is only in light weather that the tide carries you off much and in this condition you can make a pretty good estimate, but when there is a breeze and sea no one can guess very closely. We usually only have fog in light weather and then I watch very closely the buoys I pass. For instance, suppose you have a cross tide of one mile an hour and are only going ahead two miles an hour. Then you will have to make a great change in your course to come out right. The poor fisherman who has to go to sea in the winter is up against a very different proposition, for he often has snow and poor visibility in a breeze, or even a gale, so he dreads snow more than anything else if he is close to shore."

All this time, the boys were whittling away on their models and listening to the conversation, but Weldon said to Jim: "In cutting the concave in the forefoot of that model you will do best if you hold the knife rather loosely in the right hand and shove the blade along with the thumb of the left hand that is holding the model." Weldon took the model and showed Jim how the knife could be controlled in this way to take off a very small, thin shaving if desired.

In the meantime, the afternoon sun was shining strongly in the cockpit and although it must have been hot on shore, the breeze that came up the harbor kept them all quite comfortable. When there was a pause in the conversation Goddard, who had been

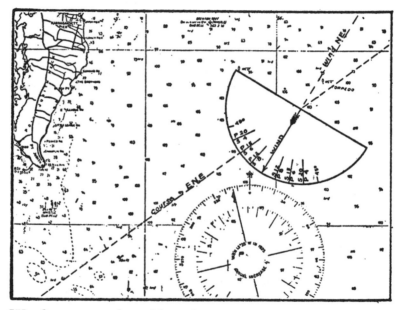

Wooden semi-circle, calibrated in minutes, to indicate correct amount of time to spend on a tack.

rummaging in the ditty box, asked: "What is this thing which looks like a protractor?"

"That," replied Weldon, "is a gadget I use to tell how many minutes to stay on a tack when beating to the windward. If your destination is dead to windward, you stay on each tack the same amount of time (say ten minutes a tack), but if the course is not dead to windward you have to stay on one tack longer than the other." Weldon then put the semi-circular piece of wood on the chart. "There is a pin point near the center of this piece and I will put the pin into the chart right on this pencil course line which runs about E.N.E. Now suppose the wind is N.E., then I rock the flat side of the semi-circle around to right angle from the wind like this. Then you can read on the curved side the numbers and letters S—6, P—15, which of course means you stay on the starboard tack six minutes and the port tack fifteen minutes." Weldon then shifted the gauge around so the flat side faced the east and went on: "Now, if the wind had been east instead of northeast it would have been the same amount on our starboard bow as it had been before on our port bow, and you see the gauge now reads S—15 and P—6. If you are at sea, you can double or quadruple these times or, if in constricted waters, halve them."

Goddard then inquired how Weldon had laid off these angles and times and Weldon answered: "I only laid them out for each compass point of wind angle higher than a sailboat can point. As you know, a good sailing yacht can point up to four points of the wind. I did it by geometry on a chart. You may think me queer, but I would rather do that sort of thing on a winter evening than listen to the radio. If you would like to have such a gadget I will send you one when I get home." Goddard replied that he would like it very much for he had a high appreciation of simple gadgets that did not get out of order, and a still higher appreciation for those who could think them out.

This made Weldon feel pretty good. It was said before that it was very comfortable sitting in the cockpit of *Rozinante* but it now seemed even more so and the men became very talkative. As Goddard was lighting his pipe Weldon said: "You know, in the old days, a slate or blackboard played an important part in navigation. The deck officer wrote the compass course on a slate for the quartermaster, and most of the notes that later went into the deck log were noted at once on the slate. Also, notes were made of the times a change in course was made, or if the wind headed or let the vessel up. On the *Rozinante,* we have a sort of slate and find it very handy for many things."

Weldon then went into the cabin and lifted one corner of the mattress and took out a piece of semi-flexible fiberboard about 18 by 12 inches. It was painted on one side with a dull black paint called blackboard paint and on the other side several tables were pasted to it that were varnished over. He explained: "When we are tacking to windward on these long and short tacks that we have just spoken of, I make a diagrammatical sketch of our course and jot down the time we come about, so if we are in somewhat restricted water and there is a fog we can tell approximately where we are."

"Yes, I can see that," said Goddard, "but time and distance are two different things."

"To be sure they are," agreed Weldon, "but on the other side of this fiberboard that I call my 'slate' we have tables giving the distance a vessel travels at different speeds." And he turned over the slate and showed a table with lines running horizontally and vertically. Each of the horizontal lines was for different speeds like 1/2K, 3/4K, 1K, 3K, and 5K. The vertical lines were for time in minutes like 2M, 3M, 5M, 7M, 12M and 15M. "Now, suppose we enter the table at the speed of three knots and follow along the line to five minutes. You see we get the distance of 1/4 nautical miles. By interpolation, this table can be used for many speeds and times. For instance, if our speed had been 6K instead of 3K, we would double the distance given for three knots. Or, if our time had been 10 minutes instead of 5 we would have doubled the distance given for five, and so on. A table could be given for each minute and mile but it would be so large it would be unwieldy. You see, on a small boat you do not have time to make calculations, particularly if you are singlehanded, or even if someone is confusing you with talk."

"That is very true," agreed Goddard, "but how do you estimate your speed through the water?"

"I do it mostly by the length of the waves the *Rozinante* makes," Weldon told him, "and you will note that all boats make waves of the same length at the same speed, but some models make higher waves than others at the same speed."

Weldon then showed Goddard a table on the back of the slate which gave the distance between the crest of waves at different speeds—1K, 1/2 ft.: 2K, 2 1/4 ft.; 3K, 5 ft.; 4K, 9 ft.; 5K, 14 ft.; 6K, 20 ft.; 7K, 27 ft. He added: "You see, there is such a difference between the lengths at the various speeds that it is really possible to make a good estimate. The best thing about it is that it can be done almost instantly, whereas streaming a log or even reading a log is only practical on long courses." He said he had known men who could estimate the speed of small sailboats very accurately by simply looking over the side and watching the wake, but that was an art that took several years to acquire, and that changing from one size of yacht to another, particularly if there was a difference in freeboard, threw the guess out. "Our blackboard has several other uses and some of them are to make rapid calculations on. We also use it for signal purposes. Power boats often come alongside and ask a question, and while we can hear the question they cannot hear the answer on account of their noise, so we write the answer with chalk on the slate and hold it up. Quite often the answer is simply 'yes,' or 'no,' and so it can be written quite large. Sometimes a course or bearing is asked for and this much can be written in three large letters. The last-but-not-least use of the slate is to draw on and the boys have produced some pretty good drawings with chalk. Perhaps we use it the most to make diagrams of things which I am explaining to the boys."

Goddard said he thought a waterproof outfit like the *Rozinante's* slate was a most useful thing on a small yacht, but inquired of Weldon what he allowed for leeway in laying out courses.

"I usually make no allowance," replied Weldon, "for the modern smart sailing craft with a sizable keel makes little leeway under normal conditions. Many of them will make good four points from the wind or fetch practically as high as they point. It used to be customary to study the wake of a ship to guess at the leeway, and some people used to take the angle of the log line but the wind sometimes affects this. However, if the wind has been blowing for some time, the whole surface water moves to leeward so fast that a deep keeled yacht often makes a wake that sags to leeward as if the yacht were fetching even higher than she is heading. In heavy weather, the sea for some distance down is moving to leeward, and under this condition a small vessel that is well reefed down makes considerable leeway (at least a compass point.) Under this condition, I always give lee shores or other dangers considerable leeway and I think all sailors instinctively do so. Sometimes, on a shore tack, you can take a bearing ahead, as you would if you were estimating the tide, and gauge the leeway quite accurately. Often, when reefed down, you will only make good on an angle about as the helmsman sees by the forestay when he is sitting in the normal weather position for steering. This means that the craft is making more than a point of leeway. The best thing is always to be conscious of leeway and realize it is greatest in a sea and wind."

Goddard said: "I believe I have learned more useful tricks in small boat piloting this afternoon than I would have if I studied three or four big books about navigation. I want to thank you very much."

Weldon then asked: "I believe you are starting on a cruise in the *Viator*, and may I inquire what your first port will be?"

Goddard answered, "We are going south of the Cape and our first run will be to Provincetown, starting early tomorrow morning."

"By Jove!" exclaimed Weldon. "With your permission, I would like to accompany you as far as Provincetown."

"Good! Come by all means," replied Goddard, "for that will make the long, straight and rather uninteresting run much more fun."

"What do you think of that, boys?" inquired Weldon. Jim and Dan both answered together: "Gee! Maybe we will see some of the fishing fleet there."

"Yes," replied their uncle, "particularly if bad weather is threatening, for Provincetown is one of the best harbors near Georges Banks or the fishing grounds."

Just then Dan noticed that someone was hoisting the meal pennant on the *Viator,* and when he spoke of it Goddard asked: "By George, what time is it?"

When they looked at the *Rozinante's* Chelsea clock they were all surprised to see it was a little after six. As Goddard hurriedly climbed into the dinghy he said, "This afternoon has certainly slipped away quickly and I have enjoyed it immensely."

Weldon replied that it certainly had been a great pleasure to have him aboard and he hoped they could continue the gam when they got to Provincetown. "By the way, what time are you starting in the morning?" asked Weldon. "As early as I can; about seven," replied Goddard. "Well, if the weather is light I'll start before that," said Weldon, "and you can use your motor till you catch me." "O.K.," said Goddard, as he started to row briskly toward the *Viator.*

Goddard had told his wife that he wanted supper early so when he got back he was in for a little teasing from the three women, but they made a merry supper of it and all turned in by eight o'clock with everything ready for an early start.

The crew of the *Rozinante* had their supper ashore and made purchases which filled the various storage places for food on board with a supply that would last them several days. They also succeeded in turning in soon after eight bells.

Next morning in Provincetown Harbor the wind was still northeast and, although it was lighter, it often veered enough toward the east to make the horn on Peaked Hill Bar very perceptible. As the darker clouds passed overhead, they were often accompanied by a light rain, and everything had that dampness that denotes proximity to the Gulf Stream. But the cabins of the *Viator* and *Rozinante* were comfortably warm and dry, thanks to their coal-burning stoves, so that everyone seemed contented and resigned to being storm bound.

After breakfast on the *Viator,* the girls and Mrs. Goddard were all wrapped up in the fashion magazines and catalogs of patterns that they had brought along. They settled down for a day of it, when Mrs. Goddard said, with a sigh: "I do wish I had brought my pinking shears and some material." Goddard thought it was time for him to beat a retreat, so donning his oilskin jacket and a sou'wester he left the women to their own devices. As he climbed the companionway steps, he said to his wife: "If you want me I'll be aboard the *Rozinante*."

As he rowed over in the tender, he noticed that several of the new diesel trawlers of the fishing fleet were in and, although some of them were quite handsome craft, he bewailed the passing of the fishing schooners which in his youth had made Provincetown so interesting when the Georges Banks fleet gathered there in an easterly.

On board the *Rozinante*, the boys were playing a game they never seemed to tire of; taking turns asking questions from a section of the *Yachtsman's Guide* that is called "A Nautical Dictionary." They were just finishing the list of questions as Goddard came aboard. Jim was holding the book and had asked Dan what the meaning of the word "yoke" was. Little Dan answered: "One of them things on a rudder," but their uncle broke in to the conversation saying, "Now, Dan, rudders can have many things on them, so be more explicit. Besides, I don't want you to say 'one of them things' for that sounds like a young hoodlum talking." So Dan tried again, saying: "A yoke is the piece of wood on the top of a rudder."

Weldon encouraged him: "That is much better, Dan, but now, Jim, you read the definition in the *Yachtsman's Guide*"

Jim read: "Yoke. A piece of wood placed across the head of a boat's rudder with a rope attached to each end by which the boat is steered."

After this, the boys came out in the cockpit to look at the fishing fleet, but they seemed restive, perhaps because it was too wet to whittle or tie knots easily, so their uncle asked: "How would you boys like to climb the Pilgrim monument?"

They both replied at once that they would like to, very much.

Weldon agreed; "Well, if you will do just as I tell you, you may."

"All right, sir; we will try to remember what you tell us."

Weldon went on: "In the first place, I want you to take your oilskin jackets. But don't wear them in the tender even if it rains, for in case of a capsize you can swim better without them. I want Jim to do the rowing and Dan can sit on the floor on top of the oilskins to keep his stern dry."

"All right," the boys agreed.

Weldon continued: "If you rowed ashore with Jim on the middle thwart and Dan on the after one the tender would be by the stern and row hard. Besides, her high bow would be affected by the wind, so Dan should try to place his weight as far forward as possible and he can do this by sticking his feet under the middle thwart and lying back on his elbows."

"How will I reach the foot braces if Dan is in the way?" asked Jim.

His uncle reminded him: "Don't you remember that when we came out last night, I straddled you with my legs and used one of the frames on each side of the floor boards as a brace for my heels?"

Mr. Goddard then spoke up: "The foot braces of a boat should be way out at the sides, anyway, for then one can brace himself against sliding sideways on the thwart. I believe, if the truth were known, that central foot braces have been the cause of many capsizes in small tenders. I cannot understand why boat builders still insist on placing them amidships, particularly when they can see many tenders with heel holes dug nearly through the planking outside of the floor boards."

"Yes, I agree with you," replied Weldon, "but to go on with the instructions to the boys: When you land, try to tell whether the tide is rising or falling. It is sometimes hard to tell in rainy weather, but a rising tide usually carries a narrow strip of spindrift or foam along with it, while a falling tide does not unless there is some sea running. However, I speak of the tide because the beaches at Provincetown shelve very gradually and in some places the tide recedes at the ebb as much as a quarter of a mile. If the tide is coming in, haul the Sancho up some distance and tie this little grapnel to the painter planted as far inshore as possible. Even then, if you are gone an hour you may have to wade out to her. If the tide is falling, leave the *Sancho* where you land with the grapnel out, and you may have to haul her some way when you come back before she will float. By the way, how will you boys go about dragging the tender?"

"Oh," they replied, "we will both get on the painter and pull."

Weldon shook his head. "That is not the best way for two to do it. It is much better if one gets on each side and puts his fingers under the quarter knees or gunwale strip. Then both lift as you pull. Both remember to pull together. If you have far to go, sponge all of the water out of the dinghy and even remove the oars or anything else of weight. I am glad you are both strong boys and the tender is light. After you have secured the tender, take the sponge, bailer, oars, and rowlocks to the barber shop where we left them last night and give the barber ten cents for keeping them for you. The land where the monument stands is quite a little above the town, so when you get there you should rest before climbing the long flight of steps in the tower. When you come back, you can look in the store windows if you want to, but if anyone speaks to you it is best to give them a polite reply and move on, for there are some queer birds around the artists' colony of the town. I do not ask you to climb the tower quickly, but the sooner you get back to the tender the less wading or lugging you will have to do. Here is some money for each of you. Don't spend all of the money for candy, but get something like cod line for towing models or picture postal cards to send home. Now boys,—Boats Away!"

After the boys had left, the two men settled down for a game in the cabin. "What do you think the weather is going to do?" asked Goddard.

"I think it will stay the same until the barometer shows signs of changing," replied Weldon.

Goddard mused: "If I were sure that it would be no worse than now, I would push on to the Cape Cod Canal. But I suppose it will be quite rough off the jetties there with the northeast wind we have had the last twenty-four hours."

"Yes, I think so," agreed Weldon, "for the seas often break there in a northeaster." Then Weldon continued, "If the wind comes out moderate southwest, as I expect it to do in the morning, I hope to take the *Rozinante* around the outside of the Cape and we will meet you at Nantucket. You know the distance from here is about the same, either through the Canal or around the Cape, but somehow or other it is a pretty and interesting sail on the outside of the Cape when there is a westerly wind and clear weather."

"I agree," replied Goddard, "but as I have promised the girls to go through the Canal, I will have to go that way. If, as you say, the distance is about the same either way, we might still make sort of a race of it."

"That's an idea!" exclaimed Weldon. "Will you be willing to start as early as I do?"

"No, probably not," returned Goddard, "but if we take the elapsed time of our separate voyages it will be nearly as interesting and instructive."

After that was settled, they sat quietly for a few minutes enjoying the companionship of two kindred spirits in a small cabin. Goddard's eyes were roving over the *Rozinante's* equipment until he saw a monocular hanging in its case near the companionway.

"I see you prefer a monocular to binoculars."

"Yes, decidedly so," responded Weldon, "especially on the water, and particularly on a small vessel or boat. In the first place a monocular costs just about one half as much as a binocular of the same quality and light gathering power. In the second place it is much quicker and easier to focus. In the third place it is more compact and easy to stow away. Also, a monocular is less apt to be damaged by a fall or have some of its parts get out of alignment."

"But how about the loss of stereoscopic effect in a monocular?" asked Goddard.

"On a small yacht or boat," Weldon said, "stereoscopic effect is of little value, as we are usually looking at a single distant object, such as a private signal or buoy, and care little if everything appears on one plane, or if there appears to be little difference in the proximity of objects. Of course, stereoscopic effect is useful in viewing landscape where each tree will stand out by itself with space around it, and a glass with good stereoscopic effect is of much value in the army or even in the navy when viewing a convoy, or even in spotting the splashes of gun fire. For these uses, the modern prismatic binocular is far superior to the older glasses. On the prismatic binocular the objective glasses are farther apart than the observer's eyes while on the old straight line, or Galilean, binocular all the lenses have to be the same distance apart as the observer's eyes."

"That may be so," remarked Goddard, "but what do you think are the most valuable qualities in a glass for small craft?"

"I think strength in the tube or body is most essential in a good glass for if the lenses get the least bit out of alignment or polarity the definition or sharpness of the image is much impaired. Few people realize this or know that the principal reason many old glasses are no longer clear and sharp is because they have had a fall or knock that has put them out of line. However, in the high grade expensive glasses the lenses are held in place rigidly in scientific mountings which, while they hold the lenses in exact place, still do not bend or distort the glasses the least amount. The Bausch and Lomb Company has even developed lens mountings and prism mountings which will spring these parts back in exact place even if they have been slightly moved by a sudden jar or by the fall of the whole instrument, and I have been told that some of the glasses made by that company for our navy have fallen from waist high to a steel deck without their optical qualities being much impaired. This, of course, would be impossible with a cheap glass."

"Is there any way to tell if a glass has gotten out of line?"

"Why yes, there are several ways to tell, but perhaps the simplest is to draw two sharp ink lines on a piece of paper in the form of a cross. The paper should be two or three feet square depending on the angle of vision field of view of the glass, and the paper should be held perfectly stationary at about 100 feet. Now place the monocular or binocular to be tested on a very steady support and look at the crossed lines. If the lines are both bright and sharp (as they appear with new glasses), the lenses are in line. But if the lines seem hazy and broader than they should, then the glass is slightly out of line. If you see two separate parallel lines then the glass is definitely out of line. If both of the crossed lines appear double the glass is out of line both horizontally and vertically.

"A still easier test is to look at a distant electric wire that is in front of a white building; if the wire looks sharp, round and black the glass is real good, but if the wire looks rather indistinct, flat and gray, then the glass is slightly out. If you see two wires where there should be only one, it is not necessarily because you have been drinking, but the lenses are definitely out of line. Now tip the optical instrument sideways and test to see if it is out in the other direction. Of course, with binoculars each tube or series of lenses must be tried separately. It is necessary in these tests that neither the glass nor the object looked at should move at all, so a perfectly calm day with the optical instrument on a firm stand is essential, particularly on magnifications of over six power."

"Speaking of power," said Goddard, "what do you think is the best magnification or power for use on the water?"

"That is a great question. I believe it depends a great deal on the size of the yacht and the skill of the observer. For instance, a six power glass is much too strong for a power boat which has vibration; it is also too strong for a small sail boat in a seaway. Six power is about right for general use on a small yacht, seven power is perhaps the best on the larger yachts if you sit down and there is little motion, while eight power can only be used to advantage by one who has practised holding the glass and himself steady by leaning against a shroud or a deck house. As for a ten power glass—even if it is in the hands of an expert well braced and he has stopped breathing (as a target shooter does in aiming his rifle), he will not generally be able to see as well as he could with a seven power glass because the ten power glass would have less light gathering power or relative brightness on account of its magnification. For example, a ten power glass with a 50 millimeter diameter objective lens will have a relative brightness of only 25, while a 7 x 50 glass will have a relative brightness of 50.4, or over twice the light gathering power. So seven is about the right all-around power for a monocular or binocular. Most manufacturers used to class their glasses somewhat as follows: 2 1/2 to 3 power for opera glasses: 4 to 6 power for bird or sport glasses: 6 to 8 power for military and marine glasses. I do not know what they called the higher powered ones but perhaps they were made for fools and suckers.

"However, a little over a quarter of a century ago the Carl Zeiss Company brought out in Germany a 7 x 50 glass called the Dinoctor model and this glass at once became the most popular of the high grade binoculars, so that now 7 x 50 glasses are being made in several countries. Some of them are very reasonable in price, but I doubt if the cheaper ones will retain polarity or crispness of vision very long. However, there is a good reason for the popularity of the 7 x 50 glass, and that reason is that the average person can see through it better than with any other combination now made commercially. You see, if the power of the glass were increased to over seven, then to retain the present light-gathering power the objective glasses would be too large and expensive to be practical. If the magnification or power were reduced it would not meet with popular appeal."

"Why would you suppose the average person wants high magnification?" Goddard asked.

"They seem to think you can see farther and better with it and believe a high-powered glass is more expensive to build, while the truth of the matter is that a high-powered glass costs little if anything more than a low-powered glass. If it were not that the high-powered glass is generally a little longer, there would be no difference in the cost of manufacture because a lens of more or less crown or curvature within reason can be made for the same cost. The thing that costs money is light gathering power, or relative brightness, and that can only be secured with a large objective lens. A large objective lens also generally increases the angle of sight or field of vision and, while that is a doubtful advantage in a marine glass, it is a most valuable quality in other glasses particularly when the glass is used to pick up or look at moving objects."

"You say," interrupted Goddard, "that increasing the size of the objective glass is the only way to increase the relative brightness of the glass. How about these new preparations for coating the lenses?"

"Coated lenses certainly seem to let the light penetrate the optical system much better, but at the present time its advantages may be somewhat exaggerated. For instance, an 8 x 25 coated glass would not be equal to an 8 x 30 uncoated glass for work at dusk."

"How would you go about testing the magnification of a monocular or binocular?"

"It is quite easy to do with the lower powers, but not so easy with magnifications of over 7. One way to do it is to use a picket fence as the target and place your glass on a steady stand 100 or more feet away from the fence. Now, with one eye, look through the glass and with the other naked eye try to look at the same part of the fence and you will see two images, one much larger than the other. Now move the glass carefully on the stand so that one image is nearly over the other and count off how many pickets of the fence the naked eye sees where the glass shows one picket and the space to the next picket. If the glass shows one picket to the naked eye's six pickets, then it is a six power glass. But I must say I believe the numbers or magnifications stamped on high grade glasses are very accurate, even if the cheaper glasses sometimes exaggerate some."

"Is there any way to easily test the illumination or light gathering qualities of a glass?"

"No, I think there is no easy or accurate way to do that. It is unfortunate because illumination is about the most desirable quality a glass can have and the principal difference between the cheap and high grade optical instruments of this kind is the difference in illumination."

"Why do you say illumination is such a desirable quality in a glass?"

"Sometimes, a glass is of the most vital help in picking up buoys in the dusk, or recognizing vessels and landmarks in poor light. A glass that can do that used to be called a night glass and had to have the lenses and prisms made of material that had high light transmitting qualities, while the cheaper glasses usually have to use glass that absorb much of the brightness of image. If Leonardo DaVinci worked out the machinery for accurate lens grinding before the year 1500 and Galileo made the first telescope in 1608, you can see it is some 400 years that man has been working on these optical problems. During that time, no doubt, as much effort was devoted to experiments with materials as to developing the design of optical instruments or the formula for grinding the lenses, so that today with the proper combinations of crown and flint glass not only is the illumination much improved but the true representation of color is far better. A high grade glass is a great help in recognizing the color of distant code flags, etc., whereas the image in a cheap glass is more or less colorless."

"It is very pleasant talking over these things quietly in the small cabin of a yacht, but what do you think is a good all around test for a glass?"

"A good test, and one that I would make in buying a new glass, is to anchor a mile or two off some city that has many waterfront signs and the glass that you can read the signs easiest with is the best glass for you. You will find that on a clear day if there are no heat waves in the air, you will do very well with a 10 x 50 glass if you rest it on something. But toward dusk, the 7 x 50 glass will be so much better there will be no comparison, especially if both glasses are used without a steadying rest."

"That may be so, but don't you think a binocular with 50 mm. diameter objective lenses is bound to be bulky, expensive and heavy?"

"As for the bulk and expense, you can cut that in half by using a monocular instead of a binocular. As far as weight is concerned, the heavy glass is much the best to use and is like the rifle and the camera in that respect. Some sporting rifles may be as light as six pounds, the military rifle over eight pounds, but the serious, long distance, unrestricted target rifle may weigh up to 20 pounds, and there have been ones much heavier. As for the camera, it is well known that a heavy one will take better pictures or allow longer exposures, for its weight will absorb the vibrations of the shutter, mirror, etc. While the heavy rifle or camera would be very undesirable to carry over long distances on foot, the heavy marine glass that is never carried except when in use is a very different proposition. I think a marine monocular and its case should both be heavy.

"Another thing that a marine glass should have is a good long visor or sunshade, for on the water one often has to look westward in the afternoon. If you can keep the sun entirely off the objective lens, the vision is much helped but it is surprising how few people use them."

Weldon then reached up and took his monocular out of its case and said: "As for the cost of a high grade glass, I bought this one 25 years ago and it then cost less than $50, so it would seem that it has cost me $2 a year. That is not quite right, for the glass is still nearly as good as new and I could probably sell it today for what it cost new, so you see it does not cost much to have a high grade glass. If I had several cheap ones during that time, which had to be repaired, etc., the expense might have been something."

Goddard took the glass and saw that it was a 7 x 50 Carl Zeiss and inquired how it had kept so well. Weldon replied: "I suppose the principal reason is that it is always kept in its strong case when not in use. I never put it away if it has salt or spray on it, but wipe it off carefully first. At first, I cleaned the lens with the lens tissue that is sold for camera lenses, but now I use the tissues that are used to clean spectacles and are called Sight Savers. I do not leave the glass out banging around the cockpit where everyone can handle it, or where the sun shines on the lens, but instead slap it right back in its case when through using it. As you see, the case is hung where it can be reached from the cockpit."

"How have you kept the case so well all these years?"

"Simply by rubbing it down with saddle soap once a year."

"Do you think Zeiss glasses are the best?"

"Not necessarily, but before World War II the Zeiss Company made a great many different models and because they had very active agents in the principal cities of the world they led in the high grade field. It is said that the optical glass made at Jena, Germany where the Zeiss Company was located was the best in the world and this gave Zeiss an advantage. However, Jena came within the Russian occupied zone of Germany at the close of the war, and it is said the Russians confiscated the Zeiss works and shipped most of its machinery to Russia, so it may be some time before Zeiss optical instruments are in our market again. But there are other German makers of glasses which are very good and being imported at the present time.

"You don't hear much about English glasses in this country, but the English camera lenses and binoculars are among the very best. Perhaps the English scientists have contributed as much as any in the development of the modern lens, and the marine glasses made by Barr and Strode are among the best in the world for naval use. They are rugged, long, and heavy enough to hold steady. Those made by A. Kershaw & Sons of London are of superb workmanship and give results comparable to any. Before 1900, France was perhaps the leader in the manufacture of medium grade binoculars, mostly of the Galilean type, but we hear little of French glasses at the present time. In this country the best known manufacturer of prismatic binoculars and monoculars is the Bausch and Lomb Company, and while they are necessarily expensive on account of the high cost of labor in this country, still perhaps in the end they are the best value for the dollar of any for they will last almost indefinitely and retain their optical qualities for 50 or 75 years, which of course makes them very cheap per year to use. Also, Bausch and Lomb binoculars can be had with very shallow eye cups which is a distinct advantage to those who wear spectacles as this arrangement allows the whole optical couple to be brought back to nearly its proper position and much increases the field of view. However, I advise the observer to remove his glasses if he can comfortably because the monocular or binocular can be held much steadier if the eye cup is rested against the bridge of the nose and the arch of the eye. Also, having the eyepiece well up in the eye cavity shuts out extraneous light and may be as important as the proper use of the shade tube at the objective end of the glass. Both of these things are important on the water when looking toward the west near sunset.

"If the target shooter supports his rifle in four places (the shoulder, the cheek, and his two hands) and has practiced to get the best results from each support, the observer with his glass should also practice the best positions for steadiness, particularly if he is using a glass of six or seven power. If it is impossible for the target shooter to make a good score directly after heavy exercise; heavy breathing and strong heartbeat also affect the steadiness of the optical instrument. If one sits quietly for some time, the magnified image in a powerful glass appears much sharper. To get the best results, one must sit on a steady seat, support the glass steadily and momentarily stop breathing. Then he can really get sharp definition at long distance, and after a little practice one instinctively does these things."

Goddard said: "That was all very instructive and interesting, but do you think it is an advantage to have a glass with a large range of focus?"

"I think it is very desirable on a sail boat to have a glass that can be focused on nearby objects, for often it is urgently necessary to examine some of the rigging and fittings which are aloft. I knew a designer who used a Zeiss 10 x 50 monocular for that purpose, for it could be focused on objects as close as twenty five feet. No doubt he also found the glass useful in studying the rigging of some of his rival's yachts, but the ability to look at close-to objects is most useful and only requires the eyepiece to be screwed in and out about a quarter of an inch."

Just then they heard voices alongside, so Weldon stepped out in the cockpit in time to hold the *Sancho Panza* off as the boys climbed aboard. The boys, however, were becoming quite skilful at coming alongside, and although the *Sancho* had a white painted chafing strip on the outside of her gunwales she was otherwise a black tender which is a constant worry to the owner of a white yacht.

After they were all in the cabin, little Dan said; "Gee, uncle, the *Rozinante* looks smaller than a toy boat when you are up in the monument."

"Yes, I suppose so," said Weldon, "but when you get used to going up in aeroplanes you will find ships and boats look even smaller than that. If it were not for the wake back of them, they would appear to be stationary. What else did you see?"

Jim replied; "The water off Race Point looked streaky."

"Yes, I expect it did," replied Weldon. "That is the way a rough sea appears from the air. I have no doubt there is a weather-going tide there with combing seas. How did you like the looks of the sand dunes over toward Race Point?" When the boys replied that they looked pretty good, their uncle said; "You ought to see them in the winter when they are frozen just after a rain-storm, for the colors of the sands are beautiful then. In the summer the sands are all yellowish brown, but at times in the winter most of the colors of the rainbow are represented there with the blues perhaps the reflection of the sky."

"Have you been up the monument in the winter?" asked Jim.

"No," his uncle replied, "but I have walked quite a lot over the dunes when they were frozen. That is the only time to do it easily. In the summer it is hard to walk there, particularly uphill, for your feet slip and bury in the sand. But when the dunes are frozen, the surface is hard and smooth, though not slippery and it is almost like walking on firm sandpaper. At these times it seems like walking in some fairyland where the soil is made up of glistening jewels of many colors with here and there a scrub oak of fantastic shape. Occasionally, you will find ancient sand-blasted pieces of wood of a very dark color which may be the remains of an ancient forest which has been covered and uncovered by the shifting of the dunes. Altogether it is a colorful and romantic place on a bright winter day."

In the meantime the wind had shifted more to the east and instead of the waves rippling alongside, the *Rozinante* began to have a pronounced bobble with now and then a moderate pitch. Weldon tapped the barometer and said: "At last, it has changed and is making a slight drop. If the wind is to shift into the southeast, I shall be glad if it does so before nightfall. But it will be interesting to have some sea this afternoon when I am trying the new anchor."

Goddard began to feel a little uneasy and said; "I think I had better go aboard the *Viator* and rig the big anchor and have it over the bow ready to let fall the moment it is wanted, but you can be sure I shall be over this afternoon when you are testing the new anchor for I am very interested in these matters."

Weldon told him that he would be glad to help Mr. Goddard with the big anchor, but Goddard said, "Thank you very much, but as it is a three piece anchor, I can easily take the parts forward separately and assemble the anchor on the bow with the help of the girls."

When Goddard had left, Weldon told the boys he would take them ashore for lunch a little early, for he believed it would be rough in the anchorage presently. Even as they rowed ashore, the waves were breaking a foot or two high along the shelving beach where they had landed before, so Weldon decided to go alongside a fishing boat that was at the wharf, instead.

The fisherman was a seiner with a low freeboard aft where there were some nets stowed. Her crew, which consisted of three or four good natured Portuguese, hailel them as they approached, calling: "Come aboard!"

So they soon scrambled aboard the seiner and Weldon asked permission to tie up there while they went ashore for lunch. The captain of the seiner replied: "I think that little cockleshell of yours would be better off hauled aboard than swinging around and bumping."

"I think so, too," agreed Weldon, "but how could it be arranged?"

"I'll show you how to arrange it," answered the captain as he reached down with a big paw and lifted the *Sancho's* bow up to the rail with one arm. Just then, one of his crew came on each side of him and lifted the tender aboard and set her on a tarpaulin that was over some nets. "There," said the captain, "I guess you can eat hearty without worrying now."

Weldon then asked the captain if he thought the oars and oarlocks would be safe in the boat. The captain did not answer Weldon directly, but instead called a large Western Island watch dog that looked like a long-legged bulldog, and said to the dog as he pointed to the tender: "Pronto, watch!" Pronto wagged his tail to show that he understood and lay down beside the tender. The captain then continued: "I guess if anyone takes anything out of that boat they will have something took out of themselves. And, mister," he added speaking to Weldon, "if there is no one on deck when you come back, you better keep away from the tender yourself until we speak to Pronto."

As they walked up the wharf, the boys said: "Gee! did you see them lift the *Sancho* over the rail as if she was nothing at all?"

"Yes," replied their uncle, "each of those men probably weigh over 200 pounds and have spent much time hauling seines and other heavy things over the rail. Their muscles are so used to lifting that the weight of the *Sancho* was almost nothing to them."

While they were having lunch, the wind continued blowing briskly from the east, so as they walked out the wharf on their return they could see whitecaps over the shallow water at the north part of the harbor. The wharves at Provincetown are very long and the one they were walking out on was nearly a quarter of a mile long, so Weldon had time to tell the boys that it would be a wet row out to the *Rozinante*. They would have to be careful in boarding the tender so he wanted them to know beforehand how he planned to do it.

"First of all, remember that when you jump into a small tender, you must try to land as nearly amidships as possible and sit down at once. I will board first and rig the outer oar and oarlock with my legs spread well apart to brace myself. Then, Jim, you jump in close aft of me and sit down on the bottom for I want you to hold the outer oar in place, which you can do by putting your hand over the oar and oarlock. The oar will be out with its blade in the water and you can let it swing where it wants. In the meantime, I will have the inner oar ready to shove off with, which will take my two hands. About this time, I want Dan to jump in close forward of where I am sitting. You should jump in facing aft so you can grab my shoulders or head if you slip. But as soon as you are on your knees, turn around and be ready to haul in the painter. After that, Dan, I want you to turn around again and sit on the floor close forward of us as we did in coming out last time.

"In jumping into a small boat when it is rough, it is best to wait until the wave has lifted the boat then your fall will be much less. Also, if you jump at the right moment or just as the boat starts to fall, the shock on yourself and the boat is much relieved. Do you understand now what I want you to do, boys?"

When they got to the seiner, the cook had his head out of the hatch and this was nearly as good a signal as a meal pennant to show that the crew was eating, so Weldon said to the boys; "What do you say if we walk down the wharf and look at the other fishing boats?"

This pleased the boys for, besides the picturesqueness of the drying nets, trawls and other fishing gear, the men themselves were romantic looking as they gathered in groups to talk over the weather. Little Dan asked: "Why do they wear hip boots and oilskins when it isn't raining?" His uncle told him: "The fishermen are so accustomed to that dress that they feel quite uncomfortable in a change of clothes. Also, fishermen throughout the world are notable for their peculiarities of dress. I can well remember when most of the crew of a Gloucesterman wore derby hats in all sorts of weather, but that was before the long-visored sword fisherman hat came in style."

Some of the new diesel trawlers were impressive looking, but when they came to fishermen which had seine boats alongside, Weldon said to the boys; "I believe that is the handsomest type of fishing craft in the world."

"Well, why don't we make a model of one to tow?" asked Jim.

His uncle replied: "We ought to make a model of one to look at. While the seine boat is one of the best towing boats at the speed it is used and will perhaps surpass all other models for towing steadily astern in a quartering sea, a model of one perhaps one-twenty-fourth size would not perform well behind the *Rozinante* for she would stand on end and jump all around."

By this time they had returned to the seiner where their tender was kept. Although Pronto still had one eye on the tender, he was busy polishing off the frying pan. However, as the crew was on deck, they boarded.

Weldon walked up to the captain and said; "How much do we owe you, sir?"

The captain replied: "Mister, you don't owe nothing, and maybe we will meet again when *you* will give the helping hand."

"That is spoken like a true sailor," replied Weldon.

The captain continued, "I don't know how much of a sailor I am but, as for fishing, I have been at it now man and boy for nigh forty years, and if you are ready we will launch your cockleshell for you. I hope you know how to handle her when it is rough or else you are all good swimmers."

"I think we can manage it," Weldon replied.

The captain said to his men; "Come, boys, we will give her

a sea toss, but, Joe, you take the painter well to weather and give it slack 'til she strikes the water." The captain took one end of the *Sancho* while one of his men took the other end and carried her to the rail where they swung her back and forth, counting "One, two, three!" when with a good heave she landed well out from the trawler's side.

Weldon at once mounted the rail with his feet outboard and, as the tender swung in, landed in her in a crouching position which seated him at once on the middle thwart. As he was rigging the outboard oar, the next wave lifted the *Sancho* and Jim landed in her almost in a sitting position, and with one hand grabbed the oar while Weldon was getting out the other oar to shove off with. As the next wave rose under the tender little Dan hesitated, but one of the fishermen, taking him by the back of the collar, lifted him out with one hand and set him on the forward thwart, while Weldon shoved off and little Dan hauled in the painter. It was all done so quickly and neatly that the fishermen were pleased and called out: "Well done!" and other things in Portuguese, while Pronto with his front legs on the rail gave them a parting salute of friendly barks.

After they were clear, Jim said: "Gee! uncle, the *Sancho* didn't even touch the seiner." Weldon was pretty busy rowing but he replied with a chuckle that the reason for it was that he had both arms free to push on the oar, and that both boys had done extremely well.

They had a quartering sea on the way out and they would have gotten wet if the tender had not been expertly handled, but Weldon kept a weather eye over his shoulder and every time a comber approached he backed up with his leeward oar so just as the wave struck the *Sancho's* bow swung off with it. He could swing the tender quickly because the weight of the crew was concentrated amidships, and because the boys were sitting on the floor or had their weight low and near the center of oscillation. The tender could rock quickly to meet the wave, for if high weights are desirable on large craft to make the motion slow, low weights are desirable on small craft to let them roll quickly enough to meet the seas. As he rowed, Weldon kept himself very flexible at the waist so the weight of his torso did not dampen the roll and the boys were fascinated to see how they went along without shipping any water, and were enjoying the row quite as much as Weldon. When they were half way out he said, looking back at the beach where they had landed last night, "I guess we would have had a hard, wet time of it if we had launched from the beach, for you see the waves are breaking a long way out on that shelving shore."

When they got to the *Rozinante* Weldon said he wanted the bow man to jump out first with the painter in his hand and go well forward on the *Rozinante* where he could hold the tender in place with a long scope that would allow her to pitch freely without the scend of the waves making her bump. The *Rozinante* was swinging slowly back and forth as a vessel at one anchor usually does, and Weldon turned his approach so that just as the ketch was finishing her tack toward them he came alongside so that Dan in the bow was abreast of the mizzen shrouds. Little Dan was nearly as nimble as a cat and had boarded and gone forward almost as soon as his uncle had unshipped the oar and oarlocks. At the next wave, Jim boarded and with the following one Weldon came aboard, pushing the *Sancho* well away with his feet and at the same time calling to Dan to slack away with the painter. This whole maneuver had been done very quickly without the tender touching the *Rozinante,* which gave Weldon much satisfaction. He told the boys that within a few years they would do all these things instinctively when they would appear like real boatmen. But the way some people came alongside these days was a caution.

There was quite a choppy sea running by this time with the whitecaps inshore running toward the beach in long regular rows. The wind was a little south of east, and as they looked at the *Viator* they saw Goddard had two anchors out with one warp tending toward the east while the other pointed to the south. Weldon remarked; "I see the captain of the *Viator* expects heavy weather from the southeast and he must have been under way to plant the second anchor so far to the south, but she certainly should lay steady with such well spread anchors. And, as they looked at her, they could see she did not veer around any although she was pitching considerably. Just then it started to rain rather briskly so they went into the cabin.

The two boys were sprawled out on the double berths and Weldon sat in his easy chair, when Jim asked his uncle if it would have been possible to launch the *Sancho Panza* from the beach with such a sea running.

"Yes, it is possible all right," replied his uncle, "but you would have to know how to do it and you would get wet to the skin all over. There are many ways to launch a boat against a head sea and the best method is largely dependent on the size of the boat and the steepness of the beach. With a small boat like the *Sancho* and a shelving beach like that to leeward of us, the best way is to drag or pull the boat out until she is in water at least knee deep. Then as one man holds her in place with ten or twelve feet of painter the other one should go inshore and climb in over her stern just as a wave has gone by. After he is in place at the oars the one who was holding the painter can throw it in the bow and walk around and climb in at the stern where he will have to commence bailing. It would be a hard row out from the beach now and would require both strength and skill for the rower could not afford to 'catch either birds or crabs,' as the saying is, which means he should not take a stroke with the blade of the oar either in the air or too deep in the water."

"Suppose it was a steep beach," pursued Jim.

"In that case it is usual for one to be on each side of the boat and when she has been dragged out enough to be waterborne then, while one holds her, the other gets in place at the oars. This is sometimes pretty hard to do for when the waves strike they will try hard to swing the boat around in the trough of the seas and may knock down the man who is holding her. The boat may even get on top of him, which is not of much consequence if it is a small, light boat."

Little Dan then asked how they launched the life boats or surf boats off the beach.

"Surf boats are generally kept where there is a firm, rather steep beach, and are launched on wheels with the crew all in place at the oars. Much of the development of the life boat and ways of launching it were developed in England, and perhaps the greatest experts at putting out in a sea were the pilot boats that launched off the beach at a town named Deal in England.

"You boys, of course, understand that in all these cases we have mentioned the boats were launched bow first so the oarsmen could pull hard at the oars and get through the surf as soon as possible. I must mention to you that in coming ashore through the surf it is best to keep the bow facing the sea and back in. In this way you can control the boat and stop her from swinging around side to it, which is always disastrous."

"Why does the boat want to swing around?" inquired Jim.

"You know that close to the beach or shore there is what is called an undertow, which is nothing more nor less than the water of a spent wave running to sea again. This undertow is strongest between the crest of the waves. As a boat comes in with a sea, her end is being impelled toward the beach while her landward end is being forced outward by the undertow. Thus, if she is not kept right head to the sea she will be swung around and rolled over."

Both the boys then asked their uncle to tell them more about the Deal pilot boats, but Weldon said he expected Mr. Goddard over soon so he would tell them that story in the evening after supper.

Jim looked out the side light and cried: "I see Mr. Goddard coming now," so they went out in the cockpit.

After Goddard was alongside and waiting for the *Rozinante* to swing toward him, Weldon reached over with a boat hook and gaffed the painter in the bight where it came up over the bow. He then gently pulled the tender toward them while Goddard was removing the oars and oarlocks. As Goddard stepped aboard with one hand on the mizzen shrouds, he said: "This will be a dandy time to try that new anchor."

"Yes," agreed Weldon, "but tell me how the women-folks on the *Viator* are making out."

"Why," replied Goddard, "since I put the second anchor down they are very contented; in fact they are very busy with cooking and dressmaking. It seems that being away from home has awakened a new interest in these things and I might say they are as happy as meadow larks over a new mown field."

"Don't they mind the pitching?" asked Weldon, and Goddard replied, "No, not at all. In fact, they have so much female gear spread all around that there was hardly room for me to sit down for lunch so I was glad to escape to the *Rozinante*."

They were all sitting out of the wind in the lee of the *Rozinante's* deck house when Goddard asked; "How do you propose to try the anchor?"

Weldon said he simply meant to haul ahead until his present warp was well up and down and then let the new anchor fall, but Goddard argued that most of the stockless anchors require much scope to take hold and he doubted if this one would catch on bottom that way.

"Well, we shall soon see," said Weldon as he bent the new anchor on the second warp and went forward with it. He let the anchor over the bow and put the warp in the chock, but because the *Rozinante* was pitching considerably he took a bight of the warp around the shrouds and secured it with a half-hitch. Then, undoing the warp that was on the mooring cleat, he called to those aft to haul in smartly. When the warp was nearly up and down he called out; "That will do," and let the new anchor go.

The *Rozinante* soon payed off and started to leeward, beam-to the wind and sea. After Weldon thought there was a reasonable scope out he belayed the warp of the new anchor, but there was no need of it, for the warp never became hand tight although the *Rozinante* was quickly settling to leeward in the troughs of the seas. Finally, when the old warp had run out some distance beyond where it was wet, or had been belayed before, he jumped up and took a bight of the old warp around the mast, when the *Rozinante* at once came head to the wind.

Goddard simply said: "I told you so," but Weldon called aft: "Pull in on the new anchor warp," which the boys soon did for the anchor came home very easily.

After the anchor was up to the bow, Weldon took the warp out of the chock and brought the anchor aft to the cockpit, muttering: "I have been told that this sort of anchor required a chain or other sort of weight at its head to make it take hold, but as I do not have a chain aboard we shall have to lash some sort of weight to the head of this anchor." He then raised a piece of the cockpit floor and took out of the bilge a piece of lead ballast that weighed about ten pounds, explaining to Goddard that the *Rozinante* had been designed with some inside ballast aft in case some later owner wanted to install a kicker. He lashed the small pig securely to the head of the anchor with cod-line.

When this was done, Goddard, with a wise look, hefted the anchor and asked, "How much do you think it weighs now?"

Weldon replied; "At least as much as a sensible anchor would," but he was taking the stops off the mizzen by this time and added, "I mean to give this anchor a real test this time for I intend to tack to windward a half mile and let go with this patent thing alone and see what happens."

After hoisting the mizzen and unstopping the jib, the boys and Goddard hauled up the present anchor while Weldon ran up the jib. They took a tack toward Long Point and, after coming about, stood on until they were half a mile to windward of their previous anchorage where the *Viator* was. Weldon then lay the *Rozinante* to under mizzen alone and she settled back very steadily about four points from the wind, but this had brought them into over eight fathoms of water and where there was a soft mud bottom. Nevertheless, Weldon went forward and let the anchor go. He then let out what he thought was a good scope, but the warp being dry and having a tendency to float, and because they were sagging to leeward, the scope down at the anchor may not have been more than what a good anchor requires, which is some 2 1/2 to 1. So the *Rozinante* worked off to leeward about as she had before the anchor was let go. However, occasionally she came up in the wind a little, but after a wave or two lifted her bow and straightened the warp she would swing off again.

Weldon was mad and said some terrible words to himself, but on account of his nephews he only remarked: "By bell, book and candle, I never saw an anchor like that. I believe a bag filled with stones would hold on better."

"Well, come aft," called Goddard, "for we have plenty of time and space to talk it over," so Weldon came aft to the cockpit and, although it was blowing pretty fresh with a choppy sea, it was sheltered and comfortable behind the *Rozinante's* deck house.

"What do you think is going on down on bottom?" inquired Weldon.

Goddard replied; "I believe most stockless anchors require a very great scope to enable the flukes to take hold. While the anchor seems to hold occasionally now, I believe every time the warp tightens and our bow is lifted by a wave, the head of the anchor comes up parallel with the warp and the flukes slither through the mud with little resistance. But we shall soon see if more scope will allow the flukes to dig in, for we are dragging back into shallower water."

Sure enough, after they had sagged back until the warp tended well out ahead, the anchor took hold and the *Rozinante* came up in the wind so the mizzen shook frantically and Weldon took it in. He then got the sounding lead and took a cast, getting only three and a half fathoms with a bottom of sandy mud.

"No wonder the hook took a'hold on this firmer bottom with a warp out of over four times the draft," he said. "All right, boys, get the anchor and we will coast back under bare poles."

With all hands on the warp, the anchor was soon at the bow. The *Rozinante* swung off, and with the help of the rudder took up a course wind-on-the-quarter where she did some very deep rolling for the waves were just the right distance apart to coin-cide with her period of roll.

Weldon remarked that he could soon reduce the roll if he swung or bore off more, but he would like to anchor this time in a more southerly part of the harbor if Goddard did not mind the longer row to the *Viator*.

"That is all right," returned Goddard, "for the row will do me good."

So they stood on, casting the lead until the depth suddenly reduced to one fathom, whereupon they let go their regular anchor and came head to the wind.

Goddard remarked that he knew this spot would soon be in the lee when the wind shifted more to the south but he wanted to warn Weldon that the bottom was very steep there and if he dragged only a short distance to the northeast the warp would be straight up and down. Weldon answered that he had so much confidence in his regular anchor that he did not expect to drag a foot, particularly after the wind shifted enough to make a lee there. Weldon then went forward and brought the stockless anchor aft to the cockpit and was removing the warp and weight when he asked Goddard if he wanted the anchor.

Goddard replied: "No, thank you, sir."

Weldon was sitting with the anchor across his knees at that moment, but suddenly rose up and gave it a sea toss, at the same time saying; "To the bottom I pitch it!" which made the boys double up with laughter.

Goddard asked; "Why did you do that?" for he was a canny fellow of Scottish descent.

Weldon replied: "I tell you, I don't think much of an anchor that requires a scope of four or five to one and that will hold practically nothing with less scope."

Goddard suggested; "You might have sold it for junk."

"Yes, I know," was Weldon's reply, "but I would hate to think that some unsuspecting person might get it and lose his boat or even his life with such an anchor."

Goddard scratched his head, and said; "There must be some good in those types of anchors or there would not be so many of them."

"Perhaps it is because they break out easily," Weldon offered. "I have no doubt that is one of their selling points, but when someone invents an anchor that does not break out easily he will have made a worthwhile invention for then you can use it with a much shorter warp, or if the tide rises you won't just float away."

Goddard scratched his head again, and said, as if he were thinking aloud; "It might have been used to take ashore some time to hook over the roots of a tree if it were good for nothing else."

"No," said Weldon, "most of the stockless anchors have such thin shanks that they will bend over sideways if a strain is taken to them on an angle, and it is not a very uncommon sight to see these anchors with collapsed shanks in boat yards."

By this time the wind had shifted to south-southeast bringing with it a light rain, so they all went into the cabin. Little Dan remarked: "I wish I had an anchor for some of my models." His brother asked him; "Do you want a stockless one?"

At this Dan sat up straight on the berth and replied; "No, not by the bell, book and candle!" This made all hands laugh and Weldon thought to himself, "I am glad I didn't use any worse words in front of that little parrot."

After they had settled down, Goddard asked if it would be against the rules and regulations of *Rozinante* if they had a little refreshment. Weldon quickly replied: "Even if it is, I feel like something to cheer me up after making a fool of myself with that anchor, but I should have known that anything with such exaggerated claims would be almost no good." After a few minutes they became relaxed and Goddard said; "It is high time that someone made a scientific test of the action of anchors on various bottoms. I realize anchors have been proof tested for strength in various ways for some 150 years, and tried in various ways under water where the testers could not see what was going on, but I believe there is little real, authentic data about the actual holding power of different types."

"How would you go about making such a test?" inquired Weldon, "and don't you think the equipment would be very expensive?"

In answer Goddard pointed out: "If someone acquired the use of a headland or cliff which had different sorts of shore or beach around it it would not be too difficult to make some good tests."

"That might be so, but how would you measure the strains on the warp and estimate the angle of scope?" asked Weldon.

"I would make the set up about like this:" Goddard went on. "First, arrange a strong crab or windlass on the top of the cliff, and have it placed so it could be canted around to take a strain from the beaches where the anchors are to be tried. I would use a wire rope in place of a warp and, near the anchor, attach a spring scale that would weigh or indicate the tension. Back of this rig I would have a strip of cloth about thirty feet long plainly marked off in fathoms and strung on stakes a foot or two above ground. Now if you should take successive photographs of the anchor, as it is being dragged along, the pictures will show how the anchor buries, what the angle of the warp is, and how much the anchor holds at each successive fathom of drag. I would not test anchors that weighed more than fifty pounds or so for it would be heavy, hard work, and I would not make a complete photographic record of anchors which did not pass an elimination test of general usefulness."

"What would that test be?" inquired Weldon.

"First, I would have the anchors dragged by a tackle or automobile away from the cliff until it was well buried. Then reverse the direction of pull toward the cliff and as the anchor came over, or capsized to take a new hold, I would have men throw kelp and rocks on top of it and in its new path. I think you will find that all of the stockless anchors with swinging flukes will come over so loaded that they will not take a new hold for a long while, and those which have flukes that swing near the shank will be so choked with kelp and stones that they will not take hold at all, while the usual anchor, when it is reversed, will come over with its other fluke all clear and go down through any amount of kelp and stones without moving perhaps its own length. Of course, I would eliminate all anchors which did not take hold with a scope of 45 degrees."

Weldon interrupted to ask if Goddard thought many anchors would hold with such a steep scope.

"Yes, decidedly so, and I believe an anchor that will not take hold with the warp well up and down is a pretty useless thing, for often one has to anchor where there is little swinging room. Of course, you understand, I do not think any anchor will develop its maximum holding power with the warp well up and down, but a good anchor should take a hold at 45 degrees and approach its greatest holding power when there is only about three times the draft paid out in warp. With a chain in a seaway, an anchor will hold most with about five times the draft of cable out, but that is mostly because the bow or sag in the chain cable takes up the jerks when the vessel rises with the sea."

Weldon then asked: "How do you think it possible for an anchor to take hold with the warp as steep as 45 degrees for most anchors have the flukes at even less than 45 degrees from the shank?"

"Yes, I know," Goddard replied, "but there is such a difference in the way that an ordinary anchor lays on bottom from that of a stockless anchor that the ordinary anchor will take hold on most any bottom while the stockless, or light headed, anchor with a scope of 45 degrees will slide over the bottom with little resistance.

"I remember well the first time I tried a stockless anchor. It was in shallow, clear water with a shingle bottom that would be fine holding ground for the usual anchor, but the stockless anchor did not give resistance enough to bring the yacht's head to the wind, and it was ludicrous to see how it slid along bottom with its shank in line with the warp. The regular anchor would have its head down and its shank on nearly the opposite angle from the stockless anchor."

Weldon then queried: "I wonder why the usual anchor holds its head down so well?"

Goddard answered: "You see, the stock makes the usual anchor heavy at its head, so its center of weight is nearly half way up the shank. When on bottom, the stock develops considerable resistance so that the angle of strain or pull is changed materially. The resulting angle of pull may at times be nearly parallel with bottom. This is one of the reasons the usual anchor will hold with a steep scope, but the principal reason is that one of its flukes has to be at a good biting angle no matter what happens."

The boys had been trying to follow the talk about anchors and Jim now spoke up, saying: "Uncle, why do they make stockless anchors anyway?"

Weldon told him that large steamers had used them for years because they could be hauled into the hawser pipes without being fished or handled, but after this afternoon's experience, he told them, "I see no earthly reason why they should be used on small craft."

It was blowing pretty fresh from the southeast by this time so Goddard thought he would return to the *Viator*. Off he went with a quartering sea while those on the *Rozinante* stayed up in the cockpit to see that he boarded safely. Then they went below and, while the boys sprawled out on the bunk, Weldon shook down the stove and opened up the drafts to get the little stove hot for supper.

While they were waiting for the fire to come up Dan asked: "How about that story about the pilot boats that launched off the shore?"

His uncle replied: "I was to tell you that story after supper, but maybe while supper is preparing I can tell you about the place where these famous pilots and seamen came from."

So, after opening a can of corned beef hash and placing the

contents on a sizzling frying pan, flattening it out with a spatula, he went on: "The town of Deal is on the southeast coast of England at a point near where the Straits of Dover join the North Sea. It is half way between what is called the North Foreland and the South Foreland; it is also ten or fifteen miles south of the entrance to the Thames estuary and therefore a favorite place for sailing ships to anchor until a favorable wind and tide will take them up to London. You must understand that between the years 1600 and 1800 there were many more trading ships than after steam came into use. That was because the modern steamer often has one hundred times the carrying capacity of the usual merchant vessel of that time. Whereas today many of the large vessels run to Liverpool or Southampton, in those days most of the traffic was up the Thames. As the shipping of southern Europe and the Mediterranean passed Deal, the anchorage there was often crowded with several hundred vessels of all sizes and nations. The anchorage off Deal was called The Downs, and while it was somewhat sheltered in westerly winds it was a rough and dangerous place at other times and perhaps the scene of as much shipwreck as any place in the world."

Weldon paused to turn over the hash in the pan which he did neatly by cutting it into three slices and turning each one separately. He then continued: "About five miles off the beach at Deal, or the other side of the anchorage in The Downs, was the dreaded Goodwin Sands."

"What are the Goodwin Sands?" inquired Jim.

"In very ancient times this was said to have been a prosperous island owned by an Earl Goodwin, and this seems probable because although much of the Goodwin Sands are dry at low water, still at the border of the sand banks the depth increases rapidly. However, this is one of the most dangerous places off the coast of England because the strong tide running through the Straits of Dover will carry a vessel much off her course, particularly in bad weather, when trying to reach The Downs to exchange a channel pilot for a river pilot. It used to be said in old times that the value of shipping that was lost on Good-win Sands was worth several kings' ransoms, however much that might be."

Weldon paused to lift the slices of hash off onto the paper plates and partly filled the frying pan with water which soon came to a boil, into which he dropped three eggs. The tea kettle at the other end of the stove was chuckling a merry tune, and as he poured the hot water over the tea in the pot the cabin began to have a very interesting smell. Both the boys sat up in pleasant anticipation. Weldon now lit the cabin lamp and if it had not been for the waves rushing and gurgling alongside, the cabin would have been very quiet as the boys watched their uncle lift the eggs out of the pan and carefully place them on the hash. He then poured the tea, and putting a little more brown sugar and milk in little Dan's than in the others they were soon settled down to a good warm supper. For dessert Weldon gave the boys a couple of pieces of sweet chocolate while he lay back in the easy chair and enjoyed his second cup of tea. But little Dan hardly got through munching his chocolate when he said: "I don't see why the Goodwin Sands is so dangerous if it is only soft sand."

"It does seem strange but there is a reason for it. The sands there are of a certain consistency of water and sand that is called quicksand. As soon as a vessel strikes, she is held im-movably in place so as the seas strike her she is soon smashed to pieces. You see, the peculiar type of sand that is there makes a sort of suction under the bottom of the vessel, and even when it is calm it is said a vessel cannot be towed off if she is imbedded in the sand. In rough weather, the seas there are terrific for they suddenly race from deep water into shoal. Moreover, this region is said to never have a slack, dependable tide because the tidal streams of the North Sea and English Channel are meeting there. In a gale of wind, when the barometer may be different in the North Sea from the English Channel, the tide may be very strong and treacherous by flowing as much as five miles an hour."

A Deal galley punt, as drawn by Sir Bevil Warington-Smyth.

Weldon had finished cleaning up around the stove and adjusted the drafts for the night. He had lit his pipe and settled back in the chair and he went on: "I speak about the Goodwin Sands mostly because the Deal boats of one kind or another became very famous on account of the heroic rescues they performed on ships as they were breaking up on the Sands. But I must get back to the town of Deal. In old times there were three small castles there within about two and a half miles. They were named Sandown Castle, Deal Castle, and Wilmer Castle. They had probably been built to defend the coast during some of the wars with France, but the town of Deal, as it developed, stretched along the water front most of the way between these three. It was a straight shingle beach with no cove or harbor, so the boats had to launch off the shore and be hauled way up the beach on their return. This called for boats of remarkably strong but light construction. After several generations of experience, the boat builders of Deal built remarkably fine craft. Perhaps they were the lightest for their strength of any in the world around the year 1800. But even the best boat must be well handled to put off and beach in a combing sea, and the fine class of Englishmen at Deal seemed to make the combination of building and handling their craft that allowed them to perform this miracle. Fine, light, rowing boats had been built on the Thames for several centuries, perhaps by the descendants of some of the Danish invaders who had perfected lapstrake construction for small craft. But while the Thames was some 40 miles northwest of Deal, the French coast was even closer, so the Deal boats in model and sail plan very much resembled the Chasse Marée of the French coast but were of course smaller and much lighter, thanks to their excellent construction."

"What is a Chasse Marée?" inquired Jim.

"A Chasse Marée is a fast type of small lugger that was used much in France for smuggling and they would usually outsail the English revenue cutters of before 1800. The Chasse Marées had two or three masts on which were set lug sails. They had a long running bowsprit which could be run in during heavy weather, and a long boomkin over the stern to sheet the loose-footed mizzen. Some of the early Deal luggers were three masted, but as time went on they all left out the middle or main mast and the smaller craft only had one mast. The Deal boats were all of lapstrake construction, built with very narrow planks made of elm, and a boat as much as forty feet long only had about half-inch planking. They had small frames closely spaced. The frames were natural crooks of English elms that grew in the neighborhood. The keel, which was large and strong, was often of Canadian elm, so you see the Deal boats were mostly built of elm. They also had good sized bilge keels which were necessary for launching off the beach. The bilge keels also helped them to hold on in going to the windward, and no doubt contributed to the remarkable seaworthiness of these craft. The Deal boats were built under cover in good boat shops which were often beside the builder's residence. But I speak of the Deal boats because some of them went to the south coast and became, I believe, the first small English yachts. One of the reasons the Deal builders were so skillful at light work was because they built long, narrow eight-oared rowboats which were used for smuggling. These craft were said to be nearly as fast as the University outriggers on the Thames, and it must have been some risky work to cross Dover Strait in them with a load of contraband. However, in light weather they could outfoot anything else at the time and, with their light draft often crossed parts of the Goodwin Sands and so eluded all pursuit. So you see the Deal watermen, besides being famous pilots and life boat men, were at one time skillful smugglers. In fact, they eluded the customs officials so successfully that in 1784 the War Office sent a regiment of soldiers there who burned many of the Deal boats on the beach. But the Deal watermen could also be useful to the government, for in 1799 they embarked an army of five thousand troops to transports anchored in the Downs. This was done in one day without accident, although the wind was on shore and accompanied by considerable surf. The boats were loaded with soldiers at the top of the beach and launched out through the surf as I will describe to you later. This embarkation compares favorably with any modern amphibian operation although performed at slight cost. It does, moreover, demonstrate the skill of the Deal boatmen, and W. Clark Russell, the nautical writer of around 1850, says of that time, 'The men of Deal had become the best boat builders and boat sailors in the world.'

"The three principal types of craft launched off the beach at Deal in the old days were the Deal luggers, which were high-sided, burdensome craft about 40 feet long, with a beam of about 12 feet. They had a sunken deck forward under which was a small cuddy with stove. These craft were locally called 'hovelers' which is an old English name for coastguardsmen. They were used to take supplies out to the ships anchored in the Downs, and often took out heavy anchors and cables to ships in distress. Their principal income was from salvage work. When not thus employed they were dragging for anchors and cables in the Downs, and wrecking on the Goodwin Sands. They were quite heavily ballasted, but it is presumed they removed some of the ballast when taking out a large anchor or heavy chain cable. These 'hovelers' were very profitable between 1800 and 1850 and a share in one was a very desirable piece of property to have. But, after the steamers and the improved windlass came into use, the Downs were less used for embarking passengers and the mails and they gradually went out of existence. However these Deal luggers were the craft which are so often mentioned by the writers of novels and romance between 1800 and 1850. Captain Marryat's *Poor Jack* is the life story of a Deal pilot. You see, boys, there were no life boats stationed along the coast in those days, and few aids to navigation such as lighthouses, buoys or beacons. So, in the dangerous region of the Goodwin Sands these luggers became very famous for saving the lives of thousands of people from wrecked or stranded vessels.

"The next important type of boat launched off the beach at Deal was the so-called galley punt. These were enlarged row boats which had one mast with a lug sail. They were entirely open and they were the craft used by pilots, as they could be brought alongside a vessel under way for embarking or disembarking. The galley punts were between 21 and 30 feet long, and 7 feet beam. They, too, carried ballast which enabled them to use a good size lug sail, and they were all-around fast boats with varnished topsides. Perhaps one of the reasons the Deal boats were all fast was because they were kept out of water when not in use."

Jim here interrupted and asked his uncle what a lug sail was.

"The lug sail was the first step in the evolution of the square sail to a fore-and-aft sail. The square sail on either tack carries the wind on the same side, its afterside, but the lug sail, as it is tacked, carries the wind on one side and then the other. There are several types of lug sails which are set or carried in different ways, but the Deal boats used the simplest rig of all. It was a rather square-headed sail, that is, the yard was not peaked up much. These sails were lowered away at every tack and hoisted again with the yard and sail to leeward on the new course. These boats did not have shrouds, but instead the halyard was taken to the weather rail. If they were close hauled, the halyard was carried a bit forward, and in running or reaching it was taken aft. It is said the Deal boats could lower away and hoist so quickly that they did not lose steerage way in tacking. This simple rig was the best for launching off the beach, for there were no shrouds in the way and the sail, if handled right, could be very quickly set. However, this type of lug sail might be compared to the violin inasmuch as it is capable of miracles when in the right hands but it is very difficult to learn how to use it, so it is not often seen today.

"The third type of famous Deal craft was the galley which was a long, narrow, light, rowing cutter using eight oars, and although this type had been developed before 1800 there were still some of them left up until about 1900, but were then only used for rowing regattas. I do not know the dimensions of these craft but imagine they were from 40 to 50 feet long with 5 feet beam. I speak to you boys about these craft because I believe the Deal boat builders and watermen had a great deal to do with the development of the light boat, the oar and the oarlock as we know them today."

As Weldon paused, little Dan asked: "Uncle, when are you going to tell us about launching off the beach?"

"Oh, yes, I forgot about that," said Weldon. "Well, the Deal boats were kept hauled out on the rather steep beach with their bows toward the sea, all ready for an instant launching night or day. They rested on greased skids, but the shingle beach being composed of round, smooth pebbles, the boats would slide well if they ran off the skids. The boats were held up on the beach by a short length of chain, fastened to their deadwood near the rudder. The chain ran to a trip hook or pelican hook. When all was ready and the crew aboard at their stations, mizzen set and rudder triced up, someone on shore tripped the hook and the boat slid down the beach. Although they went slow at first, it is probable that a speed of 10 or 15 miles an hour was gained as they struck the water, and this carried them out through the first few lines of breakers, when sail and the oars took them into deep water. If there happened to be an on-shore wind and sea, they used a rope called an outhaul that was attached to an anchor a little distance off shore. The outhaul ran through a snatch block forward, and after the launching boat had struck the water all hands hauled on the outhaul until they were clear of the undertow on shore. Then the outhaul was cast out of the snatch block and let go.

"The Deal boats landed or beached in the roughest kind of weather and this called for even more skill than the launchings. But their method of beaching can only be done where there are a number of men on shore to help. In moderate weather and a side wind they sometimes sailed right up on the beach, when the man in the bow would throw a long, strong painter to the waiting men who soon tailed out and hauled the boat beyond danger, and then a line from a capstan was secured to the boat and she was hauled to her place on the skids and turned around with her bow facing the sea again. In rough weather, they landed under oars but waited close to shore until what is called a 'smooth' occurred."

"What is a 'smooth'?" inquired Jim.

"Occasionally when large waves are breaking, two of them will get together and form what is called a master sea. After this, there is a momentary lull which is called a smooth and that was the moment when they pulled for shore as fast as they could. It took great skill on the part of the coxswain or helmsman to time the landing just right. In rough weather they generally came in with the mast stepped. If the boat was swung side to the beach by the waves, a man would jump out with a halyard and run up the beach. Then with the help of others he could hold the boat heeled toward the beach so the next wave only drove her higher up, whereas if she had been allowed to heel outward the next wave would have swamped her and she would soon be pounded to pieces on the beach. Also, in rough weather men from shore ran out in the surf with ropes that had large hooks on the end and, after these were fastened over the breast-hook in the bow, a great many men could tail out to haul them up the beach."

"Were there always men ready to help?" inquired Jim.

"Oh, yes," his uncle replied, "there were said to be about 800 watermen on the beach at Deal in the 1850s, and each person who helped in hauling up a boat got a fixed sum for his services. In those days, there were about fourteen stations or capstan grounds where the boats of Deal were launched."

"What is a capstan ground?" asked Dan.

"The most suitable places along the beach for launching and hauling were called capstan grounds because each boat of any consequence had its capstan with a little shanty beside it where the spare gear of the lugger was kept. These capstan grounds were at uneven intervals for about two miles along the beach. The capstans were large affairs with eight or so wooden capstan bars about 14 feet long. With two or more men on a bar, they must have had considerable power."

"How was the hauling rope attached to the boats?" asked Jim.

"There was a hole in the keel," Weldon told him, "under the forefoot and a large shackle was attached there. In this country our Block Island boats used the same arrangement, for in the old days there were no breakwaters or harbors at Block Island and the boats were beached every night except in nice summer weather. The Block Island boats were hauled out with oxen instead of using a capstan, and I believe were never launched excepting in good weather.

"But to get back to the town of Deal. The waterfront there was very picturesque, for at the central part of the town there were several watch towers and signal masts which kept up communication with the anchored fleet that was spread out over several square miles. Deal was connected to London with a line of semaphore signals, and each ship as she arrived at the Downs was reported to her owners who often sent back orders for the captain."

"What is a semaphore line?" inquired Dan.

"Before the electric telegraph was invented, several places in Europe and England had semaphore lines for quick communication. They consisted of large upright posts with swinging arms, and where the land was level these could be some distance apart. The railroads still use them to some extent as signals, as a semaphore is a reliable way to transmit messages to the engineer of a moving train.

"But as I was saying, the waterfront of Deal was a scene of much activity in bad weather for there might be several ships dragging and signaling for anchors or cables."

"How could such small boats take out ship's anchors?" inquired Jim.

"Back of the town was a field where anchors and cables of most all sizes were kept, so if one of the luggers got an order to deliver an anchor of a certain weight one would be selected and slung under the axle of a very large pair of wheels that horses drew down to the capstan ground. After the anchor and cable had been hoisted aboard the lugger, she launched in the way I have described to you. When the lugger was some distance to windward of the ship that was dragging, they let the anchor fall and then paid out cable enough to let them come back to close under the ship's bow. There, by passing a heaving line aboard, the bitter end of the cable was hauled aboard the ship. The lugger then made her escape as best she could. This was rough, hard work and called for the highest kind of seamanship, but the luggers often received considerable salvage pay when a valuable ship was saved. The waterfront at Deal was so interesting under these conditions that several artists of the time either painted or drew it, and among others was J. M. W. Turner.

"After about 1860, the town of Deal had hard times, for the steamer was taking the place of the sailing vessel and few vessels were detained in the Downs waiting a change of wind and tide. The sidewheel steam tugs from the Thames also came way down to the Goodwin Sands and picked up sailing ships. The chain cable with improved windlasses had taken the place of the hemp cable and wooden windlass. At this time hundreds of Deal watermen were hard up, and, to relieve this condition, free passage to New Zealand and Australia were offered to them and their families. It was important in these regions to have good boatmen before the wharves were built there, and it is interesting to note that the last of the Deal luggers were built to be taken to these colonies. Some people say the reason the New Zealanders and Australians are so fond of yachting and sailing is that many of them are descended from the watermen from Deal who were the most skillful in the world."

5

Ashore on Nantucket / The Tranquilo
On Leeboards / The Boeier Hawk

It was six-thirty next afternoon when the *Rozinante* came to anchor under Brant Point, a little northeast of the town on Nantucket, and as the western sky turned to rosy pink the white houses of the town told in the shadows of the afternoon sun. It has often been said that contrast or variety is the spice of life, and after the buffeting the *Rozinante* had had in rounding Cape Cod and crossing Nantucket Sound in a northwester, the quietness of laying at anchor with only ripples alongside was most welcome.

As soon as the sails were furled, Weldon took out the slate and, half thinking aloud, said: "We sailed 73 miles in a little less than 13 hours." After a little figuring, he told the boys that they had averaged about five and one-half miles an hour which was remarkably good speed for such a small boat over a long course.

As he looked up at the boys he could see they were both sun-drunk and dizzy from the continuous quick motion of the sail in choppy water. He knew the best cure for that was a light supper and rest, so he went below and heated a couple of cans of chicken soup.

On the other burner of the Sterno stove he heated some water lukewarm, and getting some absorbent cotton had the boys carefully rinse the salt off their faces and other places that were sunburned. He told the boys that on a small boat, where the spray was flying most of the day, the skin can get caked with salt. This will produce a bad sunburn that washing in cold water would aggravate but warm water, carefully applied, would remove most of the sting. At first, the boys thought the warm water was painful, but as they got used to it a pleasant throbbing sensation followed. After they had applied some sunburn lotion they were surprised how much easier it was to open and close their eyes.

The boys were too tired to have a good appetite and after taking the warm soup they were ready for bed. In fact, little Dan almost fell asleep before he was undressed and had to be helped by his brother; and both boys were sound asleep as soon as they lay down. Weldon himself was pretty tired after being at the helm for the better part of 13 hours. As he sat in the cockpit enjoying his last pipeful, the setting sun had changed the whole western horizon to coppery red while the nearby sky seemed of a transparent cold green that overhead changed to robin's egg blue. The town to the south was silhouetted in darker shades while the church steeple reflected the last light of the setting sun. The colors were like a winter sunset but the warm, balmy air from Nantucket Island gave that feeling of well-being so noticeable in a summer evening south of the Cape.

It was nearly calm now and the sounds from the shore seemed like distant echoes while the restful chortle of the tender astern mingled with the sounds of the evening. These scenes and sounds are not noticed by one who goes for a few hours' sail only to return to the same harbor, nor do they impress the sailor who returns from a cruise on a larger vessel. But to one who has been buffeted by the waves all day in a small boat, the harbor sensations at nightfall are truly enchanting.

The stars were appearing one by one as the heavens darkened, and as Weldon looked toward the harbor mouth he saw a distant gray object which, as it neared, seemed like a silently moving ghost. As it rounded Brant Point Light and stood toward him, its red and green lights were shown and Weldon could recognize the *Viator* coming up the harbor under power as her sails reflected the gray and white of the starlight. Soon the splash of the anchor was heard, and after the whiz and rattle of her descending sails had died down, the ghostlike apparition changed to a merry thing with lighted cabin, and the cheery voices of the girls came across the water. Although the *Viator* had anchored within hailing distance, Goddard did not call over because he saw the *Rozinante's* cabin lights were not lit and rightly guessed that they had gone to sleep early after the long run.

It is a great satisfaction to know that your running mate has made port safely, so Weldon turned in beside the boys in a very pleasant mood. He was enjoying that agreeable sensation of healthy sleepiness that comes from a long sail. It is not recorded whether anyone snored on the *Rozinante* that night, but as the stars twinkled overhead in the dying northwester the time passed rapidly and in what seemed a matter of minutes the sun was pouring in through the companionway. Weldon turned over to face away from the sun and said to himself: "I'll take another snooze for a few minutes," but he was surprised when aroused by Goddard's cheery voice alongside calling "Ahoy aboard the *Rozinante!* Isn't it time for you to get up? I've been up two hours and had my breakfast." Weldon was still in his pajamas but he quickly stepped out in the cockpit and invited his friend aboard to watch him make breakfast for the boys.

As Goddard was climbing aboard, Weldon shook the boys and told them that if they could do it, a swim before breakfast would be good for them for they were now in water warm enough for a pleasant morning dip.

The boys were soon in their trunks and they dived off the stern while Weldon lowered a bight of the anchor warp over the side near the mizzen shrouds for them to climb up on. The boys had never been swimming south of the Cape before, or had an early morning dip, so they were delighted with the warm water and played around the two dinghies astern before coming aboard.

In the meantime, Weldon put the boys' clothes out on the cockpit seats in the warm sunlight, together with two large towels. He said to Goddard: "One of the advantages of our deep cockpit is

that swimmers can rub down and dress out there without bringing any salt or water into the cabin." Weldon told the boys to
towel every bit of water and salt off of themselves but to be careful in the places that were sunburned. After a good rubdown the
boys were pink all over and suddenly became conscious of the
smell of bacon and eggs that was coming from the cabin.

Weldon asked Goddard: "Are you sure you can't take a cup of
tea with me?" When Goddard refused, he gave the boys some
slices of orange and told them that they were to eat out in the
cockpit and brush their hair after breakfast.

Goddard watched little Dan as he held his orange up to his
mouth with his shivering pink fingers, and remarked to Weldon:
"I can plainly see that Dan is at the right age to get the most out
of cruising."

"Yes, I think so," replied Weldon, but when they asked Dan
what he thought he only replied by nodding his head for he didn't
want to remove the orange from his mouth for an instant. After
the bacon and eggs were dispatched and Weldon sat back in the
morning sunlight sipping his tea he said: "It took us about twelve
hours and fifty minutes to sail from Wood End off Provincetown
to the breakwater here and I would like to hear how you on the
Viator fared."

Goddard answered, with rather a sheepish look: "It took us
almost two hours longer to make the run than it did you, but on
the way down I measured off the two courses roughly and I think
that it is over three miles longer going through the Canal than
around the Cape. While that would only absorb about half an
hour, we lost time in other ways. In the first place, we had a slow,
wet beat from Provincetown to the Canal; as you know the wind
was shifting from southwest to west at that time so it was almost
dead ahead. We went across under jib, mizzen and motor. Mrs.
Goddard and the girls stayed below most of the time, for we
pitched heavily and threw a lot of spray. In fact, soon after leaving Long Point it was so rough that I slowed the motor for a
while. But as we approached the Canal and the sun came out, all
hands were much revived and we had a belated breakfast while

running the canal under power with all sail down. It was blowing pretty hard in Buzzards Bay and we made the run to Woods Hole under jib and mizzen. As the wind was northwest by then, we made good time. When we got to the Hole there was a fair tide and as I did not want to run through with a fair wind and fair tide we stood back and forth in front of the opening to wait for the tide to slack up. You know, it can be rough off there in a northwester."

The boys had been listening to Goddard with much interest and Jim asked him why he disliked a fair tide in going through Woods Hole.

"With a fair tide, Jim, and a fair wind you are rushed through a channel without an opportunity to slow down if you feel uncertain of your position, but with a head tide you can stop or move sideways without advancing. If I were accustomed to Woods Hole and knew all the shore ranges, the fair tide and fair wind would be as desirable there as anywhere else; but as it is I prefer a slack or light head tide in passing through. While the channel had been widened of late years, still the velocity of the tide seems as great as ever. Another thing about a head tide is that it gives good steerage way or control with the vessel stopped, but if you stop or back up with a fair tide you may lose steerage control altogether and be carried sideways toward dangers.

"Well, we went through the Hole under power with all sails down and it seemed very tame with a light head tide and all the buoys standing up straight. When we were off Nobska Light, we came up in the wind and put all sail on her, but from there on the wind was almost dead astern and although it was blowing a good breeze it was a mighty pleasant sail. As you know, there is just navigation enough between the shoals to keep the run interesting, and on a clear day like yesterday there are few prettier places to sail than the Vineyard and Nantucket Sounds.

"By 6:30 the wind began to go down, and it was nearly calm when we got to the breakwater, so altogether we did pretty well and must have at times gone through the water as fast as you did."

"I have no doubt of it," replied Weldon, and asked what his plans were for the day.

"Mrs. Goddard and the girls are going to spend the day ashore sightseeing and looking at gardens," he said. "They are busy now prinking up to go ashore."

"Can you take them all in the dinghy at once?" inquired Weldon.

"Yes, I can, but they may get splashed with spray if a power boat passes us."

"Well, I'll tell you what I will do if you approve," responded Weldon. "I will put the boys ashore on the beach here and let them walk to town, then I will row the girls up to town in the *Sancho* with you and Mrs. Goddard alongside in your dinghy, for I know a place where we can haul the dinghies onto a float. You see, I have to do some shopping so we might just as well all go to town together."

It was one of those calm, perfectly clear days that follow a northwester, and had every indication that it would be a scorcher, for it can be hot at Nantucket at times even if it always cools off at night.

After Weldon had landed the boys on the beach, he told them: "When you get down to town you will come to a rather wide street that is paved with cobblestones and has a row of nice looking houses on both sides. If you wait for us at the end of the street that is nearest the water we will soon be along."

The men then rowed both tenders alongside the *Viator* and soon after Mrs. Goddard and the girls came on deck. They looked very fresh and neat and no one would have thought they were cruising on a small sail boat. Weldon was proud to row such pretty girls ashore, and careful to get them there without a drop of spray. Soon after landing, they met the boys and all walked up Main Street together but, as Weldon and the boys were not very well dressed, they kept a few paces in the rear.

The girls, however, attracted quite a little attention and Weldon heard one old timer say to another: "That looks like old times!" for the natives were becoming a little fed up with the throngs of vacationing women whose desire to look risqué had taken the place of wholesome feminine beauty. Those who admired them would have been amazed if told that Mrs. Goddard and the girls had just landed from a small sail boat and that the girls had slept several nights on top of those apparently freshly starched dresses.

Weldon told them that if they walked a short distance to the south they could get an unusual view of the church on the hill. As seen up a narrow lane called Cat Alley, the church and foreground are very charming. Mrs. Goddard and the girls were to have lunch on shore and then take a drive around parts of the island. They might even visit Sankaty Head where the view toward Spain is interrupted only by the combers on Nantucket Shoals and where the invigorating air is fresh from the Gulf Stream.

So the men and boys were on their own and felt nearly as fancy-free as any sailors on shore. However, there was much shopping to be done, as their several days' cruise had depleted their larders. After the purchases were made, Goddard said: "Phew! things are no cheaper here than north of the Cape." For, although Goddard had spent about $30, the whole lot weighed less than 40 pounds. They had their groceries put in separate cartons marked with the names of the yachts to be delivered to the steward of the yacht club.

In the meantime, they had spotted a restaurant and said to each other: "Now that we are foot-loose and fancy-free what do you say if we have a regular dinner?" So they ordered steaks smothered in onions. It was quite a hot day and, although both men took no dessert, the boys each had large slices of huckleberry pie, so all hands felt well fed as they sauntered down to the yacht club. It was a relief to be afloat again after the heat on shore. As they rowed back with a boy on the after seat of each tender, and the bows piled high with groceries, the men were in a very happy mood, so Weldon suggested that they take a row around the harbor after stowing away their purchases.

This seemed to meet with the great approval of both Goddard and the boys. The reason for their enthusiasm for the row was that all understood it would be principally devoted to looking over the yachts and boats in the harbor. A row boat is the best possible way to do this as one can stop, back up, or turn around to examine the craft from any desired angle, while all the time he is comfortably seated and thus at an advantage over the pedestrian sightseer.

They took a circuitous course to avoid some anchored wide-sterned power craft that were draped with chromium plating and inhabited by strange beings of unnautical aspect. Little Dan who was with his uncle in the *Sancho Panza* asked: "Why do you and Mr. Goddard hate power boats so much?"

His uncle answered calmly: "We don't hate *all* power boats, Dan. It is only those modern freaks that look like the result of a collision between an automobile and a dining car, with the whole mess superimposed on a float stage. The motor boat designers have to design craft down to the taste of foolish and uncouth individuals. I suppose it will be impossible to educate them beyond red-stained wood and chromium plating. It's a shame that they are not compelled to anchor away from the yacht club for they spoil the looks of the waterfront."

Most of this talk went over the head of little Dan, but it allowed Weldon to get rid of some spleen. By this time, Goddard was headed for a long, lean sailboat that was in the southern part of the harbor, and when Weldon came alongside he asked, "What is she, one of the old P boats?"

"No," replied Weldon, "she is one of the Larchmont O boats that were designed by William Gardner and built by Wood of City Island, just before World War I."

"Why do they call them Larchmont O boats?" inquired Jim.

His uncle told him: "They were a one-design class built by members of the Larchmont Yacht Club. Six of them were built and they cost $12,000 apiece, which certainly seems remarkable today, for they were built of the best materials and now, when about thirty-six years old, look in very good shape."

The yacht's name was the *Celeritus* and as no one was aboard they rowed close up to her. Weldon remarked: "Her planking looks almost like new." The boys were much interested in this long, rakish craft and their uncle said to them: "You see, boys, what a difference there is in the looks of yachts. This craft was designed by a real artist and is a good example of the saying that 'a thing of beauty is a joy forever,' but I am sorry to say there are few, if any, men alive today who can design good looking yachts."

"She may be good looking," remarked Goddard, "but I shouldn't think she would have much room below deck, and would be wet with such low freeboard."

Weldon answered: "You would be surprised how much room below deck some of these old Universal Rule boats had. If I remember right, these O boats had four berths aft and three in the forecastle. As for the wetness, these boats with long, fine bows throw little spray and, as they heel, the windward side becomes high enough. A yacht like these O boats can run along at some nine knots in a strong beam wind and sea and be very comfortable. But a power boat, like the abominations we have just passed, would have to slow down to eight knots and be most uncomfortable, if not unsafe."

It had been rather hot rowing around in the bright sunlight, but the afternoon southwest breeze was springing up and the southerly part of the harbor was ruffled with the dark fingers of its first zephyrs. Soon they could feel the warm fragrant wind which had passed over the varied shrubbery of the island and absorbed the peculiar spicy odor that is noticeable there on hot days.

While the two men were still enjoying the beautiful curves of the O boat, Jim, who was facing the other way, cried: "Oh, look! There is a yacht with lee boards."

"So it is," replied Goddard, "and that ought to be something worth looking at."

As they approached this yacht they saw her name was *Tranquilo* and aboard there was a middle aged man sitting in the cockpit under an awning. After they had rowed around the *Tranquilo* and the dinghies had approached each other so the men could carry on a quiet conversation, the man in the cockpit turned his head toward them and said: "You seem interested in my craft. I should be happy to have you come aboard if you care to."

Weldon and Goddard were a little surprised, but Weldon an-

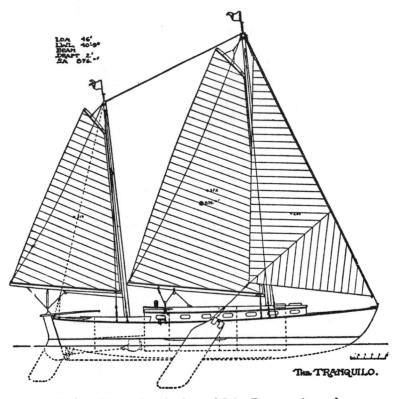

The profile and sail plan of Mr. Brewster's yacht.

swered him: "I would like to very much, for I am very much interested."

Weldon and Dan boarded first and the owner of the *Tranquilo* introduced himself. "My name is Brewster," he said, so when the others boarded Weldon could make the introductions all around. He told their host: "We are cruising on the two small ketches anchored down near the lighthouse."

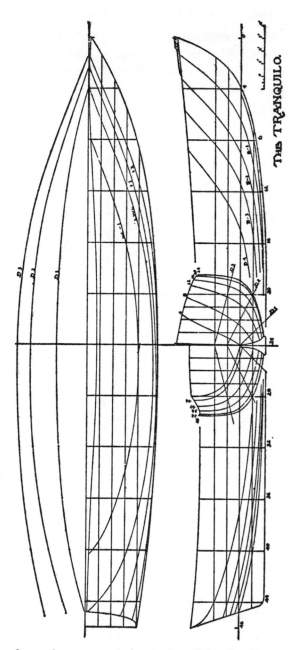

The lines drawings of the leeboard ketch, *Tranquilo.*

"I had rather supposed so," answered Brewster, "for if I had thought you were some of the cowboys who mount the flying bridges of yonder red motor cruisers, I never would have invited you aboard. But I might have known that such characters would not get into a small boat until an outboard noise-maker had been attached to the stern. I am delighted to meet two sailors who can bring a tender alongside properly under oars."

There was a little pause in the conversation, for this compliment not only pleased Goddard and Weldon but it let them know they were talking to a man who knew the niceties of seamanship. Weldon then asked: "Sir, what is the draft of the *Tranquilo* and what is the meaning of the name?"

Brewster answered, "The two things are more or less connected, for the name *Tranquilo* is a Spanish name which means quiet, or the equivalent to our word tranquil. Her draft is exactly two feet and she, thanks to her lee boards, can lay on bottom so that if the usual anchorages are crowded or noisy we can lay where none of the noise makers can come very close. We also can sail over vast regions where nature is pretty much undisturbed, and if it were not for the outboard motor boats we should be perfectly tranquil most of the time. So perhaps now you can understand why we dislike those outboard noise-makers so much."

The *Tranquilo* had a very comfortable cockpit which was large enough to accommodate two or three very comfortably in folding chairs. To sit quietly under an awning is very restful after being out in the sun on a hot day. Brewster then remarked: "This is the kind of an afternoon when I like to sip a cool glass of lime juice, but if you gentlemen prefer something else, perhaps it could be found." He then turned to the boys and asked: "How would you like some lime juice, sugar and water?" They all thought the lime juice sounded very refreshing, so Brewster called for five glasses with ice in them. His captain soon appeared with a tray and all the necessities, for the captain had been with Brewster several years and could tell 99 times out of 100 what he wanted in different temperatures or at different times of the day.

The afternoon breeze had carried away the sand flies; and now it gently flapped the leech of the awning as they sat with sweating glasses in hand. Weldon raised his glass and said: "Here's to being aboard!" and after they had all crooked their elbows, little Dan laid his glass down disgustedly without more than tasting it, which made everyone smile.

Mr. Brewster said: "Perhaps, young man, I put too much lime juice in your drink. If you pour some of it down the cockpit scupper I will put more sugar and water in your glass." After that was done Dan liked his drink as well as the others.

The conversation now became less restrained, and Mr. Goddard inquired about the general dimensions of the *Tranquilo* and who had designed her. Brewster informed him; "She is 46 feet on deck; 40 feet 6 inches on the waterline, and 11 feet beam. As the captain says, she can go most anyplace there is a heavy dew, but with our lee boards down she takes a whole fathom of water. She was designed by old William Taffrail Garboard-Strake himself, who, as you know, can produce something a little out of the ordinary, for he does not belong to that fraternity whose members copy one another and are only in business for the almighty dollar."

"Well, he seems to have pleased you, sir," said Weldon.

"Yes, he did," agreed Brewster, "for the *Tranquilo* has more room for the dollar than most any yacht I ever saw. She is comparatively fast and a good sea boat, but best of all I like to lay on bottom whenever I want to and she can do that almost as well as the Dutch boats. You see, I have taken her south several winters and shallow draft more than doubles the cruising area there, particularly in Albemarle Sound where there is still good shooting."

"Aren't you afraid of scraping off the paint and letting in worms when you ground in the south?" inquired Goddard. Brewster answered: "No, not at all, for two good reasons. First, the *Tranquilo* is sheathed with rather heavy copper and has some hard-rolled phosphor bronze sheets in places where she is apt to bear on bottom. The second reason is that it is easy to run up in some creek or river every few days where there is fresh water which kills the worms. After all, it is the centerboard boat that the worms attack most often, for where the centerboard rubs the paint off the center-board box is an ideal place for them to enter. Yes, the shallow draft has many advantages."

Weldon then asked if the *Tranquilo* carried sail well with such shallow draft, and if she were not hard to handle with the lee-boards up. Brewster replied: "As far as the sail carrying is concerned, all I can say is that I never have had to reef her yet and have never been knocked over more than 30 or 40 degrees. She usually sails with much less heel than other sail boats. You see, her model is quite similar to some of the good sailing dinghies before the sailing dinghy was spoiled by length-measurement rules and had to adopt the plumb bow and stern. You know, a good sailing dinghy is quite able if there are a few sandbags secured on her bottom so they can't shift. Well, the *Tranquilo's* very heavy bottom, and the slab of lead which is outside, seem to make her self-righting and unusually stiff. In fact, she could have had more sail area, but it would have only been a nuisance where we depend on power in light weather. As for her handling qualities, all I can say is that you have to get used to her. Of course, the only way we can go to windward in shallow water is with the engines. Also, even under bare poles, she is apt to slide off on you if there is a side wind but, usually, lowering the lee boards a little makes her mind the helm well. Twin screws help maneuvering at slow speed. Although the *Tranquilo* has ample power, her engines are very compact. They are a pair of Universal Unimite Fours."

"Why did you select those motors?" inquired Weldon.

"Principally because they were compact, economical and quiet running. Although the engines are very small they give around 50 horsepower apiece at 2500 revolutions a minute, and with a reduciton gear of about two to one the propellers are about the right size for this type of boat. Of course, the engines are not often run over 1400 revolutions a minute, when the two of them together develop some 50 horsepower. It is nice to have the extra power sometimes in maneuvering for a breeze."

"How fast will she go with both engines wide open?" queried Weldon.

"I don't mean to give you a short answer, but I don't know and I don't care what her maximum speed is, for I prefer the convenient navigating speeds and the *Tranquilo* will do six miles per hour at 1200 revolutions per minute. I suppose with the engines opened up she will go up to nine or more miles per hour."

"What do you mean by convenient navigating speeds, sir?" inquired Goddard.

"Why I mean six and 12 miles an hour, or the speeds which take even minutes to run the various miles," answered Brewster. "For instance, at six miles per hour it takes one minute to run each tenth of a mile and ten minutes to run each mile. At 12 miles per hour, naturally, it is one-half that time, or five minutes per mile. Of course, three miles per hour is also a convenient speed when it takes 20 minutes a mile, but that is too slow and as we can't make 12 miles per hour, why, we generally run at six when we can usually estimate the speed of the *Tranquilo* by the revolutions per minute of the engines if the wind is light. But when the sails are helping, we slow the engine so she brings the crest of her bow wave somewhere abreast the after side of the deck house. I must note that there are very useful tables in the last part of *The Yachtsman's Guide* that give the time and distances for other speeds. One of these tables is called 'Distance Run in Given Time at Various Speeds.' The other table is called 'Time Required for Given Distances at Various Speeds.' Brewster then reached in the after hatch where there was a handy shelf for binoculars and other navigating equipment, took out *The Yachtsman's Guide* and explained: "You see, I have an index tag pasted to these pages so I can refer to them at once, for I think this is one of the best parts of that good little book."

While the men were talking in the cockpit, the boys had wandered up forward to look things over. They were quiet at first, but finally little Dan called aft: "Gee, uncle, she has short gaffs like the *Rozinante*."

Mr. Brewster spoke up: "You bet she has short gaffs, and they are one of the best things on the boat." He then turned to Weldon and said, "I noticed when you came in yesterday afternoon that you had a similar rig."

"Yes," replied Weldon, "and I think many cruisers will adopt this rig in the next few years for not only is a quadrilateral sail easier to cut but, as Captain Fritz Fenger says, 'Why go so high?' "

"Do you think Fenger is much of an authority on such matters?" inquired Goddard, to which Weldon replied: "I think if actual experience is any qualification, he should be one of the greatest authorities we have."

Brewster remarked, "Yes, perhaps he has cruised in as great a variety of craft as anyone, and certainly he said something when he asked, 'Why go so high?' "

After this, the men began looking at the *Tranquilo's* rig. Goddard remarked, in an inquiring way: "I see you have no backstays and I suppose you can't have standing backstays with a gaff."

Brewster answered: "The *Tranquilo* seems to get along without backstays most of the time, but there are some on the mizzen that can be set up when required, although we generally carry them, as you see, stopped up to the mizzen shrouds. We only use them in strong wind and sea and, as they are on the mizzen which is generally sheeted quite flat, it does not matter much if they are not tended at once in tacking ship."

Goddard then inquired why it should be that the *Tranquilo* did not need backstays most of the time?

"The *Tranquilo's* masts, as you see, are quite large at the deck in their fore-and-aft dimension. The masts were stepped with considerable more rake than they now have but the heads were sprung forward about eighteen inches before the forestay was shackled in. You know, most of our older American sail boats, and this includes the Gloucester fishing schooners, got along without backstays by springing the masts forward and that is what we do. But the mizzen backstays are always ready to use as preventers if the mastheads jump in a seaway." After a pause, and sipping his lime juice, Brewster continued: "You see, the reason we did not want backstays to tend was because we have a rather large jib to sheet on tacking, and, what with the lee boards, the *Tranquilo* is not what you might call a single-hander. Nevertheless, she can be handled by one man under power or under the mainsail alone. The lee boards, however, are not as much bother as you might suppose. In short tacking, like sailing up a harbor, we leave them both down. It is only on long hitches that the weather board is raised. Our jib sheets are rigged with a jig, but the captain is so expert at hauling in the main part at the right moment that we seldom use it. While winches of various types may be necessary or best on a racing yacht, the old fashioned jig is best for a cruiser. It is the cheapest and neatest, and when rigged with a nylon tackle does not twist up much."

"Well, I should have thought a self-tending jib would have been more convenient," said Goddard.

"It certainly would be in tacking," agreed Brewster, "but on carefully considering the matter we thought the loose-footed jib had important advantages. For instance, it can lap by the mast so it has the most area. It can be backed to windward if the yacht gets caught in stays. It is easily removed for stowing below deck. It leaves a freer foredeck in working around the anchor, for the bunt of a loose-footed jib can always be pushed to one side, while the jib on a boom or club hanging in lazyjacks is always in the way up forward."

After a pause, Goddard said he thought the *Tranquilo* had very much of a Dutch look with her short gaffs and lee boards. "Yes, I think so," replied Brewster, who was becoming very talkative. After clearing his throat he continued: "I had thought very seriously of importing a Dutch yacht, for I was determined to have a shallow craft that could lay on bottom, which none of our centerboarders can do satisfactorily, and I did not want a centerboard case that spoiled the best part of the cabin. Besides a centerboard box or case always leaks, more or less."

"You certainly sound as if you did not like centerboards," interrupted Weldon.

"That is right, young man," replied Brewster, "and I will tell you in more detail just why. I think there are six good reasons and, although I have mentioned some before, we will review them now. One; in laying on bottom the slot invariably gets jammed with sand, gravel and shells and not infrequently gets damaged. I suppose this is the reason the centerboard never was popular in England. You see, most of their small yachts take the bottom at low tide, or, as they call it, 'lie on the hard,' for the rise and fall of the tide is so great there that many of their sheltered harbors almost dry up at neap tide. Two; the centerboard case is difficult to paint on the inside, so it makes a favorable entrance for worms, and while I know that in the south they pour crankcase oil, kerosene, etc., into the box to keep out the worms, and try to anchor in fresh water; still, these things are a nuisance to keep on your mind. Three; leaking. No matter how heavy and strong a centerboard case is built, the shrinking and swelling of the boards at the side of the case cause leaks at the forward and after ends of the box. You see, the grain of the wood in the risers or end pieces is up and down and so cannot swell and shrink with the side pieces. Although there are several methods of mortising the end pieces into the keel and fastening them to the centerboard logs, the case invariably leaks some and generally is most difficult to recalk. Four; as for spoiling the space in the cabin—on what is called a bulb keel centerboarder, or a boat which has some outside keel, the centerboard case can be mostly below the floor or cabin sole, but on a very shallow boat like the *Tranquilo* the centerboard box would come up nearly on a level with the sheerstrakes unless the case were made unusually long. The long centerboard slot, however, has disadvantages which I will speak of later. While it is true that on a much larger yacht than this you can have a fore-and-aft partition at the case or box, no matter what you do a centerboard will spoil the cabin of a yacht of this size and draft. My fifth objection is cost. On a yacht of about this size the centerboarder will cost at least $1000 more than the keel boat. The sixth and last, but not the least, objection is that the centerboard slot very much weakens a boat. You see, the floor timbers cannot be carried across from side to side, so the very part of the vessel that takes bottom is weakened, and that is why a long centerboard slot is bad."

Weldon here broke in to inquire: "What happens when a centerboard boat grounds?"

"At first," replied Brewster, "only sand, mud, gravel and shells are forced up between the board and the slot, but as the vessel begins to bear hard on the bottom the slot closes against the board and inbeds the sand and shells either in the board itself or in the slot, or both."

"Why does the slot close?" asked Weldon.

"On a flat-bottomed boat like a Connecticut sharpie it doesn't close. But on a round-bottomed boat when you press upwards in the region of the slot, the slot will surely try to close. Yes, the boat or yacht with a long centerboard case is a continual nuisance, for it has to be blocked up right in the winter and even then, at times, there is trouble with the calking of the garboard seam abreast the box. If you calk hard, you will start the fastenings, or split something, for where the floor timbers are not continuous from side to side nothing but a wide keel can stand this strain. If you don't calk hard, when the boat goes afloat or is waterborne, she will leak here because the keel is no longer pressing upward. I have seen some older boats that were a perfect mess around the centerboard logs, what with repeated calkings and repairs."

Goddard then remarked: "I have heard that the late Commodore Ralph Munroe in Florida did away with centerboard troubles by using much thicker boards than usual."

"Yes," returned Brewster, "I have seen some of the craft he designed, but I believe it was because they had strong keels and well-made centerboard logs that they were successful, for one of the troubles with a centerboard is its own swelling and shrinking so that a wide or thick board has to have more clearance. While it is true that some of the Cape Cod cats had very thin centerboards in about 1900 (and they gave trouble from getting bent or twisted,) it is likely that a centerboard thicker than is necessary for strength is a disadvantage. They have to be heavily ballasted to make them sink and thus are hard to hoist out of water."

"What do you think should be the proportion of length to width?" inquired Weldon.

"That is a pretty technical question for me, but I have heard that three-sixteenths of an inch per running foot of length was about right if the board was fastened with good drift bolts of from one-quarter to one-third the thickness of the board. But you will find that the average small board is a little thicker than that; while the large board is often a little less than three-sixteenths inch per foot of length. But, gentlemen, I don't even like to talk about centerboards, so let's get back to the Dutch cruisers."

Brewster than shook the ice in his glass and saw that the tide was getting pretty low, so he freshened the glasses all around and continued: "I nearly purchased a Dutch yacht of the boeier type, for it seemed to be about what I wanted, but in my case the pleasure of watching the craft being built was an important consideration so I decided to have her built where I could visit her on weekends. This necessitated a quite different model from the usual boeier for we in this country, at the present time, are not used to planking up sharp bends or using cant frames in the bow and stern where the boeier is very full."

Brewster then got up and said: "By the way, I have the plans of a boeier below and will bring them up."

While he was below, Goddard remarked to Weldon: "I believe this is one of the most useful cruisers I have ever seen. I hope he shows us below deck."

The boys were forward watching the captain who sat on the deckhouse making a shallow-water sounding line. As Brewster's captain liked young ones, all hands were in a pleasant mood as the freshening southwester carried away the heat of the day.

When Brewster returned on deck, he spread some plans on the cockpit floor and said: "These are the plans of the famous little boeier *Hawk* which made very extensive cruises in Europe; one of which was described in the article published in the *National Geographic* of May 1937. The article is called 'By Sail Across Europe' and is one of the best illustrated cruising stories ever written. On this trip, the *Hawk* passed through eight countries and spanned Europe from the English Channel to the Black Sea. You may be astonished at the full lines of these boeiers but they are a

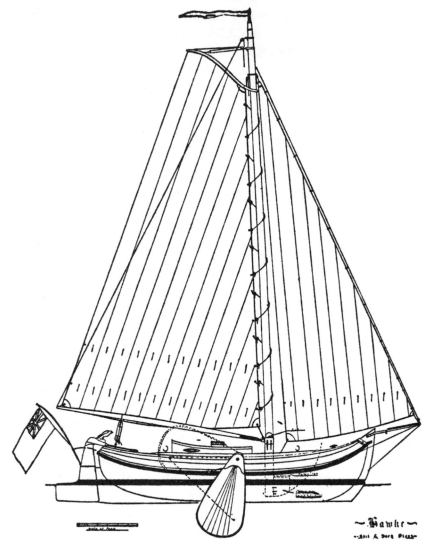

The profile and sail plan of the Dutch boeier yacht, *Hawk*.

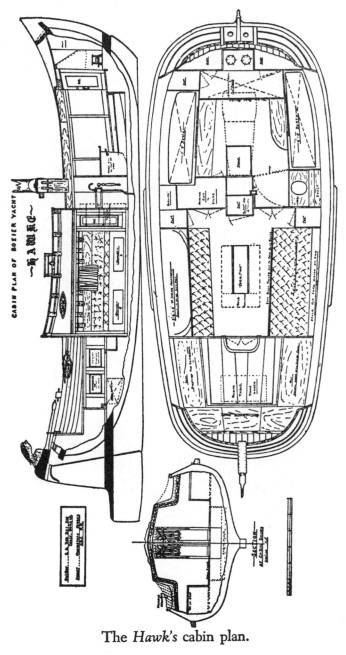

The *Hawk's* cabin plan.

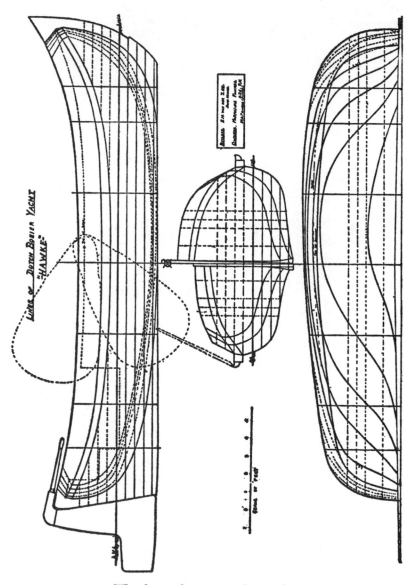

The lines drawings of *Hawk*.

very perfected ancient type and descended from the first yachts, or 'jaghts,' in the world. The general type has not changed much in three or more centuries."

"That may all be so, but how can such a full bow be forced to windward through a choppy sea?" inquired Weldon.

"It does seem amazing," said Brewster, "but these fine little vessels seem to tromp the waves under them instead of cutting through them, and they really go to windward remarkably well in a sea. They also have an easy motion and the larger ones have high bulwarks, so that altogether this type of craft is well thought of by the yachtsmen of Great Britain as well as Holland. However, their model and construction, to a great extent, is planned for canal work and lying alongside wharves, so it is much heavier and more expensive than necessary for an American yacht. While the bottom and bottom framing of the *Tranquilo* may be as strong as the Dutch boats, her topsides are far lighter and she only has a slight chafing strip at the sheer strake. Altogether, the *Tranquilo* combines some of the good qualities of the Dutch craft with a model that can be built in this country."

"By the way," asked Goddard, "what do you think of having yachts built abroad?"

Brewster replied: "I very much approve of it for that may in time make the American builders listen to reason in the way of cost."

"Aren't you afraid our boat builders will be driven out of existence?" queried Weldon.

"No," answered Brewster, "I only think the ones who want big profits will be squeezed out, and it may be a good thing if the poorly managed yard that has no interest in nice workmanship is lost, for the high prices they have been asking has encouraged the other yards to high prices until yachting is almost impossibly expensive. I believe the principal reason the Dutch, German and Swedish yards can now outbid the American ones is that they are better managed. They have men at their heads who really know and love yacht construction. Between 1890 and 1916, we had several yards which were well managed and content with reasonable profit, and during that time we could build yachts as reasonably as anyone. Some say it is the cost of labor in the United States which has made the great rise in building cost, but while the wages are only three or four times what they used to be, the cost of yacht building seems to have increased some ten-fold. No, I think the principal cause of the high cost is poor management and the poor spirit of the workers. When the workman again puts his mind on his work and likes it enough to temporarily forget TV, baseball scores and pin-up pictures, he may do as much and as good work as his father did, or the European worker is now doing. Even if the United States' worker's wages are high, in the yards where there is good management (and I mean by that where the boss understands both the men and the work, as they used to do) the workman has many labor-saving and time-saving power tools to help him. You know, in such highly competitive businesses as automobile and hardware we can still underbid the foreign market. But if these businesses were run like the modern boatyard, then automobiles and hardware would cost ten times as much. Most of the yachtyard owners seem to think the yachtsman is a sucker and ought to be charged $25 for a five dollar job and I, for one, will be glad when foreign competition has brought them to their senses."

Following this lecture Brewster was a little dry, but after sipping his lime juice he went on: "I must show you around below deck, but as there is a watertight bulkhead between the forecastle and the after cabin we must go forward to see the forecastle."

As they looked down the forward hatchway, Brewster explained that the forecastle was about eight feet long with full headroom in the after three feet of it. "As you see," he said, "it has two pipe berths, a table and a watercloset, together with good light and ventilation."

They all then went aft, including the boys who seemed much interested, and entered the cabin through the companionway at the cockpit. Brewster remarked: "We have the galley away aft because we often eat in the cockpit and, while the galley is only three and one-half feet long, it seems to be big enough because it runs the full width of the yacht." Then they moved forward to the next compartment and found themselves in a double stateroom, seven feet long, which had folded-up pipe berths back of transom seats and a folding table amidships. Brewster explained that they generally ate there in rainy weather and, if it grew a little cool, the nearby galley stove kept it a dry, snug place to spend an evening. Next forward, he showed them the toilet room which ran clear across the ship. While generally used as a passageway to the forward stateroom, still that room had another entrance or escape. He then took them into the forward stateroom which was a double one, almost like the after one, but the mast came down through its forward part. There was a ladder and hatchway opening near the starboard side of the house. "You see," he said, "if anyone in the forward stateroom wants to go on deck, he can do so without passing through the toilet room and the after stateroom. We have altogether 23 feet of headroom running fore and aft which, as you know, is remarkable on a yacht of this length and draft. We have good light and ventilation without opening skylights or leaky portholes for, as you see, there is a whole row of removable sidelights in the house sides. As these plate glass shutters set in a gutter that drains outboard, there is no drip over the berths. Not only is this arrangement much cheaper than the metal parts of various kinds, it looks more shipshape for, since the chromium plated noise-makers have adopted the square metal port in large quantities, it no longer has a nautical aspect. Of course, you know the port light that swings sideways or opens upwards is a continual nuisance as it restricts headroom. Also, when being opened they invariably let fall a few spoonfuls of very salt water that usually lands in the middle of a bunk or transom cushion so that with repeated openings there are damp spots under each part which last all summer."

"Don't you get any drip from this arrangement?" asked Weldon.

"No," replied Brewster, "not at all, for the gutter drains it all outboard. We have 18 of these sliding sidelights in the deck house and on a hot day like this, when they are all open, it is very airy below deck. What do you suppose 18 opening metal ports of this size would cost today?"

Goddard said he couldn't guess, but supposed it would be considerable. Brewster informed him: "They would cost close to $30 apiece, if they had this amount of clear opening—a total of something like $540."

"Phew!" said Goddard. "No wonder boats have inadequate ventilation nowadays."

As they walked aft again to the cockpit, Brewster said: "You might think I have shown you all of the cabins, but I haven't. Under the after deck is a little stateroom that I am proud of and, while it only has about four feet of headroom, it has one of the most comfortable berths in the ship."

They all went to the after end of the cockpit and looked down into this little cuddy which had a berth running athwartships against the transom. Brewster said to the boys: "You can go down if you want to." So the boys did and sat on the bunk with plenty of headroom over their heads.

Little Dan spoke up and said: "Gee, uncle, there are two portholes through the stern." His uncle remarked: "Yes, I remember that when we were rowing around I noticed them."

Mr. Brewster then said: "You see, the *Tranquilo* can sleep seven people comfortably, but if each person wants a separate compartment or state room, then four can be accommodated, and you must admit that few boats of this size can do that."

He then told them that one winter he had gone south to Albemarle Sound to do some shooting. That winter they had a colored crew. One was a sort of deckhand and the other an excellent cook. "We three aft had our own separate sleeping compartments, which is almost necessary when you have guns and gunning clothes. We worked south slowly that winter and spent the fall in the Chesapeake to avoid the hurricane season. We certainly had a good time."

Goddard remarked that he had heard it was pretty rough at times in Albemarle and Pamlico Sounds.

"Yes, it is," Brewster agreed, "but there are many shallow water shelters in the western parts of each bay that a shallow draft boat can take advantage of. If you can lay on the bottom as we often did in the many small inlets, you are perfectly protected in the worst storm. You may be high and dry while a northwest gale is roaring overhead, for there are often low tides in those conditions. In the long winter evenings it is pleasant to watch a canvasback duck being basted in the oven, while outside the gale roars. Our cabin seems particularly snug as the coal crackles in the stove. We knew that those cold snaps would soon be followed by moderate weather, and so we rather enjoyed them. The best part of it is that there are still some wild places there that abound with game, for deeper boats cannot navigate much of the bay."

Weldon inquired if they shot from the *Tranquilo*, and Brewster said: "No, we had two duckboats which we towed much of the time, but they could be hoisted on deck if desired for the *Tranquilo* has a long deckhouse unobstructed by skylights."

Goddard inquired if the *Tranquilo* had ever been to Florida and Brewster told him: "No, she has never been south of Pamlico Sound, although I have always wanted to cruise in the northern part of the Gulf of Mexico. A shallow craft that can lay on bottom can find many shelters there as well as passing through innumerable inland waterways. In fact, with a boat of this draft you can pass in sheltered water now most of the way from Florida to the Rio Grande River in Texas, a distance of some 1,000 miles."

Brewster said he thought shallow draft was nearly as useful down east as it was in the south, for it lets you take many short cuts. Besides, you have these many shallow bays, marshes, and lagoons that are fun to explore. "It is nearly as much fun on a summer day," he said, "to be high and dry at low tide, to get out and walk around your craft or follow along high water mark with an axe in hand to gather a supply of kindling. Yes, a craft like the *Tranquilo* allows a quite different type of cruising from that forced on the deep yacht which usually keeps outside the three fathom lines on the chart, and thus is generally out of sight of the best coastal scenery."

By that time, the men were again comfortably seated in the cockpit when Weldon, to make conversation, said: "Sir, you said you had visited Nantucket when a boy. Can you tell us if it has changed much?"

"Changed! I'll say it has changed! Why I can remember well when the sidewheelers ran here and when Nantucket had its cute narrow gauge railroad running to Siasconset. It was a passenger train with its quaint locomotive and open cars; perhaps not so different from some trains on the mainland around 1850. The rails of this line were taken up and shipped to France during World War I. Then, there were the prairie dogs which used to inhabit the level land in the central part of the island."

"What do you mean, prairie dogs?" interrupted Weldon.

"It seems that about 1890," Brewster answered, "there was a plague of rats, or some other meadow rodents here, and to check them or exterminate them someone imported some prairie dogs of a small species. But, in turn, they became almost as much of a pest as the rats, and as you rode over on the narrow gauge railroad you could often see them in places as they sat near their burrows or dived underground as the train rattled by. Perhaps the great change has been in the type of boats and yachts. For before 1900 hardly anything but sail and steam ventured out here. Cat boats could be seen in every direction on Nantucket Sound, many sailing for pleasure or trolling for the bluefish that were then plentiful. While Nantucket may not have had as many cats as Edgartown, still there were several quite large ones here, and I remember one that used to be kept down near the lighthouse that had a very striking design painted on her sail. It was the picture of a setting sun done in red and yellow, and gave a very Venetian effect. The summer people in those days were a more substantial lot and came for all summer, often staying late in the fall, for no place is pleasanter than Nantucket at that season when a restfulness settles on the island."

Weldon then asked how Nantucket had acquired the prosperity to build such fine houses in colonial times. Brewster explained: "It might be a long story, for Nantucket was settled very early. It is said the first settlers here were driven out of the Puritan colonies because they had different religious views from the narrow Puritans. Although Nantucket was never very fertile, still the Indians, being a constant menace west and north of the Puritan settlement, caused the move. Of course, there were Indians at Nantucket and Martha's Vineyard, but there were Quakers among the first settlers here and not only could they get along with the Indians but they were also thrifty and industrious. Nantucket made her money almost altogether by whaling, and the story is told that they took up that industry because the whales often grounded on the shore here. I can well believe it, for I myself have seen a whole school of perhaps 20 whales stranded only a little to the westward of the harbor entrance."

"Why do you suppose the whales were so often stranded on Nantucket?" inquired Goddard.

"They say it is on account of the complication of Nantucket Shoal. A school of whales seems to have a leader or navigator and if he or she gets confused and runs ashore, most of the school will stubbornly follow. The variety of whale which does this most is called the blackfish. It is among the smallest of whales and seldom grows to a length of over 30 feet. However, it is a pitiful sight to see them slowly dying in shallow water, for the old bulls, which may be 100 years old, seem to take several days to die and the little six-foot calves are most pathetic."

"Do whales live to be a hundred?" asked Jim.

"Yes," Mr. Brewster told him, "they say some of the larger varieties live to be 600 or in other words there may now be whales alive that were born at the time of the battle of Cressy and were grown up when Columbus crossed the ocean blue.

"Well, in the early days they set up their try-works where the fish were stranded. As the oil business became profitable, they developed a light double-ended row boat modeled somewhat after the Indian canoes of this district and went after the whales with harpoon and lines, in which case they could land the fish somewhere near their try-works. In those days, they had stations or crow's nests on spars where men kept lookout along the likely parts for whales, as I believe they did on the south of Cape Cod and Long Island, for this shore-whaling was one of New England's early industries. However, it is believed a Nantucket blacksmith forged the first improved irons for harpoons, and this no doubt gave them an advantage over others. But the art of catching and killing whales was learned from the Indians who perhaps had been doing it for centuries before New England was settled. The Indians harpooned the whales from their canoes, using a bone-headed harpoon attached to a rope made from the bark of trees or the bark of grapevines, which had a 'drug' or drag of some kind attached to it. After the whale was tired out they shot and killed it with bow and arrow. It seems that many of the famous harpooners of the next two centuries had Indian blood in their veins, for they seemed to enjoy the excitement of the kill and whaling was about the only industry that the Indians took part in.

"About the year 1700, a sperm whale was stranded on the island and the quantity and quality of its oil much impressed the Nantucketers so they began fishing farther offshore. At first, they used small sloops and only took cruises of a few days, towing one or two whaleboats. They cut in the fish at sea and brought the blubber home to try out in their shore try-works. But, as the whales became scarce along the coast, whaling ships with the try-works on deck were built and long voyages were undertaken in which the oil was brought home in barrels. Thus the great New England industry of whaling was started, and other colonial cities and towns, such as Sag Harbor, New London, Newport, Bristol, R. I., and New Bedford sent out whaling fleets. It was during this time that Nantucket captains became famous as expert navigators and usually brought their ships home safely after wandering all over the globe on cruises of a year or two in duration. In 1715, there were but six sloops sperm whaling out of Nantucket, but by 1775 the sloops, brigs, and schooners, all told, numbered around 150. I think Nantucket was considered the greatest whaling port in the world at that time.

"Before about 1756, most of the oil was sold to agents in Boston, but after that Nantucket ran her own ships to London and made substantial profits up until the Revolution, when most of the Nantucket whale ships were captured by the British. Nantucket came back for a short time after the Revolution, and I think by 1820 had some 80 ships at sea, but as whaling voyages became longer the ships necessarily became larger until the draft of water over the bar at Nantucket was not sufficient. So, even before the Civil War, most of the whaling business was transferred to New Bedford, where it was to flourish for another 50 years, and some of the fortunes made in it were to be invested in our early mineral oil business at even greater profits."

"Why was there such a demand for sperm oil?" inquired Weldon.

"In the beginning, sperm oil was used principally for illumination and was the fuel of the first practical lamps. The font of these early lamps was often made of glass and had a spud at the bottom that fitted into a candlestick. Sperm oil is not easily ignited, but will burn steadily when fed to the flame through a wick, so it was quite safe and could be used in a simple burner. After the burners for mineral oil were perfected, then sperm oil was used in large quantities for lubrication, and our early steamships and railroads used much of it. I believe it is still the best oil to prevent rust, for when well refined it has no acids in it which etch or discolor steel. Today, sperm oil is much sought after as a base for soaps and cosmetics."

After taking a sip out of his glass, Brewster continued; "I must tell you, before finishing this short history of the island, that the early natives were as fine a lot of people as could be found anywhere. They were mostly Quakers—industrious, law-abiding, and peace loving. It is said that Nantucket got along without police or lawyers up until about the time of the Revolution, and while many New England towns sent out colonial privateers and ran slave ships, Nantucket was as prosperous as any other region of its size until the last of her whaling." Brewster concluded: "I think that should answer your questions about the early prosperity of Nantucket."

"Yes, it does, sir," replied Goddard, "and I found it very interesting."

"Me, too," chirped in little Dan. "I liked the part about the Indians hunting whales in canoes, and the 600 year old whale."

By this time, the afternoon was rather waning and Weldon said, preparatory to their leaving: "We expect to sail to Edgartown tomorrow, and, sir, I can't thank you enough for having us aboard."

"Well, young man, it has been a great pleasure to have you and your nephews aboard and it is a coincidence that I intend to make Edgartown my destination tomorrow. But I expect to sail around the south side of the Island, and while most yachtsmen keep away from the south side on account of the outlying shoals, there is really good water close to shore the whole way except over the shoal off Great Point which my captain knows a way through. I should be pleased to have you accompany me around, but it will mean an early start for both of you will have to cross the bar off the Point at high water, and there is a small rise and fall there so we shall have to be on time."

"What time is the tide high?" inquired Goddard.

"Nine thirty-five a.m.," Brewster told him, and Weldon asked, "What do you say, Goddard?"

Goddard quickly replied: "It sounds good to me, for I never saw the south side of the Island. How far is it to Edgartown going that way?"

Brewster answered, "It is just under 50 miles, but as we shall have to make an early start to get to Great Point at high tide we should get to Edgartown before dark."

"Well," said Goddard, "I can be ready to start at seven in the morning, but what shall we do about the *Rozinante* if it is calm?"

Brewster told him: "If it is calm, or light weather, I will tow her to the Point, which is about seven miles from here, and if it is calm on the east side of the Island, I will tow her until a breeze springs up."

As they climbed into the dinghies Goddard and Weldon both thanked Mr. Brewster for the pleasant afternoon he had given them. There were broad smiles all around, for there is nothing pleasanter to contemplate than a long run in company where the time and destination are agreed upon.

As they were pulling away in the dinghies, Weldon inquired of Mr. Brewster why the *Tranquilo's* waterline was painted so high. Brewster told him: "That is only so we shall have to wash the topsides less. You see, scum and other dirt does not show on a high waterline."

It must have been later than they thought, or else the time had flown fast over the lime juice, for as they were passing the yacht club they saw Mrs. Goddard and the girls. So, landing the boys and telling them to be at the restaurant at six o'clock, the men rowed the ladies of the *Viator* to their floating home. After supper, although Mrs. Goddard and the girls were healthily tired, there was much talk of gardens and island vistas aboard the *Viator*.

6

At Edgartown / Dinghy Handling

The Cedar Bucket / Some New England Fishing

Boats

The next morning was not transparently clear like those following a northwester, but instead was one of those opalescent mornings which are not uncommon in August, south of the Cape. The sky was cloudless, but as it approached the horizon, the colors gradually changed to pink and gray, as the varied tints of Nantucket lent their soft tones, the whole spectrum of color was represented.

It was dead calm as Weldon came on deck, but he saw that Goddard on the *Viator* was already astir and had his anchor at the trip. The morning was so still that they could converse easily and Weldon said: "It looks like a beautiful day."

"Yes," agreed Goddard, "it is beautiful enough, but I think it will be calm, and maybe very hot, for even the morning sun has considerable warmth."

"Do you see any prospects of a breeze?" inquired Weldon.

"Why yes," Goddard answered him. "When I came on deck, there was a heavy dew, and I believe a good southerly breeze will spring up by afternoon."

While the men were talking, the girls came on deck in their bathing suits and, after saying good morning to Weldon, dove overboard together. It certainly was a morning for color for as the girls came to the surface gasping for breath, the ripples that ran in every direction reflected the morning tints of pink and blue and the girls' limbs made zigzag golden streaks in the clear water. The girls started to swim toward the *Rozinante* but had not gone far when Mr. Goddard called out that he could see the *Tranquilo* was under way, so they hurried back and climbed aboard the *Viator,* quite out of breath but with strength enough to tail out on the warp and help Goddard bring the anchor to the surface. It was loaded with sandy mud, so he decided to leave it submerged a while and let it wash itself off as they slowly steamed toward the breakwater.

In the meantime, the girls had stretched out on deck for a sun bath. When Goddard was on his way aft to start the engine, Prim had asked him if it would be all right to wear their bathing suits until after breakfast. He replied: "I don't know why not, if you stay on deck." The morning dip had given the girls a keen appetite and the pleasant odors of preparing breakfast were coming up the companionway, so Prim leaned over the hatch and called: "Ma, I'm awfully hungry." She was a little disappointed when her mother's only reply was: "That's good!"

By this time, the *Rozinante's* anchor was up and stowed and Weldon was rowing her toward the harbor entrance when the *Tranquilo* came alongside and handed him a long, strong towrope. Weldon took a turn around the stemhead with the rope so it came in one chock and went out the other, then after rounding the face of the stem, it came back under the towing part to the mooring cleat. As he straightened up he said to himself: It is calm now but there may be a ground swell outside.

The three boats were now headed out through the channel beside the breakwater. On the *Tranquilo* the captain came up in the cockpit and said, "Sir, breakfast is on the table. Let me relieve you at the helm." On the *Rozinante,* Jim was steering while his uncle was preparing breakfast and trying to get little Dan up and under way. But on the *Viator,* they were having a real feed, for as Prim remarked: "No one can prepare breakfast like Mother!"

At first, they had shredded wheat with huckleberries and light cream; then two dropped eggs apiece that were flanked with a few slices of Canadian bacon. But the girls were not entirely filled up until they had topped off with strawberry jam on pilot crackers. They all ate in the cockpit and, although the sun was strong, they were moving at some five knots through the still air which made it ideally comfortable.

After breakfast, Mr. Goddard said to his wife: "If you take the helm, I will clean things up," but she replied, "No, I can do it easier and quicker."

"Well, suit yourself," he answered as she went below.

All this time, the steady rumble and drum of the engine, the good breakfast, and the warm sun had had their effects on the girls and they were soon happily sleeping on the fore deck as the warm sunlight sent pleasant sensations through their bodies. Mrs. Goddard came up again and she, too, was overcome with a sort of drowsiness for the slight roll caused by the ground swell, as well as the monotonous purr of the motor, were very enervating. She put a pillow up against the deck house and lay down. Goddard soon saw her head nod as she fell into oblivion while the shadows of the spars moved back and forth across her face.

Goddard said to himself: I believe one of the best things about a cruise is the opportunity it gives for sleep, and when you can sleep all night and part of the day with thorough enjoyment, it certainly is good for you. When I hear of people who can't sleep, I am sorry for them, but I can't help thinking they ought to go on a sensible cruise for they would soon be cured. Goddard's greatest pleasure was to see others happy and contented, but he also had a great capacity for enjoying landscapes and the colors of nature, so during this long trick at the helm, when the others were happily resting, he was content to watch the changes of sky and sea as the morning progressed. The morning no longer had the soft translucent effect of its earlier mists, but off to the northwest over the mainland there were the feathery clouds of a dying west wind. The perfect calm made the distant water almost like molten silver, while the close-to water was such a transparent green that the *Viator* seemed to be floating in space. The long stretch of beach toward Great Point was dazzling white; the lowland behind, prominent in green and brown. Overhead, the sky had turned to turquoise blue as the terns wheeled about giving their plaintive cries and diving from one transparent element to the other, so that the borders between the two was wrinkled with circular ripples.

It was a Sunday morning and Goddard gave thanks that there were still places where one could worship in temples not made by human hands. Steering a boat of this size in a calm is quite different from driving an automobile, for, when there is nothing near, you can be partly lost in contemplation, as only a slight consciousness is required to steer toward a distant mark. Thus many pleasant thoughts passed through his mind as he sat steering toward Great Point in the sunlight. He often said to himself that this was the kind of a day that made up for all the trouble and expense of the *Viator*, for, not only do several people get lasting pleasure from such a day, but the salt air, sunlight, and opportunity to relax and sleep, are healthful.

In the meantime, the *Tranquilo* and her tow had pulled somewhat ahead but she now slowed down so the *Viator* could follow her closely over the shoals off Great Point, for there is only a narrow gulley there that shifts from time to time. The chart only shows three feet of water there but in the right place, which is quite close to shore, there is usually a fathom and a half at high tide. Brewster knew approximately where the channel was, but he slowed down and steered a zigzag course with the captain up forward making quick casts with the short sounding line. The captain finally said: "That is about right now, sir, if you steer due east." In a short time they got over two and a half fathoms, when the captain reported: "We are clean through now, sir."

On board the *Rozinante* the boys were fascinated and surprised that the shoal they had passed over was the place the seas were breaking so heavily on the day they approached the Island. Their uncle explained to them that there were places farther out where there were only two feet of water, and when there were tide and wind, the conditions were quite different. They bore off to the south, now, and ran close along the Island's east shore. There was no wind in sight so this would have been a monotonous hitch if the beach had not been close at hand. As they got abreast Sankaty Head, the cliffs were very interesting, and time passed quickly enough until lunchtime. Everyone was surprised that there was no ground swell and the water was so clear that they could see bottom in two or more fathoms.

They had lunch off Siasconset, where there were many people bathing. Goddard told the girls that Siasconset had been a famous bathing place for over 75 years, as almost nowhere else was the water cleaner or more bracing, for there is nothing but sand for several miles around. When they were all through lunch and off Tom Nevers Head, a slight breeze sprang up close under the cliffs so they all hoisted sail. Although the breeze soon petered out, they could see dark patches on the ocean out to the south. In a short time the dark patches covered most of the water out at sea and the silver gray water was only close to them. The sails now began to rattle in earnest and the cool ocean breeze was a relief after the heat of the morning. The coming breeze was due south-west and as their course along the south shore was a little north of west, they had a good rap full. The motors were shut off and the *Rozinante* let go. The quietness was amazing at first. By the time they had become accustomed to talking in their natural tones of voice, the yachts had heeled perceptibly and the sensation of being noiselessly propelled was very refreshing. Everyone now got into his favorite position and looked forward to a good sail, for there are few places pleasanter than the south side of Nantucket where you can skirt the shore very closely if you want to.

At first, there was little difference in the speed of the yachts but, as the breeze freshened and they bore off to almost a close reach, the *Tranquilo* romped away from the others. It was not only her size, but she had straight lines under water together with long waterline length, and thus was fast in anything but beating to weather. Goddard and Weldon were amazed and thought she must have a motor running, but they found out later that that was not so, and from that time on, Goddard and Weldon looked on the *Tranquilo* as a most remarkable boat.

Mrs. Goddard remarked that it was too bad that some of this wonderful air could not be canned and taken to hospitals and sick rooms for she was convinced it would cause many cures.

"Yes," said Goddard, "I quite agree and I think this air would make one forget old age, failure, or any sorrow he might have. Nevertheless, I believe it would be necessary to take the air in a small sailboat to get its full benefit, for complete relaxation is one of the conditions which lets the good air do its work. I am also convinced that there is something in ocean air close to the surface of the water that is the best of all. For instance, if we were on the top of one of Nantucket's south shore cliffs, the air would be good, but nothing like as rich and soul satisfying as it is down here." He paused, and then continued: "Most modern conveyances travel at such high speed that they have to be enclosed, so that after a ride in an aeroplane, automobile, or an enclosed motor launch, one's condition is not improved. But in a slow moving object like a sailboat, where you can move around and lie out in the warm, pleasant wind and sunlight, the conditions may be nearly ideal. This has been so for a thousand years in the past and will continue so in the future. However, to really get enjoyment and improved health from sailing and cruising, one must have confidence in his boat and skipper, for otherwise one will not be able to relax. So it is the duty of skippers of cruising craft to avoid all dangers, and this can usually be done if they understand seamanship. While I believe a short race with a good-natured skipper is a healthy recreation, still most of the boys who come back from an ocean race are so nervously exhausted that they require a week of rest to recuperate. This, of course, is the direct opposite of one's condition when returning from a sensible cruise. Then one is completely rested and improved in health."

Perhaps Goddard did not realize it, but one of the reasons for the feeling of well-being in the crew of the *Viator* was that they were leaving the *Rozinante* behind, for these little informal brushes are ever so much more fun than the tension of a sched-

uled race. The good natured competition of a cruising race without time allowance is nearly as much fun to the loser as to the
winner, and is usually the source of much pleasant conversation
later.

They were now all headed for Cape Poge, which is the point
northeast of Edgartown. The *Viator* rounded Cape Poge at 6:30
p.m. with the *Rozinante* close astern, for she seemed to have
picked up some in the broad reach of the last hour. However, the
Tranquilo was almost hull down ahead and they saw her make
the zigzag course for entering the inner harbor at Edgartown
where she lowered her sails.

The girls on the *Viator* were unusually hungry and spoke of
it a couple of times, so Goddard said: "Ma, don't you think we
could have supper before we come to anchor?"

"Well, I suppose so," she replied, "but it is not just what I had
planned."

He said: "You know, Mum, one of the pleasures of cruising
is to have the regular schedule broken up. Unexpected changes,
if they are agreeable, are all the more fun, and the thought of eating soon sounds agreeable to me, too. Besides," he continued, "if
we only have some sandwiches now, we can have a snack before
turning in."

Miss Prim added: "Ma, if you will let Va and I make the
sandwiches, you can stay on deck."

"I'll tell you what we can do," Mrs. Goddard answered. "If you
girls get a can of tongue, a can of chicken, and the bread, I will
see what I can do on deck." So the girls went to work with a will
and laughingly brought up the bottle of pickles, some ginger ale
and the carving knife. They would have brought up much more
if Goddard had not called out: "That will do now. Belay!"

The afternoon breeze was dying as they tacked toward the harbor, and the sun approached the westward enough to make the
water toward Oak Bluffs shine with red and gold. It was refreshing to have a light head wind after the long reaches and runs of
the day. As they sat munching their sandwiches in the dying
southwester, with prospects of a snug harbor ahead, all were

wrapped in silent contentment. By the time they were abreast of
the lighthouse, at the entrance of the inner harbor, Goddard was
aware they were stemming a bow tide, so he started the motor and
said: "Now, girls, see what you can do at furling the sails."

It was the first time they had done it alone, so they felt quite
important as they gave each other orders on sticking the sail stops
and lowering away. Prim had helped her father so many times at
furling that they now did it neatly and quickly. This was fortunate, for Goddard was fully occupied in passing up the narrow
harbor in a tideway. They anchored just beyond the town in the
stillness of the twilight.

The girls thought Edgartown Harbor was the prettiest place
they had ever seen. Although it was twilight, they wanted to go
for a swim, but Mr. Goddard told them the tide was so strong
where they were anchored that they might be swept away and he
would have to go after them in the dinghy. "Besides," he said,
"you girls are likely to have all the swimming you want in the
next couple of days."

"Why is that?" they both asked, but all they could get out of
Goddard was: "You wait and see."

The lights and sounds of the town were just distant enough to
lend enchantment to their anchorage. As they sat in the stillness
of the evening, the moon rose over the Chappaquiddick Island
shore, and they felt the contentment of those who were happily
tired after a long sail. Although it was one of those calm summer
evenings when all nature seems to respond to the moonlight, the
girls began to yawn and soon after Mrs. Goddard caught the habit.
Goddard said: "I think all of you children had better turn in."
Which they did very quickly and willingly without even lighting
a cabin light, for there was enough moonlight in the cabin to see
by.

The only sound on the *Viator* now was the slight murmur and
ripple of the slowly running tide and, now and then, an almost
imperceptible vibration as the anchor warp trembled in the
stream. These things had quickly lulled Mrs. Goddard and the
girls to sleep, for the murmur of a slowly running stream after a

long day's sail makes sleep irresistible. As Goddard sat smoking his pipe in the moonlight, he felt one of those waves of thankfulness that are experienced by those who have spent a day in the open, close to nature. He was as contented as the camper or farmer who is far from the tension of the city. But as he sat wrapped in these pleasant thoughts, he heard the soft rumble of oars and saw Mr. Brewster being quietly carried toward him on the tide.

As the tender swung alongside, Mr. Brewster said very quietly, "I hate to disturb you, but do you think the *Rozinante* is all safe?"

Goddard replied: "I think she is about as safe as anything in this world can be. I believe she is anchored just outside the entrance to the inner harbor. When the tide turns, I think you will see Weldon rowing in, for he loves to work the tides. But won't you come aboard and join me in a nightcap, for I want to ask some questions about the *Tranquilo?*"

These two things were a temptation to Brewster, for he loved to talk about the *Tranquilo,* so he replied: "Thank you very much," and, softly unshipping his oars and oarlocks, he climbed aboard.

Goddard took the painter and the tender went astern without touching the side of the *Viator*. He said, apologetically: "Today's wonderful sail has pleasantly exhausted my crew, and they have all turned in, but we are all much indebted to you for suggesting going south of Nantucket, for, it turned out one of the nicest sails we have ever had." As Goddard was backing down the companion way, he asked what Brewster would have to drink, and his reply was: "Whatever you are having."

They settled down with their backs against the deckhouse, and their feet drawn up under them on the cockpit seats. In the silence, a line of spindrift neared them, then the tenders swung abeam, and the *Viator,* after slowly running up on her warp, veered so gradually, that instead, the moon and stars seemed to be moving. Finally, she took up her position stemming the coming tide, and the moon which had been to starboard, was now broad on their port.

The swing had brought the *Tranquilo* into the men's range of vision, and Goddard said: "I have been thinking about your boat and have wondered how such a round bottomed boat would set level, when grounded on various shores."

Brewster answered: "I don't think she would sit very level on most shores if she didn't have a set of legs to keep her upright."

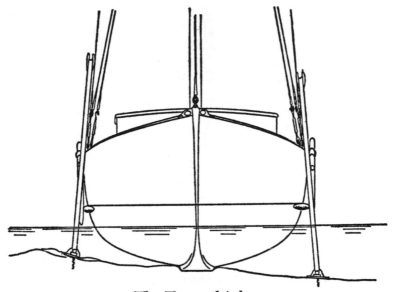

The *Tranquilo's* legs.

"Oh," said Goddard, "I didn't know she had a set of legs. I wish you would tell me about them, for I have often read of English yachts using legs, but never saw a set."

"Well, when the *Tranquilo* was built, I had some of her chain plates made wide enough to have an extra hole at the top where we could secure a shackle. Most boats only use one pair of legs, but the *Tranquilo* has four that are put down abreast of the shrouds. It is true that other yachts have used a strong flange eye near the rigging for this purpose, but nothing is as strong as a chain plate to stand an upstrain."

"Is it necessary to have the legs at the shrouds?"

"No, some sloops which only use one pair of legs, and have the mast rather far forward, put the legs down somewhere near the greatest beam, but it is sometimes convenient to have the legs at the shrouds so you can lock them in an upright position. The *Tranquilo's* legs are round spruce spars about 2 3/4 inches in diameter, and 9 feet long."

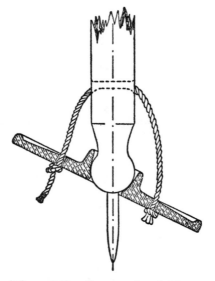

The self-leveling pads of *Tranquilo's* feet.

"What determines the length of the legs?"

"In most cases it is the draft of the yacht, plus the freeboard, plus enough length to use a tackle or seizing at the upper end. But the legs for the *Tranquilo* were made a convenient length to stow under the deck at the side of the cockpit. Sometimes, I wish they were longer for at times when you lay on bottom in a river the offshore depth is more than that under the keel."

"What are the bottoms or feet of the legs like?"

"They somewhat resemble the ring at the bottom of a ski pole. That is, there is a pad at the bottom that can swivel around and has a spike passing through it. The foot, or pad, at the bottom is generally made of thick wood. But this has the disadvantage of trying to float up when you are rigging the leg, so I worked out a shape made of cast iron, heavy enough to keep the leg on end while you are securing it in place. Some of the wooden feet have required a rather complicated joint to let them rock and still not become detached when you pull them up, for the feet certainly stick down hard at times if you have been laying on a clay bottom. The *Tranquilo's* feet are held on by ropes which pass through holes in the legs, and thus the feet can rock some 45 degrees in any direction, but are securely attached."

"Why must the feet rock so much?" asked Goddard.

"They usually do not rock much, but if you happened to place one so that one side bore on a rock, or other hard surface, it would bring a bending strain on the leg if the foot could not rock freely."

"I see, but tell me about the spike that goes down through the foot."

"Oh, there isn't much to it. The spike is simply of five-eighths inch steel, and extends below the foot about six inches. I will show you the whole rig the next time you are aboard."

As Brewster paused, they heard a faint groaning noise which started with a thud and ended with a grunt. It recurred at even intervals of about five seconds. Goddard looked around and chuckled: "Here comes the *Rozinante,* and, just as I said, he is rowing up with the first of the flood."

As the *Rozinante* passed along, Goddard asked Weldon to come aboard after he was anchored, but Weldon declined: "Thanks very much, but I'll see you in the morning."

"I guess he thinks we are making a night of it," remarked Brewster.

"No doubt," agreed Goddard, "but if he knew we were talking about cruisers and cruising he would be over quick enough. By the way, you haven't told me how you secure the upper end of the legs."

"The top of the legs are made like a crotch, or very narrow boom jaw. We take two or three turns with a rope between the shackle at the chain plate, and this crotch, and thus have a strong but quickly adjusted rig."

Goddard remarked: "That sounds simple enough, but isn't there quite a strain on the ropes at times?"

"Why, no. You see, a wide keeled boat like the *Tranquilo* would sit level by herself on most bottoms. The legs are simply to stop her from starting to heel when struck by a side wind, or if thrown off balance by people moving around on deck. You know, when a boat is laid on the beach to have her bottom cleaned and is held up by her halyards running to anchor warps, there is seldom much strain shown on the halyards."

"Yes, I know," replied Goddard, "and it used to be a common sight to see boats laid on the beach that way. But now you almost never see it."

"Well," Brewster replied, "it is just another of those deplorable signs of the times, for people seem to want to do everything the hardest and most expensive way. It will cost you from $20 to $50 now to have a boat hauled and her bottom cleaned and it is a dirty and messy job for the yard men as they struggle around on the poor footing of the ways and cradle. Often, through poor management (and that is the rule in the modern yard) they let the weeds or growth dry on, and then it is hard to remove anyway. But, worst of all, your boat will have been dented or scratched, not to mention the combinations of grease and cinders they will smear on your decks and ropes. If you had laid your boat on the beach to scrub her, as we used to call it in old times, then you would have a pleasant time of it without expense or damage. I say, 'a pleasant time of it,' because it is a real pleasure to walk all around your boat with good footing, and no poppets or shores in the way. When the tide is down to knee depth around your craft, you can go to it with the ingredients for the work plentifully at hand. These ingredients are sand and water. With a good broom or scrubbing brush, after it is dipped in one and then the other, the soft weeds will come off easily, and the whole bottom will be scrubbed smooth in a short time. You will notice, as you dip your broom in the water, that a lot of the bottom paint is coming off. That is a good thing, for most bottom paints are improved by having their outer surface removed to expose the anti-fouling chemicals. This is the reason a bottom will resist fouling better after a scrubbing than before. So, outside of having a few shrimps and fiddler crabs run over your toes, there is little inconvenience in acquiring a clean bottom when laying on the beach. If there is some under-water painting to be done, this can be accomplished on a bright day by simply rubbing the salt off the dried place with a rag and slapping on the paint. Several of the good bottom paints set best under water.

"I have heard that many of the small sailboats of a hundred years ago were laid on the beach for cleaning at each change of the moon, for they seemed to do things easier and better in those days. Yes, even up to the horse and buggy days, when I was a boy, one could keep a boat at a trifling expense for they still knew how to do things in a simple and easy way."

Goddard broke in to say: "I suppose in the old days there were no good anti-fouling paints, and the bottom had to be scrubbed often."

"Well, now," answered Brewster, "I don't know. The paints certainly were not advertised as much as they are now, but they may have been pretty good, or at least were made from pure materials. The way bottom paint used to be made was to put scraps of brass and copper into a glass jar with some nitric acid. After this had stood a month or two and become a green liquid concoction, which they called verdigris, some of it was mixed with white lead paste, linseed oil and turpentine. It was supposed to be dangerous and poisonous, I suppose, on account of the nitric acid, and perhaps the style of green bottom paints has descended from these early mixtures. A little later, or perhaps 70 years ago, there were several so-called copper anti-fouling paints that were made of the shavings or dust of finely ground copper or bronze, mixed the same way as the older green paint, with sometimes the addition of banana oil. These paints were bright copper or bronze color when applied, but soon after the boat was put in the water, they turned to a brownish green. Of course, there were several brown and red bottom paints in the old days whose principal ingredient was, no doubt, red lead. In different parts of the coast, various other powdered chemicals were added, and these paints to a great extent, depended on erosion for their anti-fouling qualities. In other words, as soon as a weed or minute barnacle attached itself to these paints, the powdery surface came away."

"Do you suppose everyone mixed his own paints in the old days?" queried Goddard.

"Yes, I think so to a great extent, but no doubt they had help from house painters at times. When you think how easily the artist mixes his colors or paints as he goes along, you can see what a simple matter it is, although few people think they can mix their own paint today. In reality, they could save money, and protect the wood better if they mixed their own. It takes little intelligence to mix paint, though it does take an experienced eye to match colors. About all you have to do is to get some white lead powder or paste, or zinc powder or paste, and stir it with linseed oil (and they generally use boiled linseed with paint) until you get the consistency of heavy cream. Then add the coloring materials and thin with turpentine until the brush will carry a load without dripping too much. If you want the paint to dry quicker, you can add a little Japan dryer, but if this is overdone the paint will crack later on. My captain mixes most of our paint, and he thinks it neater to keep the ingredients separate and mix them as required, for there is much less waste that way, and it does away with storing a lot of half used-up cans of paint, that will skim over."

"You certainly must have a good man," remarked Goddard.

"No better than the average used to be," Brewster told him, "before the Florida winter racket had taught most of them to be two-faced crooks whose principal delight was to increase the cost of yachting."

"Why do you call them two-faced crooks?" inquired Goddard.

"You house them; you feed them, and clothe them, and pay them to help you. Instead, most of them try to run the bills up so they can get more commission. If that isn't being two-faced, what is? Did you ever consider what an easy time the average yacht captain has?"

"No, I don't know as I ever thought of it," replied Goddard.

"It is about like this: you pay him to share with you the pleasure of yachting for the summer and, as he is under no expense since you have housed, fed and clothed him, he has his wages clear to live on during the winter, when many take a six-month vacation."

"That does sound pretty soft," agreed Goddard, "but don't most of them work pretty hard during the summer?"

"My observations are, that they work little, if any, more than the owner does. You see, most boat yards, today, do all the fitting out and that only leaves the ship-keeping during the summer, which can usually be accomplished in a few hours a day. I must say, I have often envied my captain, when I have had to head back to the city to get together a little money to keep things going while he was anchored in a cool, pleasant place without any worries, excepting to be prompt in stuffing his gut three times a day.

"In the old days, there were men who had a real love of the water, and their yacht. They were content to be aboard most of the time, and enjoyed cruising as much as the owner and his party. Some even had an appreciation of the beauties of nature. They stayed with one owner year after year, and almost became members of the family. But today, there are so many attractions on shore that, as a class, they dislike being afloat and have acquired some tough, City Island ways, and look on an owner as an enemy to be plundered. Of course, the principal reason for all this is that they try to live beyond their means and seem to think the world owes them as much as someone who has created a well-paying business. So, after they have gambled their wages away, the only easy way they can pay the installments on their auto, TV and other extravagances, is to rob the owner. There are still good men to be had, and I am glad I have a good one."
Brewster here knocked on wood before continuing. "My man has

a little age on him, and has been through most of the snares that entangle the young ones. He seems thankful to have a steady job, after what he has been through. He's a good cook, and gets along well with my wife in the things which have to do with the galley."

Goddard then spoke up: "Don't you think the class of people who have taken up yachting recently has had a very demoralizing effect on the paid hand?"

"Yes, I suppose so, or it must be pretty tough to work for some of them."

Goddard asked Brewster which of the nationalities he considered the best for sailormen on small boats.

Brewster answered promptly: "I think a middle-aged, old-fashioned Yankee much the best. Some of the Scandinavians are good shipkeepers, and clean, but after they have been with you awhile, they get morose and moody and you can't tell when they will turn queer and do something to hold up a cruise. The worst thing about it is, you can't find out what is biting them, for they don't know themselves. Apparently, the change of the moon affects them."

"How about the down-easters?" inquired Goddard.

"Those from 'way down east, the bluenoses, are good seamen, but do not take to yachting naturally. They are never very neat and, while not morose like the so-called squareheads, still they are disagreeable at times. The men from Maine, whom some call Maniacs, are much better. If it were not that they are natural liars, they would be, perhaps, the best of all."

"Why do you call them natural liars?"

"Because they are great talkers and always tell exaggerated stories about their prowess as hunters. When you have heard for the twentieth time about the time they shot ten geese with one shot, you begin to get terribly bored."

Goddard said: "I would like to hear the story once, if not twenty times."

"I can't take off their down-east drawl, but one captain I had, used to tell a story many times, that went something like this, and

I will have to adopt the first person. 'I was nearing home one evening, after cruising the woods all day, when I saw a whole row of geese roosted on a fence. So I hauled the ramrod out from under the barrels of my old gun, and tied a string on it. I worked the string down on top of the charge and tamped it down well with the ramrod. The birds must have been real tired for they sat perfectly still while I took aim. But when I let fire, blessed if the gun didn't knock me clean over. When I got up, what do you think I saw? Well, there, sure enough, was ten geese, all laying dead beside the fence with the ramrod half through the last one, and the rest all strung up for carrying home.' Every time he told that story I felt that he was trying to string another goose."

"You shouldn't have felt that way," said Goddard, "for the Maine stories are only a sort of Baron Münchausen humor, with a people whose ancestors were hunters."

"I know it," replied Brewster, "but it is tiring to be cooped up on a small boat with a glorified liar. I don't mean that you should think that the Maniacs are dishonest in money matters, but it is hard to tell when to take them seriously."

"Where do you think the best men for yacht crews *do* come from?" inquired Goddard.

"The east end of Long Island during the last hundred years has produced some remarkably good men, and there have been some good ones from Connecticut, Rhode Island, and Massachusetts. What I call a good man for a cruiser is one who makes it pleasant for you, when you are aboard; one who tries to keep down expenses and is reliable and able to take the yacht from place to place if you are called away. Last, but not least, he has to be housebroken enough to be helpful in the cabin and galley. It was quite different in the old days before the income tax, when yachts were larger. Then you could have a whole forecastle full of snuff-eating squareheads and only the steward came aft. But on our present small yachts, where you might say the cabin and forecastle are all together, the conditions are trying for both owner and crew."

"How is it you have had experience with so many sorts of men?" inquired Goddard.

"You see, my father and grandfather, were both yachtsmen. In my youth, I went on my father's steam yacht which had a crew of six. They were; captain, steward, engineer, fireman and two deck hands. From my childhood, I was in contact with yacht crews and often heard about those of a generation or two before. There used to be many good men in those days who very much appreciated a berth on a yacht during the summer after their hardships of the previous winter in the merchant marine. Sailormen were paid $45 a month, then, and no one thought of keeping them through the winter. But times have changed. It is rather remarkable that I have about the same income that my father had, but can do less than one-fifth as much with it."

"How do you suppose that is?" inquired Goddard.

"In the first place, the income tax takes two-thirds of my earnings, then the wages of the workingman have gone up, and on top of that the general value of the dollar is much less. Whereas my father had a country estate and a steam yacht, I live in an apartment and have only a sand dab to cruise on, with a crew of one. But as they say, 'it is better to have had and lost than never to have had at all.'

"I don't know why we talk about the crew problem on such a beautiful night, but it is the principal factor that determines the size of boat one can have. When you are young, perhaps you can take care of a boat 35 feet overall if you have the boatman at the club look out for her during the week. But when you get to my age and are no longer supposed to do heavy lifting, a man becomes necessary. Also, at my age, you appreciate the luxury of good meals and a comfortable cabin, so when you take a man aboard you have to jump the length of your craft about ten feet. Many of the boats between 35 and 45 feet are impractical cruisers for that reason."

Goddard said: "The *Viator* is well under 35 feet, and I find her about all I can swing. So I have often thought of a boat large enough to require a paid hand. This talk has been very interesting and I would like to know how much you think the expenses jump when you take a man aboard."

Brewster replied: "The difference in first cost will not be so much, for your 45 footer will only cost about 50 per cent more than the 35 footer. Often, today, the larger boat will be cheaper if bought second-hand. But it is the annual expense that jumps. The 45-footer with the man may cost three times as much to run, although you will not begin to get three times the pleasure, for the modern man is a nuisance some of the time. For instance, I suppose my man would like to go ashore tonight, but as I took the dinghy, he can't. That reminds me, I had better be returning to see how he is getting along, so he can turn in if he wants to.

"Before I leave, I must tell you that if a light wind comes up tonight, running against the tide, your dinghy will annoy you. When I anchor here, as I often do, we put two good sized fenders down and tie the dinghy alongside with bow and stern ropes. It doesn't seem to get choppy here very often, although it does in midstream. The fishing launches don't pass here early in the morning, so a dinghy properly secured alongside is all right in this anchorage."

"I'm very glad you reminded me of the dinghy," Goddard said, "for if you had not, I would have been on deck at four tomorrow morning, swearing terrible oaths, as I floundered around in the dew."

After Brewster had left, and Goddard was securing the dinghy alongside, he said to himself: A man may be expensive, but it must be nice to see a light burning in the forecastle when you return at night, and have someone to help you with the dinghy. But $3,000 a year, wages, food, and clothing, is too much for me.

Goddard was up early in the morning, and rowed away quietly, before the others on the *Viator* were awake. He had made arrangements with an Edgartown boat builder to hire a sailing dinghy for a few days and, while Mrs. Goddard was let into the scheme, it was kept a secret from the girls. As Goddard sailed back in the dinghy, towing the *Viator's* tender, the girls were curious to know what was up, but the only satisfaction they could get out of him was another: "You wait and see!"

As soon as breakfast was over, Prim said: "Pa, you promised that we could wear bathing suits all day when we got to Edgartown."

"Yes, that's right," he replied, but as the girls started for the stateroom to make the change, he added, "Wait a minute, now! Who is going to help Mother clean up after breakfast?"

"Oh, we thought *you* were!" they replied, but Goddard smiled, "No, I am going to be busy getting the *Viator* under way."

So the girls helped Mrs. Goddard get things straightened out below while he went on deck to take down the riding light and start the motor. However, the girls made a lightning change and were on deck soon enough to tail out on the warp as the anchor was broken out. Goddard only hauled the anchor up to the chocks and, although the crown was still slightly submerged, he left it that way for the short run they were to make to the head of Katama Bay. As they steamed along in the morning sunlight, the girls sat on the bow with their feet dangling in the spray sent up by the anchor, while the sailing dinghy and the *Viator's* tender tailed out astern. Much of Katama Bay is shallow, but in the southwest part close to a sandy bluff called Katama Point, there is seven or eight feet of water. Here they anchored.

Goddard had chosen this place to give the girls some lessons in sailing a dinghy, because there is quite a level sandy bottom there with about three feet of water. It was also a pleasant place to sail, for with a southwest wind there is a stretch of about a mile where you can reach back and forth under the lee of Norton Point, a low sandspit making the southern border of the bay. The girls had both steered larger boats but were not acquainted with the peculiarities of a dinghy, so they watched with interest as Goddard stepped the mast and arranged the halyard and sheet.

There was a light, steady breeze as they cast off, and took up their first tack with Goddard steering. At first, he showed them how the sheet was made fast by taking a turn around a pin that was under a thwart, and then held in one hand. He explained that this was the proper way to hold the sheet in a breeze, but in light or steady weather it was permissible to tuck a short bight of the sheet between the thwart and the downcoming sheet. This arrangement made a quick-releasing belay if the loose end was kept in the hand ready to jerk.

Prim remarked: "I noticed you made the halyard fast the same way."

"Yes," Goddard said, "that pin hitch has been used for centuries all over the world, on most of the ropes of unballasted craft. The pin is easier to make than a cleat, and the quick releasing feature of this hitch often saves time on small craft, where things sometimes have to be done quickly."

The dinghy had an oarlock socket at the stern and, after sailing a way, Goddard slacked the sheet so that the dinghy lay to with only the after part of the sail full. Then he unshipped the rudder and put an oar over the stern to steer with. This made the girls laugh, but Goddard explained to them that an oar was really the best way to steer many small boats and that most life boats and whale boats of the past were steered with oars.

"Why?" inquired both the girls.

"There are many reasons for it, but first of all an oar is a scientific lever arrangement that cannot be improved on for simplicity. It can do several things that the rudder cannot do well. It can be used to row the stern around if the craft is moving slowly. It can be used to scull with, or to pole on bottom. But, best of all, an oar properly handled is a powerful lever that will keep a boat from broaching-to in a following sea, and when landing on the beach it is nearly foolproof. I suppose the last two reasons are why the oar is used to steer life boats and surf boats. An oar is very much the best steering arrangement for small sailing tenders, for if you can do away with the rudder and tiller you have made a desirable simplification, for these parts are always a nuisance to store, and the rudder hangings on the stern of a tender are a perpetual nuisance."

"Yes, Pa," said Prim, "but isn't the oar harder to manage than a tiller? Won't it get away from you if you let go of it?"

"The particular oar and rowlock that you are now using is planned for rowing only, but for a steering oar, a round rowlock is best. Then there can be a strip of leather, called the 'button,' tacked around the loom of the oar, which stops the oar from running out of the closed rowlock. In steering with an oar, it is usual to carry it much further inboard than when rowing for this gives greater turning motion to the boat with less exertion to the helmsman."

The girls had been a little puzzled by some of the terms Goddard had used, so they asked him to tell them the proper names of the parts of an oar. He explained: "In the first place, oars were divided into three classes: the short ones, which are used in pairs (one in each hand like those in a dinghy) are called 'sculls.' The next longer class, are properly called 'oars,' and the word 'oar' also designates this instrument when the rower only uses one, which is pulled by both hands. The longest rowing instrument is called a 'sweep,' and is used by the larger boats, with often two or more men pulling. While the sweep is seldom seen nowadays, it was a very important instrument 500 or more years ago. The word 'rowlock,' is preferable to the word 'oarlock,' for designating the pivot of the scull, oar, or sweep.

"The early rowlocks were depressions or notches in a boat's rail, while the non-swiveling oar attachments above the rail were called 'tholes,' or 'thole pins.' The word 'row,' is derived from the Anglo-Saxon 'rowen,' while the word 'thole' is from the Anglo-Saxon, *thol.*

"The rowlock, swinging thole, or metal crotch, came into use in about 1819. As for the names of the parts of the scull, oar, or sweep: the wide, thin part that goes into the water is the blade," Goddard explained to them. "If it is concave on one side, it is called a spoon blade. The small part of the instrument next to the blade is the neck, while the larger part that plays in the oarlock or thole is the loom, and the part that is held in the hands is the grip.

"While it is true that some whaleboats had rudders to steer with, when sailing, they always shipped a steering oar when nearing a whale, because the oar was much the best for quick turning. This was particularly true when backing up." He showed Prim how the oar was held on a slight angle to hold it down in the oarlock, and then shifted places with her while she tried steering. The story about the whale boats and life boats had made the girls interested in steering with an oar. That is what Goddard wanted, for it is best always to learn to steer with an oar first of all.

By this time, they had almost reached the beach, or opening between the ocean and the bay which had been broken through in the hurricane of 1938. As they looked out to sea, they could just see Skiffs Island to the southeast. The water is very shallow in this part of the bay and as the centerboard had scraped the sand in places, it was hauled well up.

After coming about, Goddard said: "I am going to show you now how to steer the dinghy without an oar or rudder." This made the girls open their eyes, but Goddard explained to them that while the sail was pushing the dinghy sideways, the underwater part of the hull was resisting that movement. So, if they made the dinghy draw more water forward by moving their weights toward the bow, the sail's side push would bring the dinghy up in the wind. If they moved their weight aft, the side push would head her off because then the stern would have more draft or resistance to side movement.

He then explained that a short, wide boat like a dinghy is hard to steer, anyway. If she heels, the under-water shape becomes more curved on one side than the other. They could obviate that by keeping the dinghy nearly upright. Also, it will be necessary to haul the centerboard nearly all the way up, he told them, so that the dinghy will make considerable leeway. This will allow a difference in draft, either forward or aft, to be more effective.

He told the girls to sit just a little to leeward of the centerline, and that he would do the moving fore and aft to get the balance. After the centerboard was hauled up and the oar taken in, Goddard moved a little aft of where he had been sitting and the dinghy paid off to wind abeam, with the *Viator* right ahead of them. As they sailed along, Goddard slowly moved fore and aft, in a crouching position, with both of his feet under him. He used his hands also in moving around, for the sheet was belayed and there was no tiller to handle. Goddard told the girls that long, narrow boats like a canoe were much easier to steer that way, and that racing two rudderless canoes was great sport, particularly when tacking to windward.

Now they were close to the *Viator,* and Mrs. Goddard was sitting comfortably in the cockpit reading, but Prim called to her: "Gee, Mother, we are steering without a rudder!"

Mrs. Goddard replied: "I think you have all lost your rudders."

The dinghy, nevertheless, kept a steady course close under the stern of the *Viator,* and was headed for the shore beyond, when Prim asked: "Pa, how will we come about?"

Although they were approaching the shoreline quite rapidly, Goddard said very calmly: "When I say One, Two, Three! we will all move well forward in the dinghy, and when I say All Right! I want you to come aft again."

They were very close to shore when he called: "One, Two, Three!" As they all moved forward, the dinghy made a slow but graceful luff, with the stern swinging enough to bring her by the wind's eye. When Goddard said: "All Right!" they moved aft, the bow payed off and they were on a new tack. All they had to do was shift the sheet over. The girls now wanted to do the balancing, or trimming, so Goddard took up a position to leeward, so they had room to shift their weight fore and aft. At first, in their breathless excitement, they steered a very crooked course, but after a while only one girl had to move to keep them on course.

By this time, the sun was rather hot and the excitement of sailing the dinghy had somewhat subsided, so Prim said: "Pa, I thought you said we could have all the swimming we wanted."

Goddard answered: "I feel like swimming, myself, so we will go back to the *Viator,* while I put on my bathing suit. You girls can lower and furl the sail, and get the *Viator's* tender ready to go ashore in, but see that your bathing caps are on tight."

While Goddard was on board, he had a chance to tell his wife not to be surprised if the girls did some screaming, for he was going to tip the tender over to show them how to right it and let them get used to being capsized. So after they rowed toward shore, a little way, Goddard quickly pulled in his oars and moved over to the rail.

The girls must have suspected something of the kind, for they as quickly sprang to the opposite side and set up piercing screams which much amused Mrs. Goddard on the *Viator*. Goddard put his toe under the thwart, and leaned away out on his side, but the combined weight of the girls was too much for him, so they all laughed again. Just then he made a sudden move and came over to their side, so they all went over with the loudest screams of all. At first, the girls started to swim, but soon realizing the water was only about four feet deep they stood up, laughing, while Goddard was collecting the floating oars and bailer.

The tender, of course, was bottom side up, and as she had tipped over slowly, she was water-logged, or had little air in her. After the girls got their breath, he told them to right her. They both went to one side and tried to raise her rail above the water, but they couldn't quite do it, although they had their feet on bottom.

Then Goddard explained to them that any raising movement on the tender created a suction from the entrapped air inside and, as the tender tipped, the flotation of the immersed side resisted tipping. He then threw his body upon the tender's bottom, and hooked his fingers over the further rail. The tender then came over easy enough, while he explained that the weight of his body had made the air inside the boat want to escape, so there was no suction to hold her down. The girls then had fun turning the tender over and over, which they could do quite quickly after they had become accustomed to using their hands and feet at the same time.

Goddard then said: "I want to show you what it is like to be trapped in the air under a boat." They tipped the tender bottom side up, with quite a lot of air in her. Goddard dipped his head under the rail, and stood up inside the tender. The girls were a little alarmed at first, but as he proceeded to talk to them in a calm voice, they began to laugh, for his voice had a very strange, muffled tone to it after passing through the bottom of the tender. After awhile, Goddard came out from under the tender, whereupon, Prim asked him what it was like under there. He told her: "You just try it and see."

Prim seemed to hesitate, but when her father said; "That little dip shouldn't be much for a girl like you, who can swim under water 50 feet," she went under, and they soon heard the muffled sounds of her voice calling Veronica to join her. Veronica took a long breath and she, too, went under. The voices of the two girls were amusing as they talked to each other and marveled at how light it was under the boat and how plainly they could see bottom. The water was about shoulder deep where they were, with a clean, sandy bottom. Goddard encouraged them to stay under, until they were thoroughly used to it.

During this time, the *Rozinante* had sailed up, and made fast alongside the *Viator*. The two boys came rowing over in the *Sancho Panza* to join the swimming party. The reason Weldon had made fast to the *Viator* was that he had just come from town where he had purchased seven fair-sized, freshly boiled lobsters. Now, in the absence of Goddard, he proposed to Mrs. Goddard that they work together and make up a large lobster salad for all hands.

Weldon was full of enthusiasm as he said: "I stopped in at an antique shop this morning and purchased a blue Staffordshire platter that took my eye, when all at once it occurred to me that the platter would look nice dressed in the various colors of a large lobster salad. You know, the lobsters south of the Cape are delicious. I also brought along some fresh lettuce, mayonnaise, potato chips, fresh rolls, and island butter. Now, if you and I go to work and boil a few eggs, I think we can make something good."

Mrs. Goddard replied: "You are as welcome as the flowers in spring, for I was just worrying about how I would fill up those hungry girls of mine."

So we will leave them busily working over the salad, while we go back to the swimmers. Goddard was just showing the girls how to shove some of the water out of a swamped boat. He explained: "With most boats, it is best to do this from the bow because a large, or wide, stern cannot be shoved through the water quickly enough." He then got at the bow of his swamped pram tender and pushed it down in the water until he could put his feet on the bow with his legs doubled up under him. He then sort of rolled over backwards and, at the same time he straightened his body out, pushing very hard with his feet so that the tender gave a quick jump backward with the stern well up in the air. When she settled down again, she was more than half free of water. The next time he jumped her, he did it with his hands, after depressing the bow just to the water level and waiting until the inside water had surged well toward him. While the second jump did not rid the tender of more than a few buckets of water, he said: "It will save much time in bailing, anyway."

"But how are you going to bail her out if you are on the outside?" inquired Prim.

"That is the hardest part of the whole thing, particularly if you haven't got a good bailer. A hat sometimes makes a fair one. However, it is best to get one arm over the rail, like this." He showed them that by pressing the rail down nearly to the water level, you can scoop or bail the water out quite quickly, but it becomes hard and discouraging work if there is a sea occasionally lopping in.

"After the water is more than three-quarters out of the boat," he told them, "you should climb in over the middle of the stern. This is a hard thing to do quickly, and it takes what seems a lot of strength if you are tired. At any rate, you should try to squirm in over the stern, without tipping the boat. After you have your hips beyond the stern, it is not as hard as you may think, although you are face downward. As soon as you are in the boat, you should sit right on the bottom, so your weight is partly water-borne, and bail frantically until there is no longer danger of water lopping in over the side. Right here, I must tell you that some dinghies with low centerboard cases are a problem, but sometimes this leak at the top of the box can be partly stopped by a handkerchief or some other piece of cloth torn from your clothing.

"I want you girls to try jumping the swamped tender, to see which one can get the most water out." While they were doing this, Jim and Dan came rowing over in the *Sancho Panza* all dressed for swimming, so Prim asked her father if she could tip them over. "No, for they are quite a little younger than you girls and I don't want to scare little Dan. Instead, I want you to row the *Sancho Panza* over to the *Viator*, get a scrubbing brush and ask Mr. Weldon if he wants the bottom of the *Sancho* scrubbed."

"All right, Pa," said Prim, "but how am I to get into the *Sancho* when her rail is as high as my face?"

"We'll arrange that, but first we must get the boys out without shipping water."

Jim said he could get out all right and, after pushing Dan to one side, he took a flying leap over the stern, but little Dan hesitated some time before he could make up his mind what to do, for the instinct to keep in a boat is a strong one when you are young. Mr. Goddard came alongside and let Dan climb out on his shoulder. After he was in the water, he was all right for he was a good little swimmer.

The next thing was to get Prim into the tender. This they did by taking the painter over the stern, where there was a scull hole, and tying a loop in the painter about two feet below water. Mr. Goddard and the other children held the *Sancho* steady and Prim, after putting one foot in the looped painter, mounted the stern very nimbly and soon squirmed forward.

While Prim was away with the *Sancho*, Veronica who was quiet and gentle with children, showed the boys how to roll the tender over and over and how to stand under her when capsized. Little Dan had considerable reluctance to try this, for the water was nearly up to his chin. But when Veronica said they would go under together, he couldn't hesitate. In his hurry to raise his head, he bumped the midships thwart, but after that he was just as comfortable under the tender as outside.

The water in this shallow part of Katama Bay is unusually warm and one can stay in for hours without discomfort, so while the children were playing with the *Viator's* tender, Goddard spent most of the time floating. This is the most comfortable position one can assume in the water for the whole body is evenly supported.

Mr. Goddard was not a stout man but he could float without difficulty because as he breathed, he kept his lungs a little more than naturally inflated. As he lay on his back, he kept his head all submerged, excepting his face. Occasionally, his feet slowly started to sink, but then he moved his hands in such a way that they acted like two propellers and forced his body ahead in the water enough so that his toes soon appeared at the surface. The children were much interested in the way Goddard floated, and he told them that he would give them a lesson in that art if they went swimming that afternoon.

Now, Prim came rowing back all out of breath to tell them that Mr. Weldon and her mother were making the largest lobster salad she had ever seen and there were to be potato chips and she had had a handful already. This information made the young ones inclined to return, but Goddard said the bottom of both tenders had to be scrubbed.

He walked around inshore, towing the upset tender until he came to a place about three feet deep, where he stuck the oars in the soft sand and tied the bailer to them with its own lanyard.

He then told Jim and the girls to take the oars and other loose parts of the *Sancho* and secure them in the same way, when they could capsize that boat. Strange to say, the three of them had hard work to do it.

However, as soon as they had shipped some water, the *Sancho* went over easy enough. In this second capsize, the girls did not scream at all but as the rail came over, it hit one of them on the head. Since she had considerable hair under her bathing cap, it caused nothing more than a ducking. Goddard told them that they should always watch the rail of a capsizing boat and the one who was hit in the head said she always would.

They now all went to work scrubbing the bottoms of the tenders, which was done by Dan and Jim, reaching down to bottom and bringing up handfuls of sand which they put on the bottoms of the boats. Goddard used the brush that Prim had brought over, but the girls used an old sponge that they had found jammed under the floor-boards of the *Sancho*. The boats were at just a comfortable height to work on, so it was more fun than work. Goddard was glad to have it done, for neither of the tenders was painted with anti-fouling paint and the warm water south of the Cape had produced some delicate green weeds and scum that did not appeal to his sailor's eye.

When the scrubbing was over, Goddard told the children that there was a way to lift a boat out of the water so she would empty herself completely.

"Of course, it can only be done with a light boat when she is in about three feet of water. First, you turn the boat on her side, and then lift slowly and gradually until the water has mostly flowed out. Then, with a quick turn, set her on her bottom. Now, I will get at the stern and the girls can take the bow while the boys can stoop down and lift on the lower rail." Goddard had a wonderful way with young ones, for he somehow made them interested in what they were doing so that now as they all slowly lifted together, the tender came clear of the water and went over on her bottom with less than a pail of water in her. They now gave the *Sancho* the same treatment but, being a slightly heavier boat, they did some hard lifting before she was clear of the water.

In the meantime, Weldon and Mrs. Goddard had not been idle, for although it is admitted Mrs. Goddard did most everything in putting the salad together, Weldon did take the lobster meat from the shells very skillfully with a strong two-pronged iron fork. First, he twisted off the claws and, taking them one after another, pulled off the little lower claws and thrust one prong of the fork up where this little claw had been until the prong came out at the neck of the claw. With a twist and a rip, he opened that end of the claw so that the succulent white claw meat came out in one piece.

After twisting the lower end of the body away from the upper shell, he squeezed each section of this armor between his thumb and forefinger until it cracked and, turning the tail over, he opened each section until the swimming muscles came out in one piece. There were two little tabs of white flesh near the large end of these swimming muscles and as he took them between thumb and finger had pulled gently toward the stern of the creature, a long strip of flesh came off neatly exposing the colon, which was a small dark colored gut. This has to be gently lifted out if it is to be removed in one piece, but Weldon knew how to start at the forward end, and pull diagonally backward, so that it came out entire. It should be noted, for the uninitiated, that this is the most essential part of the lobster to clean thoroughly and the part that often gives lobster eaters ptomaine poisoning.

Weldon knew how to choose some of the savory parts of the lobster head or forebody and he placed these soft parts on a plate. It took him less than a quarter of an hour to remove the meat from the shells.

After that, he busied himself, stretching an awning over the cockpit of the *Rozinante,* for although they were only separated from the ocean by a narrow sand spit the sun was very hot. They had decided to eat on board the *Rozinante,* because her large, open cockpit would allow them all to sit in a circle around the platter of salad, which was placed on two camp stools from the *Viator*. While the *Rozinante* did not have an ice chest, Weldon had brought from town some dry ice that now flanked several bottles and the butter as they reposed in a bucket on the cockpit floor.

Finally, Mrs. Goddard handed the platter of salad over and followed with a good supply of paper plates, drinking cups, and napkins. After everything was arranged to her satisfaction, Weldon gave a prolonged blast on the foghorn, and the tenders came rowing back as if they were in a race. The several hours spent in sailing and swimming had created unusual appetites among the youngsters. Mrs. Goddard served the salad on paper pie plates, flanked with a freshly buttered roll, while Weldon handed around the cold ginger ale. The first part of the meal was very silent but, just before the ice cream was served, Goddard said: "By Jove! I believe that is the best meal I ever ate."

Mrs. Goddard remarked: "That is because you have been in the water most of the morning."

"Yes," he agreed, "but there is something more to it, for every day I stay on a cruise I feel better and better and to spend the day close to nature where the water and air are clean as they are here is the best tonic of all."

After the men had settled down with their pipes and Mrs. Goddard and the girls were cleaning up, putting the paper plates and other waste in a paper bag with the lobster shells, Prim asked her father when he was going to give them a lesson in floating. "Oh . . . ," he sighed, "don't talk to me about swimming for a long time, but I will tell you a story about floating."

So, after getting his pipe going well, he began: "Once upon a time, nearly 100 years ago, one of our naval vessels was passing across a warm part of the Pacific Ocean. So, many of the sailors slept at night on what was called the hammock nettings, the bowsprit nettings, or any other cool place they could find. On one calm night, one of the men fell overboard. He was not missed until the next morning, but when the accident was reported to the commanding officer he had the vessel reverse her course and requested the navigating officer to travel as closely as he could over their previous course, making allowance for leeway, etc.

"Most of the crew thought it was a foolish waste of time, but the captain said the man was an old navy shellback and might float a long while. Sure enough, after they had steamed back fifteen miles or so, the man was spotted from the masthead and, after a boat was lowered, he was picked up none the worse for his experience. When the officers questioned him, he said he had rested on his back very comforatbly and knew the captain would come back for him."

Goddard continued: "I guess the old Navy had some tough shellbacks all right, but it must have been some sensation to be overboard in the Pacific at night with your vessel steaming away from you."

"Do you think that is a true story?"

"I don't know," replied Goddard. "It is simply a story that used to go around when I was in the Navy, during World War I, but I must say I believe a man who knows how can keep afloat a long time in warm water if it is calm. Although I doubt if anyone can last long in cold, rough water, some of the cross-channel swimmers have spent as much as twelve hours afloat."

The heavy meal had pretty well sunk the grown-ups, and even little Dan was stretched out on the cockpit seat in pleasant relaxation. But the meal had had no subduing effect on the girls and they said they wanted to go swimming, but Mrs. Goddard said emphatically; "No!" and added that they should never go in swimming less than an hour after eating. After a meal like the one they had just had it was better to wait two hours.

"All right," agreed Prim, "but I would like to know why it is bad to swim after eating."

"Well, I'll tell you," her father replied. "It makes some people sick to their stomachs and they have a terrific struggle in the water when this happens. Then it sometimes gives people cramps."

"What are cramps?" Prim asked.

"Cramps are a painful congestion of the muscles that at times makes you lose control of your limbs. They are most likely to occur in cold water, and if you catch cramps, as they say, you should roll on your back and inflate the lungs while propelling yourself as best you can with the unaffected limbs. It is very important not to get panicky, for this is apparently the cause of many drownings. Instead, even if you are some distance from shore, you should float patiently on your back until the cramp has passed away. I can't help thinking cramps are bad for you and may cause some later nerve trouble, so you see it is best not to go in swimming after eating."

"I'm glad to know the real reason for not swimming after meals," said Prim, "but what are we going to do for the next hour or so?"

"I know just what I'm going to do, Prim," her father said. "I am going to sit quietly just where I am. Why don't you and Veronica take a sail in the dinghy. After this morning's lesson, you should be all right."

Mr. Weldon spoke up to say; "If Prim will sail me over to the opening, we can take along the bag of lobster shells and waste. If the tide is running out, we can throw it over there and it will drift to sea and not soil the clean water here."

"That's a grand idea," said Goddard. So, while the girls were rigging the dinghy, Weldon got the bag of waste and they were about to start, when Jim spoke up: "I wish I could go too."

"Certainly, you can go, Jim," Mr. Goddard said. "The dinghy will take four, nicely."

There was a nice afternoon breeze by that time, so they sailed to the opening in great style. Then someone suggested that if, they went out through the opening, they would be sure that the swill would drift to sea. Weldon warned them that there might be some shallow spots in the outer part of the channel, where the seas might break.

As they looked seaward, there seemed nothing but an old ground swell quietly running in, so they headed out through the opening, close hauled, with a fair tide carrying them merrily along. The seas ahead now looked much steeper than they had from inside. Soon after they had passed the gap in the land, Jim, who was sitting to leeward, reported the water was much shallower on his side, so Prim headed as high as she could. The next sea that passed under them was really quite steep, but the following one started to break a hundred feet or so to windward of them and its roar drew all eyes in that direction.

Weldon said: "Now, sit tight and brace yourselves, so you won't get thrown to leeward." But almost before he was through speaking, the wave was upon them. The dinghy made an heroic effort to meet the coamer and, with a corkscrew motion, almost stood on end but she was heavily loaded with four passengers so that much of the white water went over them.

As the wave passed, Prim was much alarmed to feel the tiller twist sideways in her hand, and looking around, saw the rudder float up sideways and then unfasten itself from the tiller to float away. It seems that when the dinghy stood on end to meet the wave, the rudder touched bottom enough to unhang itself.

For an instant, Prim was bewildered, but soon called for an oar and rowlock. However, before they could be shipped, the next wave was upon them. Fortunately, this wave did not break, and as the dinghy swung up in the wind, she only shipped a little water as the sharp crest passed them.

By this time, the oar was shipped and Prim gave a vigorous stroke, which swung the dinghy off on her course. As the outgoing tide had carried them beyond the shoal spot, the waves were no longer steep.

Weldon, who had been inwardly blaming himself for getting in this pickle, now turned to Prim and said: "You certainly are a cool one, and did remarkably well to ship the oar so quickly."

"Well," she confessed, "I wouldn't have known what to do if I hadn't seen Father do the same thing this morning, but what are we to do about the lost rudder?"

"Oh, don't worry about the rudder, for the tide stream will bring it out to us," said Weldon. Sure enough, as they looked around, Veronica spotted it on their weather beam not far away, so Prim came about, and headed for the rudder with Jim at the lee rail to grab it. She had a little too much way on as they shot for it, and so, when Jim grabbed the rudder, it made the dinghy pay off and gather way so it slipped out of his hands. Weldon now said he would like to try it, so after they changed places he brought the dinghy to a place where the floating rudder was about fifty feet on their leeward beam. Then, by slacking the sheet, he killed the dinghy's way and told the girls to haul up the centerboard. When this was done, the dinghy moved sideways toward the floating rudder, as Weldon could make her go ahead or astern by taking in or paying out the sheet. All the while, Weldon kept the dinghy headed as on a close reach. This he could easily do with the oar, although they had no way on. This time, Jim could leisurely pick up the rudder, for it slowly came to them sideways.

There was a pretty fair breeze by that time and the dinghy danced merrily over the chop as she rose to the ground swells, but they didn't mind the spray as Jim was to leeward, bailing.

After the bag of lobster shells was given a sea toss, Weldon suggested that they sail back through the opening before the tide was any lower for, as he said: "At low tide, I think every wave will break there." However, as they looked along the beach, they noticed that the only place where it broke at sea was where the tide stream ran out, so he added: "If you let me take her in, I think I can avoid most of the breakers." Prim was very glad to have Weldon run the dinghy in because she had really had a scare coming out and now felt much relieved.

Weldon went quite a little to one side of the tide stream and ran in wind-on-the-quarter, always letting the sheet run to kill her way as a sea made up behind them. They were surprised that no bottom was seen, but all of a sudden it appeared to shoal very rapidly and this time the wave astern started to break when about 50 feet away, whereupon Weldon swung off dead before it and let the sheet go until the sail was right out ahead.

When the wave was close to them, it made quite a roar, and the undertow seemed to carry them back toward it. It was not a big wave but a steep, combing one. As it smacked the transom, several buckets of water came aboard while the crest rushed by, shoulder high. The waterlogged dinghy started on a mad rush toward the beach, but Weldon by the proper use of the oar had kept the dinghy so nearly in the path of the wave that there was no tendency to yaw. They now came back on their course while the sheet was trimmed in smartly and Jim got busy with the bailer. Soon the water was reported much deeper. Although several steep seas rose behind, none of them broke so they reached the entrance without shipping more water.

The tide was now flowing out quite briskly and if there had not been a good breeze, wind-on-the-quarter, they could not have stemmed it. However, as they were steering with an oar, and had the centerboard up, they could go very close to the bank and the children were much amused at the large waves the dinghy pulled astern, while not much more than holding her own on the shore.

Finally they entered the shoal waters of the Bay and left the tide behind, but they had to sail some distance with the centerboard up. It seemed very tranquil, skimming over the calm water of the Bay after their thrashing outside, and as they approached the *Viator* the children looked forward to relating their adventures, while Weldon was embarrassed for letting them get into the predicament.

After they had boarded and the different versions of the incident had been told, all Mr. Goddard had to say was: "Where is the rudder?" After he stood up and saw it on the floorboards, he remarked: "I guess that's a good place for it, while we sail in shallow water."

Prim then asked if it was time for swimming, and Mr. Goddard said: "Sure, swim all you want to." But Prim hung back, and asked her father if he wasn't going to give them a floating lesson.

He replied: "You ought to get your mother to do that for she floats like a cork."

"Hush up!" said Mrs. Goddard. "That is all nonsense, for I don't float any different from other people."

"Oh, yes she does," teased her husband. "You just get her overboard, and you will see that she bobs up and down on the surface like a newly launched dinghy."

After the girls got through laughing, Prim said: "Come, Ma, you said you would go swimming when we got in the warm water south of the Cape." So Mrs. Goddard went below to put on her bathing suit.

In the meantime, the girls brought the tender alongside, but when Mrs. Goddard came on deck she would not get into it. Instead, she said she wanted the swimming ladder and, when the girls asked her why she wouldn't get in the tender, she replied: "No, indeed, you aren't going to capsize me!"

Mrs. Goddard, however, was a good swimmer and arrived at the swimming grounds even before the tender, but that was mostly because Goddard had decided to join the fun and jumped into the tender with Jim and Dan. He tried to persuade Weldon to join them, but Weldon said someone should watch the yachts in case a power boat went by.

This time there was little trouble in swamping the tender, for as they rocked her back and forth enough water was shipped so she went down under them as her five passengers stood up, and laughed. She soon made a move to one side, and they were all spilled out together.

Mrs. Goddard soon taught the girls to float, but Jim and Dan could not quite do it although they tried very hard, so Mrs. Goddard showed them how to scull with the palms of their hands.

This they did by holding their fingers together and swinging their hands back and forth so the palm of the hand acted somewhat like the blade of an oar when sculling, but the hands were held on an angle of about forty-five degrees with the palms downward. This not only forces the swimmer ahead but also has enough of an upward reaction to keep the body of a thin person on the surface with little exertion. Goddard then showed the boys how to swim on their backs by using their hands in this way and slowly drawing up their feet and legs when they could kick them back so strongly that the whole body was forced ahead nearly as fast as a swimmer using the breast stroke. After this, the boys had fun racing with one swimming on his back and the other with different strokes face downward. Although they found little difference in their speed, Mr. Goddard told them that while swimming on the back was very useful for resting in calm weather, it was not the best way to swim in rough water for when the head goes under the water will run up the nose giving a disagreeable sensation. When face down, the nose acts like a scupper which lets in air but allows the water to run out.

While they were having this fun in the clean water over a level sandy bottom, they were much surprised to see the *Tranquilo* approaching them for it seemed very strange for a yacht of this size to be sailing in water only about four feet deep. The *Tranquilo* was under power and had her lee boards up, and Mr. Brewster knew the shallow waters of the bay very well. When the *Tranquilo* was quite close to the swimmers her engines were stopped and she slowly coasted right up to them.

Brewster said to Mr. Goddard: "I do not want to interrupt your fun, but I have Mrs. Brewster aboard and we plan to anchor near the *Viator* so we should like to invite Mr. and Mrs. Goddard and the girls aboard for supper."

"That sounds good to me," Goddard told him while Mrs. Goddard more formally said: "Thank you very much, and what time will you expect us?" Brewster told her any time before half-past six.

By this time, the *Tranquilo* had swung beam to the breeze and was drifting into deeper water when her engines were started and she proceeded to her anchorage which was a little to the southeast of the other yachts. The *Tranquilo* could have anchored close under Katama Point but Brewster thought there would be less sand flies and mosquitoes a little further out.

Mrs. Goddard was now chock full of business and said to the girls: "Come now, we must go back at once for it will take me two hours or more to make you girls presentable for supper." Although the girls both protested, saying they could easily dress in a quarter of an hour, Mrs. Goddard had her way.

In the meantime, Mr. Goddard and the boys continued their fun. At first he gave them some sculling lessons in the *Sancho Panza*. Then he taught them to scull backward which he said was often very useful. He did this by standing up and holding the oar with the two hands at places nearly three feet apart. The upper hand was on the grip of the oar and held it quite firmly, while the lower hand only partly encircled the neck of the oar. With the lower hand he made the oar swing back and forth in the water, while with the upper hand he very slightly twisted it so that at every swing the moving oar tried to pull away from him. The boys soon learned the trick and could, after awhile, induce the dinghy to go in any direction they wanted. This kind of sculling interested them and they were amused at the eddies and whirlpools the oar made. Goddard explained to them that an oar held and used that way really made a variable pitch propeller, and in starting up or moving a heavy boat or a float stage it was best to use a very fine pitch. As the boat got under way, the pitch could be increased. The selection of the proper pitch in sculling backward was the principal trick of the thing. He told them that they should practice sculling backwards with either hand uppermost, for it is sometimes necessary to scull backwards when sitting down, as is often done in a river canoe, for that was about the best way to make that sort of craft move sideways. The boys were amazed at the power that could be produced when the oar was properly handled.

Goddard told them that a good swimmer could develop much more towing power and could even tow a boat backward against a good oarsman. The boys were so much surprised at this that Goddard said he thought little Dan could swim with as much power as Jim could develop with the oars. This made Jim give a scornful laugh, but Mr. Goddard said: "Suppose we try it."

He and Dan got out in the shallow water while Jim passed

the *Sancho's* painter under the thwarts and let it out at the scull hole aft. Goddard rove the painter under one of Dan's armpits and carried it around the back of Dan's neck and down under the other armpit, securing the end to the running part about two feet behind little Dan's back. He then stood between Dan and the tender to take the strain if one or the other of the boys started first, for he knew that if the row boat got the start she would jerk the painter with all her moving weight. Sure enough, when Jim started to row and took up the slack in the painter it nearly toppled Goddard over. By that time, Dan began to swim manfully so Goddard let go the rope and the tug of war was on. Perhaps Jim had never rowed against a dead load before and could not really throw his weight into the oars. Little Dan was a good swimmer and as soon as he saw he was winning, or beating his big brother, he made an heroic effort and towed the *Sancho* backward about ten feet. Goddard said that was enough, for he knew that if they kept at it the rower would finally get the best of it and the painter would begin to chafe Dan's shoulders and neck.

After they were all in the boat again and Jim, quite out of breath, had admitted he was beaten, they both asked at once why a swimmer could not pass a row boat if he had more driving power.

"It isn't so much a matter of power," Goddard told them, "as it is of resistance, for while a swimmer can develop more towing power than an oarsman, the human body is such a bad shape for going through the water that its resistance becomes very great as soon as it moves at any great speed. For instance, at about three miles per hour, a man would tow through the water as hard as a nicely shaped boat of ten or more times his weight. At six miles per hour, the human body might well have a resistance equal to a nicely shaped boat of more than sixty times its weight or displacement. So you see the study of underwater shapes is very interesting and man can never expect to swim very fast until he is as well shaped for that purpose as a fish."

While this discussion was going on in the *Sancho Panza*, they got a hail from Mrs. Goddard ordering her husband to return at once and get ready for supper. So Goddard remarked that he guessed the admiral had hoisted the recall signal, and rowed briskly back to the anchorage.

It did not take Goddard long to prepare for supper for about all he was going to wear were some white duck trousers, cleanly scrubbed sneakers, and a sport shirt. When they were ready to start, Mrs. Goddard sent him below for a necktie but when he returned with the tie in his pocket, she gave up in disgust and boarded the dinghy rather sulkily.

As they were rowing over to the *Tranquilo* Goddard said to Prim: "My, your hair looks nice!"

"Yes," she replied, "it ought to with the ten pounds of elbow grease Ma has brushed into it."

Mrs. Goddard frowned: "Prim, you do not speak very respectfully of your mother." But Mr. Goddard as usual defended his daughter, saying: "Never mind, Prim, Mother is always cranky when going out to supper, but after the first refreshment she can see a joke as well as anyone."

Before Mrs. Goddard could reply they were alongside the *Tranquilo* so she suddenly became very affable. Perhaps the principal reason for this was that Brewster was dressed almost exactly as Goddard was, but they were all under a slight suspense because none of them had met Mrs. Brewster. When this smiling lady stepped up from the galley to welcome them aboard, the slight tension was broken for Mrs. Brewster was a motherly lady almost old enough to be the girls' grandmother. She loved to have young ones aboard.

She said: "My, these girls are as pretty as Brewster said, and we shall all have lots of fun." As Mrs. Brewster went back to the galley, the captain came aft with a tray which, besides its usual load of glasses, had a silver plate of hors d'oeuvres which naturally took the girls' eyes after their swim. But we shall leave them even before the first plate is handed around, for with three boats in this story it is necessary to jump from one to the other rather frequently. . . .

Perhaps, Gentle Reader, you will be surprised that I have devoted so much space to swimming and puttering around on the beach with children, but you will find that these trivial scenes are the best part of cruising and may be remembered long after many a sail has been forgotten.

You will say: "Yes, but can't all this beach sport be had without the use and expense of a sail boat?" To which I will answer: "There are types of people who prefer the public beaches and the more people who are there, the better they like it. These individuals have no interest in nature, landscapes or fresh air and clean water. But some love privacy and the thrill of exploring uninhabited islands and coves is their greatest pleasure. Such a man loves to take his family day after day to new natural views; places where they can bathe in the pure water and breathe pure air, while the eye feasts on the ever-changing colors of sea and sky. For him, there has never been a better moving home than the sail boat. Perhaps the sail boat will always be the best source of pleasure to the lovers of nature for if in camping the tourist must carry his shelter and food, in sailing or cruising the boat is your shelter and carries you and your food."

But cruising of late years has become hopelessly confused with racing. Cruising is not sailing to Bermuda in competition, or taking a beating off the Fastnet Rock, nor is it spending your time changing rule-cheating sails in rapid succession. It is unfortunate that the cruising clubs of Europe and America have developed types of boats that are useless for cruising, and I say "useless for cruising" because they are too expensive to build and run: they cannot comfortably accommodate the crew that is necessary to handle them: they are too deep for the best cruising grounds and very uncomfortable in a seaway.

Perhaps you will answer me by saying: "I know, but the modern racing cruiser is fast. You will be quite wrong in that assertion, for the ocean racing measurement rules of both Europe and America heavily penalize the speed-giving qualities of a sailboat. It is true that some ocean racers are comparatively fast to windward when they set sails that greatly exceed their measured sail area. And it is true that any tub can be forced to leeward quite fast if she hoists a large enough parachute spinnaker. But, in cruising, one should not beat to windward if he can help it, and certainly would not want to set a spinnaker his crew could not handle. On the other hand, a sensible cruiser can be built for about half the cost of an ocean racer and the sensible cruiser will sail right by the ocean racer on a reach in a good breeze. On account of her shallow draft, the cruiser will often make the best time between ports and most all ports are open to her. The truth of the matter is that we have developed some ocean racing freaks that are very slow for their cost and extremely expensive to run, while they are practically useless for cruising.

If Horace Kephart, in his fine book *Camping and Woodcraft,* stresses simplicity on every page, I would just as strongly suggest simplicity in cruising, for I feel that the average small cruiser of 50 or 60 years ago is capable of giving more pleasure for the cost than the usual boat of today. In my youth, the small sailboat or cruiser had no engine, toilet, or electrical devices so that (short of a collision or severe stranding) repairs through the summer season were almost unheard of, while we could cruise in most any direction without thought of expense or fuel consumption.

Today, however, the usual small cruiser must stick to an itinerary of short trips between the boat yards that have a monkey wrench mechanic. The first stop will be to adjust the engine which cannot be gotten at; the next stop to overhaul the electrical w.c. Then, after covering twenty miles more of uninteresting coast line, there will be innumerable things to be done so the stop will require several days' delay and the shipyard bill will be a hundred smackers. At this stop, perhaps, the compass will have to be readjusted on account of the changes in electronics; two lapping jibs recut, the fire extinguishers recharged and the parachute mended, so the average speed along the coast for these new type cruisers is about ten miles a day, and the running cost one dollar a mile. In my youth, a sensible cruiser of any of the sizes between 25 and 50 feet waterline cost new about one-tenth what they do now. Yet wages, materials and other building costs have only about tripled since that time.

You may wonder why the modern cruiser costs so much. It is only on account of the ridiculous complications that the inexperienced yachtsman requires, for he will fall for any complicated mechanical device that is advertised. When someone markets a twelve cylinder toilet with dual ignition, his fondest hopes will be fulfilled. Sometimes I wonder why we used to cruise farther and faster in the old boats than now, but it is the case of the hare and the tortoise again.

Before World War I, it was not at all unusual to sail or cruise ten hours a day, day after day, at a rate of perhaps four miles an hour. While the modern cruiser with her engine and lapping jibs is admittedly faster, still if she can only run a few hours at a time away from the shipyard, her day-after-day speed along the coast is much less than the old fashioned straight sailer. While the difference in first cost between the old and new types of cruisers is only ten to one, the difference in cost per mile is something like one hundred to one, for our fuel consumption was nothing. To be sure, we would stop every hundred miles or so for a bag of coal, some oil for the lamps or perhaps a hank of marline, but outside of food the day-after-day expense was nil. The delay of an occasional calm is very little beside the long tie-ups in a boat yard. It is said that a good woodsman can make camp with little else than an axe, while the novice with several hundred pounds of equipment would fare very badly. It is much the same in cruising. If you have a little know-how, about all that is necessary is a tight deck, a comfortable bunk, and a coal-burning stove.

However, there are things other than physical comfort that are nice on a small cruiser, and one of them is the sense of complete relaxation that comes from being on a boat or vessel which has nothing that can explode and requires no fire that cannot instantly be put out with a draw bucket. The ear and nose should also be considered, and the cruiser which has no other noises than the water alongside and the wind in the rigging will give as much pleasure today as it did fifty years ago. However, on a perfectly calm, quiet night the regular tick of a

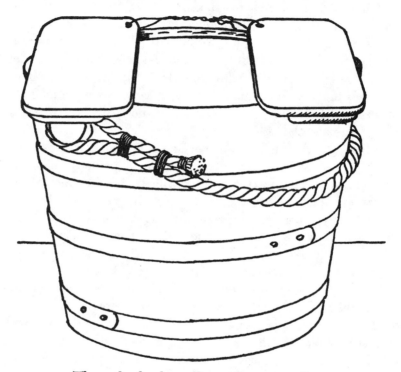

The cedar bucket toilet with seat in place.

perfectly poised clock like a Chelsea gives the cabin a very snug feeling while the varying gallop of the inferior timepiece is most annoying. As for the smells—if there is only a faint odor of oak, cedar and teak all will be well, for their combination will but enhance the ditty bag's fragrance of marline, beeswax and oakum while the fainter odors of sail cloth and manila add their soothing effect.

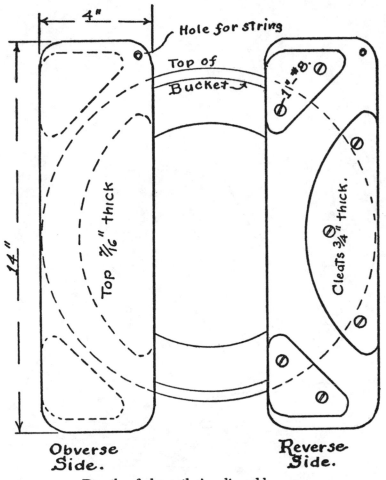

Details of the toilet's adjustable seat.

This is where the cedar bucket toilet comes in, for this arrangement can be used where desired and generally out of the cabin. It can be used in the cockpit at night or in the forepeak in the daytime. It has no everlasting odor, and for those who are affected by suggestion it may be kept hung under the after deck, when the whole ship can be as immaculate as a Greek temple. For those who have a rather tender posterior anatomy,

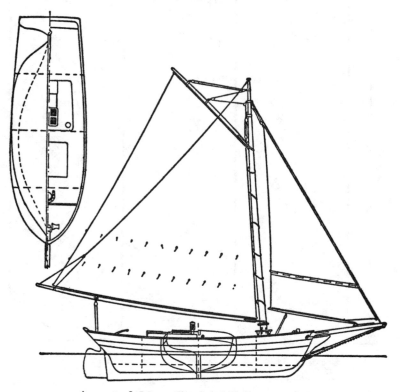

A typical New England fishing smack.

the bucket can have an attachment to increase the areas of contact, and the accompanying sketches show both this device in place and a dimensioned working drawing. The ones I have made were of unfinished teak and I suppose would function well for several generations with no other care than an occasional scrubbing or towing.

This device will also work on the usual galvanized iron bucket if you are careful to keep clear of the projecting ears where the bail is hung. One of the advantages of the device is that a fine adjustment of the aperture may be made which renders it convenient for different ages and sexes.

Some of my young readers have credited me with inventing the cedar bucket as a useful adjunct to yachting or boating, but you will find that the bucket in some form or other has been considered a necessity on shipboard since B.C., and it is likely that Noah had a whole battery of them on the Ark. If they had had the adjustable top shown they would have been quite useful for his varied menagerie. But we must get on board *Rozinante* and, while I apologize for this digression, it was partly made to give the reader a better appreciation of the Spartan simplicity of this fine little ship.

Aboard the *Rozinante,* the sun which was well into the west stole in sideways under the awning, so Weldon raised the forward side of the shelter that it might act like a windsail while the boys sat in the shade of the starboard cockpit coaming and were quite ready to eat by six o'clock. Some of us are not fond of the same food twice in succession; in fact, Weldon had no particular appetite for lobster salad the second time. The boys finished all there was and might even have eaten more, but in the first pause after the meal, little Dan said: "Uncle, when are you going to tell us about the early fishing boats of New England?"

His uncle replied: "This is as good as any time to start that talk, for one of the good types of fishing boats was built right here at Edgartown. It was called the No Man's Land boat, named, as were several of our early types of sailboats, for the

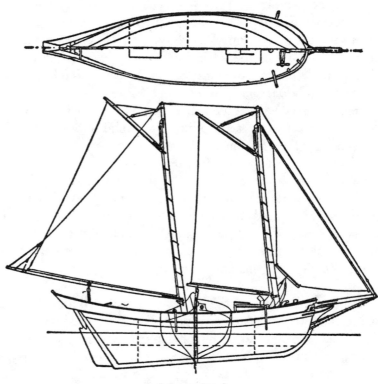

A Maine Pinky.

locality they fished in. These boats often fished around the island of No Man's Land which is some three or four miles southwest of Martha's Vineyard.

"Although most of the boats that I will tell you about were in use along the coast between 1840 and 1890, since Colonial times there had been a type of sloop generally called a shallop or smack in use all along the coast between Maine and New York. These smacks were decked over and used both for fishing and carrying cargo. They ranged in size between about 25 feet and 80 feet, and among the larger ones were the Hudson River Sloops and the Rockport Stone sloops, but most of them were smaller than the so-called Packets, which were the small schooners that carried passengers, mail and light cargo between ports in competition with the stage coaches.

"Most of the smacks had large broad sterns above water, together with a very full bow at the deckline, although below water their lines were not bad. They were of the type generally referred to as the cod head and mackerel tail model for they all seemed to have a fine run aft. Many of the early Gloucester fishermen, Nantucket whalers, and Long Island oyster sloops were craft of this type and perhaps Capt. Josh Slocum's *Spray* was an average good example of the early New England smack."

Weldon then took the *Rozinante's* blackboard and drew for the boys the lines and sail plan of a smack. He then went on: "I do not know why the smacks, generally, had such broad sterns unless it was for hauling up their jollyboat, but most of the small fishing boats which I will tell you about were double-enders with the stern generally sharper or finer than the bow. That allowed them to be good sea boats and better adapted to launching off the beach.

"Well, to start down east, some people used to say the Maine Pinky which sailed out of many of the ports east of Cape Ann was the finest sea boat of all. These Pinkies usually ranged between 40 and 55 feet on deck and made very long voyages for such small vessels for at times they went to the Grand Banks and salted down fish, in which case they would be at sea a month

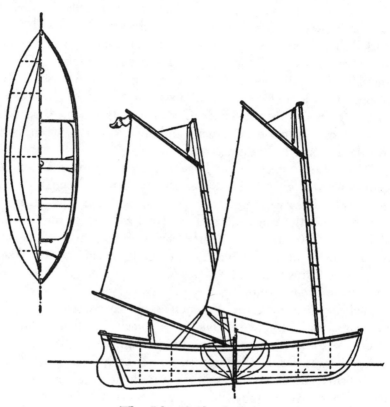

The Isle of Shoals boat.

or so. They were narrower than the smacks and, although they retained the full cod head, were so fine on deck aft that they might be said to be of 'cod head and mackerel tail' model both above and below water. One of the last of these craft was the Pinky *Mary,* which was preserved by Admiral Peary when he spent some of the summer of his retirement in Casco Bay."

Weldon drew a picture of a typical Pinky and continued: "These craft were generally rigged as bald-headed schooners, although I have seen pictures of them with a topmast on the main. They were real seagoing little ships with bulwarks all around the deck and a fair-sized forecastle which kept the stove going all the time in cold weather. These Pinkies were a step between the open handline fisherman of the coast and the bigger schooners that carried a nest of dories. For although they went to the fishing banks, they fished with hand lines from the deck. The part of the bulwarks that was carried out beyond the rudder was sometimes called a 'tail feather,' and this region of the craft was used as a toilet seat, where one could sit comfortably in the roughest weather and was a great improvement over the bowsprit shrouds that were used for the same purpose on other craft. Although Marblehead is slightly west of Cape Ann, many of the Pinkies hailed from there. These craft were called Heeltappers, for not only was Marblehead an early shoemaking town but it is said some of the crew of these Pinkies carried along some cobbling tools to work at shoemaking during the time they were sailing to and from the Banks.

"Of course, all the types of small sailboats which I will describe overlap one another in their hailing ports, but one of the prettiest of them all hailed from around Portsmouth, N. H., and was called the Isle of Shoals boat, for that was their fishing grounds. These boats were about 30 feet long, decked on bow and stern, but open amidships for about half their length. They were of light to moderate displacement and carried two gaff sails of nearly equal size but the forward, or mainmast, was slightly longer. They used a single halyard arranged so there was more power at the throat than out on the gaff, so after the luff of the

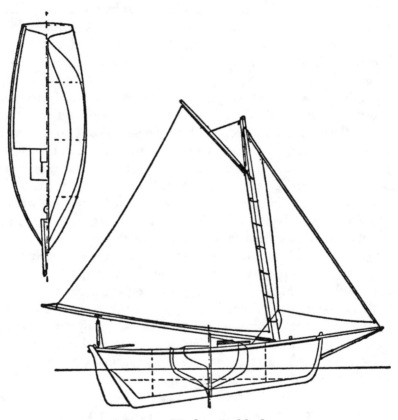

A Boston Harbor Paddy boat.

sail was hauled tight, an adjustment of the peak of the gaff could be made. The cut of their sails was rather queer, or would look so today, for the head and foot of the sails were nearly parallel. The tack of the sails was carried very low, sometimes below sheer level, while the boom was well cocked up aft as it should be on a good sea boat. As for model—these boats were moderately full on deck at the ends but very fine at the waterline and, as they were of lapstrake construction, they showed their beautiful curves to perfection. Their masts were unstayed, and usually acquired quite a bow aft with age which seemed to add to the general rakishness of these pretty craft. They could set a jib when required on a removable bowsprit but they generally sailed with two sails only."

After a pause to finish the drawing, Weldon went on: "Then there was the Paddy boats of Boston Harbor." Both the boys grinned and Jim asked why they called them Paddy boats. Weldon explained: "In about 1848, there was a famine in Ireland, so many philanthropic Boston people financed the sending of ships there to bring the starving Irish to these shores and a great many shiploads of them were brought over. They were very poor for a generation or two, but among them were boat builders and fishermen and they created and ran a fleet of small fishing boats that were known as Paddy boats because at that time the nickname for an Irishman was Paddy. These boats were very different from the Isle of Shoals boats for, as a class, they were very homely and wretchedly rigged. Their model was not so dissimilar from the small luggers of the French coast and may have resembled the fishing boats of Ireland at that time. The peculiarities of that model are a straight stem, rather high freeboard, a slight tumble-home of the topsides, together with a hard turn of the bilge and a keel with considerable drag. Also, the stern post and transom usually had considerable rake. Although this is a homely and wet model, it has a slow motion in a sea and is somewhat the shape Conor O'Brien adopted in his long distance cruiser *Saiorse*. However, the Paddy boats were rigged as sloops with the mast stepped well forward. In their

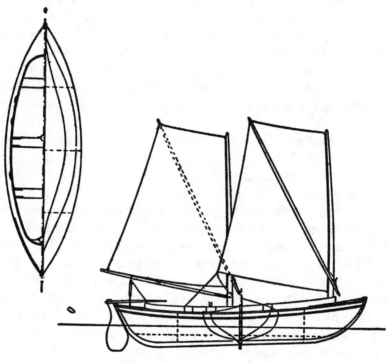

A No Man's Land boat.

day, these Paddy boats performed about the same functions as the so-called Guinea fishermen of Boston Harbor today; that is, they brought in all kinds of fish which were sold very cheap for then the poor Irish would buy anything from skate to catfish. It is interesting that the great grandchildren of these once starving Irish now run Boston's politics."

Jim spoke up: "I never knew the Irish went on the water much."

"While the Irish are not generally thought of as a seafaring race," his uncle told him, "they have always been great boatmen. It is said (by whom I don't know) that the three great miracles St. Patrick performed were as follows: First, he drove the snakes out of Ireland and they have stayed out ever since. Second, he took the hair off a poodle's tail and put it on its head as a topknot, and the Irish water spaniel has had a rat tail ever since. Third, last and most important miracle, he taught the Irish to sail to windward and they have been very good at it ever since. But I must tell you that the Irish have been great yachtsmen for a long time. One of the world's earliest yacht clubs was the Cork Harbor Water Club, established in 1720.

"But to get back to the Paddy boats. They were not a very fixed type and I would not have spoken of them except that there were quite a few of them. I believe they had some effect on the yachts and fishing boats built in Massachusetts Bay in the last part of the nineteenth century, for many of the boats along that coast had the hard turn of the bilge together with a slight tumble-home to the topsides.

"South of Boston there were no well known types of boats until we get here to Martha's Vineyard and, although the Nantucket boat builders built the fine whaleboats carried on the whaling ships, I believe they never developed a definite type of sailboat.

"The early Martha's Vineyard boats were owned by the farmers who had land along the waterfront of the island. They were used mostly to procure fish to salt down for the winter. The Indians had taught the early settlers of this region to put a fish in each hill of corn, and that is still about the best fertilizer for the sandy

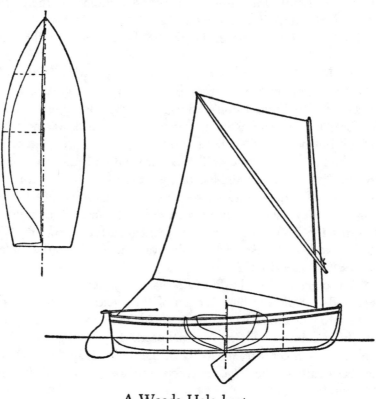

A Woods Hole boat.

soil of the island, so a good fish boat was a valuable acquisition. The early boats were quite small, probably under 20 feet in length, and launched off both the north and south side of the island. Although I have called them all No Man's Land boats, the local name for the northsiders was Vineyard boats, and southsiders Chilmark boats.

"They were kept hauled out most of the time. This was done by using an arrangement which looked like a ladder which had the cross-pieces or rounds greased. It was laid on the beach so that it extended under water enough to take the forefoot of the boat, and oxen hauled the boat ashore, with a man or two on each side to keep her on even keel. Most English and French boats that were landed on a beach were hauled up bow first then turned around and launched with the bow seaward, but the American boats were hauled out bow first and launched stern first. The Martha's Vineyard boats were straight on the keel at first, as a Block Island boat was, but the later ones had both the forefoot and the heel of the keel rounded off to facilitate launching.

"The No Man's Land boats were from 20 to 25 feet long, of a double ended model somewhat like a Block Island boat but with straighter sheer and less draft and displacement. They used a washboard or cockpit coaming all the way around which was oval shaped at bow and stern, and no doubt added to their seaworthiness. They were lightly built of lapstrake construction so as to haul out easily. They had three thwarts that were kneed out at their ends, which, together with the part deck, made a strong hull. For rig they used two spritsails nearly alike in size which were set on fairly short light masts that were unstayed so the whole rig could be quickly unshipped. Some of these boats used loose footed sails and some had a short club on the foresail and a boom on the after sail." As it was beginning to get dark, Weldon said: "Maybe we had better move into the cabin and light the lamp." As they were doing this he remarked that the sun did not set until nearly 8:30 on the Fourth of July but in the latter part of August it began to get dark by that time.

The cabin was comfortably cool now with the light south wind that was coming in from sea, but as soon as they were settled little Dan said: "What other boats were there along the coast?" What with their model making, the boys were very much interested in these talks.

"Well," their uncle replied, "there was a fine little boat built not far from here that was called a Woods Hole boat. It was perhaps between 14 and 18 feet long and of a model not so dissimilar to an old fashioned jollyboat with a handsome wine glass section stern or transom. These boats were open all the way around. Sometimes they were lapstrake and sometimes smooth seamed. Their rig was very simple and consisted of a single sail or spritsail like the No Man's Land boats. They were in vogue about 1890, so as a type they were later than the other boats we will talk about. However, although the spritsail rig is an old one, it was highly thought of in the nineties and when used with a loose footed sail was quick to rig and unrig. The mast and sprit were nearly the same length and usually would stow inside the boat, while the absence of a boom was very pleasant with a low footed sail. At that time, the spritsail was the favorite rig for yacht tenders all along the coast and I am surprised that there are not some of them now for it is a comparatively fast rig when cut high and narrow. The Woods Hole boats were used for both fishing and pleasure sailing for there used to be a great variety of fish around Woods Hole. No place is pleasanter to sail in, if you know how to work the tides and back eddies for the temperature there is pleasant and the wind often just right for small craft. These boats were also raced quite a little and some of them were light and fast. The racers were kept hauled out most of the time and, as for speed, they might beat the modern dinghy in a light wind and chop, while a native of the Hole might beat a stranger two to one. Similar boats were used in Buzzards Bay and in the inlets east of Woods Hole."

Although the boys were really interested in their uncle's stories of the older sailboats, little Dan, who had gradually assumed a reclining position, now let his head fall on the berth while Jim gave a pronounced yawn. Weldon told them to turn in so he could "douse the glim," for the light in the cabin was attracting the mosquitoes. The *Rozinante's* cabin light was in gimbals and to put it out Weldon rocked the chimney toward him and quickly blew across its top so that the flame was instantly extinguished. He then got out the ditty box and took a roll of mosquito netting; one piece of which was cut to hang like a curtain across the companionway; while a smaller piece draped over the ventilator forward. He then unrigged the awning and, as it was damp from the evening dew, he simply crumpled it up to stow under the after deck where it would be seen in the morning and given good drying.

After putting water in the cedar bucket and attaching its seat, he lit his pipe and with a sigh of satisfaction took up his favorite position at the helm with one hand on the tiller and an arm stretched along the cockpit coaming. There was a light southerly breeze which brought with it a rich smell of the ocean while the distant sound of the surf could be heard faintly as it rumbled and murmured along the south of the island. Occasionally, the voices of the party on the *Tranquilo* came to him in the still night, particularly the tinkling laugh of the girls as the Brewsters told strange tales of past cruises.

But the blissfulness of most moments seems to have its annoyances and this time it was the mosquitoes. At first, Weldon was satisfied with a few slaps and while his pipe kept the mosquitoes away from his face, he was barefooted and when they bit him around the ankles it itched unmercifully. He grumbled to himself: "I think these mosquitoes have gotten ahold of the same venom that the sand flies along the beach use, for it itches like the devil." In desperation, he retired to the cabin and lit the lamp since the boys were so sound asleep that it would take something unusual to wake them. He now settled back in his comfortable seat and read his favorite small book of poetry, but even in the cabin back of the carefully rigged mosquito netting there was an occasional exasperating buzz of a mosquito.

Weldon had taken precautions against mosquitoes and the principal thing he did every few days was to spray the woodwork of the cabin with one of the insect bombs. He would hold the bomb about 18 inches from the woodwork when the mist would deposit an invisible film on the woodwork that is very much disliked by insects and the effect will last several days. Still, if the cabin is well aired out and has good ventilation the odor of the spray is not readily noticed. This film on the woodwork will kill both flies and mosquitoes several days after an application which can be proved by the large number of dead insects that can be swept up daily below the parts that have been sprayed. Weldon found that spraying the under side of the deck and deck beams had an unusually good effect.

It must be noted that it is a little dangerous to stay long in a small cabin that is being sprayed, and some of the sprays will aggravate people who are susceptible to hay fever. These people should have someone do the spraying for them. After the cabin is well aired out, it is not disagreeable to humans unless they have a strong imagination.

7

The Squall / Reefing / Lapstrake and

Square Seam Planking / Periaugers and Point

Boats

The next morning was warm and damp although the sunrise was quite normal (neither red nor gray) and, as the day progressed, it became rather oppressive and made one feel unusually lazy. But there was much to do, for they had to return the sailing dinghy and provision up for their cruise to the westward. So they decided to only run to Cuttyhunk Island that day, which was some 25 miles on their way. Most of the morning was spent at the long wharf at Edgartown taking on water and groceries, but finally at nearly eleven they were under way with a light southerly wind that carried them out to Hatsett Rock where they changed course to nearly northwest. *Tranquilo* had accompanied them this far but now bore off toward the eastward on her way back to Nantucket and there was much waving and shouting at their parting, for all hands had become very fond of the Brewsters.

The *Viator* and *Rozinante* seemed to have about the same speed in the light southerly zephyrs that came off the island, so both arrived off West Chop together. Here they parted company, for the *Viator* took the straighter course which was north of a long shoal that was called Middle Ground, while the *Rozinante* stuck close to shore and went well south of the shoal. As this took them somewhat off their course, the boys asked their uncle why he did so. He told them that in long sounds like Vineyard, Nantucket and Long Island, the tide usually turns first inshore and turns last out in the middle of the stream. "You see," he said, "where there are millions of tons of water running in a stream, it takes some time to kill its momentum. But inshore here, where the resistance of shallow water has kept the stream from running so fast, it turns first."

For a while, there was not much difference in the progress of the two boats but in a quarter of an hour it was quite evident that the *Rozinante* was doing the better, while in another quarter of an hour, to use a sailor's expression, they made the land walk backward on the *Viator*. Weldon said: "You see now, boys, what a difference there is between a boat with a fair tide and one with a foul tide."

Soon after this the *Viator* started her engine for although Goddard was a good sport, he could see that the head tide would make them late at their destination. By this time the fitful breeze died to nearly a calm and the sky, which had been partly overcast, became noticeably darker to the westward.

After studying the sky for some time, Weldon said: "This is one of those times when you cannot see the clouds of an approaching squall, because of the general haziness of the atmosphere, but I believe the last two warm days have been making up a squall, so I am going to be prepared for the worst."

"How?" asked the boys.

"First we will stand out in the middle of Vineyard Sound to get sea room and will also reef the mainsail, so that when the squall strikes all we shall have to do is douse the jib and mizzen and carry on under the reefed main alone."

"I thought you never had to reef the *Rozinante*," said Jim.

"I usually don't," agreed his uncle, "but one reason I am doing it is to show you boys how to put a reef in, and I thought this calm spell a good time for the lesson for it may be a quarter of an hour before the squall strikes, if it does at all."

So saying, Weldon turned the helm over to little Dan and told him to steer toward the lighthouse which they could see at Tarpaulin Cove on Naushon Island. This brought the course to about northwest and although Dan said: "Aye! aye!" promptly, he had been following their course on the chart and could not help remarking: "But, Uncle, that course will carry us over the Middle Ground shoal."

"Yes, I know," Weldon replied, "but the *Rozinante* can pass over the shoal anywhere and at the west end where we are there is three or four times our draft." Weldon was much pleased at Dan's observation and told him he would make a real sailorman some day.

By this time, the wind was very light so the *Rozinante* had little more than steerage way and Weldon remarked to Jim that if the wind were stronger he would lower the mainsail and sail under jib and mizzen for he thought it was usually easier to reef a lowered sail. As the wind was so light, if they only lowered the sail a little more than to the reef eyes, or grommets, it would be best for giving a lesson in reefing. Some people always reef that way.

"With a racing sail, or a new sail," said Weldon, "it is best to lower away, for then the leach will not get damaged from flapping."

After they had lowered the mainsail the proper amount and put the after end of the main boom in the wire rope sling that was attached to the mizzen mast and was generally used as a boom crotch, Weldon reached under the deck along the side of the cockpit and pulled out four pieces of cord which he kept tied up in hanks and jammed between the shelf and deck in a certain place where he could reach them instantly, day or night. One of these pieces was for seizing the tack of the reefed sail to the gooseneck. It had been cut the right length and had its ends whipped after a trial in place.

Weldon stuck the other hanks in his pocket and went forward with Jim. He very quickly seized the sail in place, for it had a good sized grommet at the luff. They then went to the after end of the boom, where Weldon took out of his pocket a hank of a little larger cord which had a stopper knot at its end. He rove this cord through a block of wood that had been screwed to the boom at the right place for reefing, and then rove it through the reef grommet on the leach. The cord was then hooked over a hook-shaped piece of wood on the other side of the boom and again led up through the leach grommet.

At this point Weldon paused to say, "This particular way of reeving off a reef pendant is very old and was once universal, but few boats today have the proper wood cleats on the side of the boom simply because the boatyards and the young sailors know little about seamanship. You see, each move or turn of the pendant has its reason. Right here, where I have passed the pendant the second time through the reef grommet, or reef cringle, is where you pull aft to adjust the tightness of the sail along the foot. You may not think at first that this adjustment is important, but if the sail is not hauled out moderately tight on the foot it will be baggy when hoisted. If it is hauled too tight, it is very apt to ruin the set of the sail for the next week or so, so many people will not reef if they can help it." After Weldon had hauled the reef pendant aft to his liking, he took two or three turns of the pendant around the boom, sail and all, and made the end fast to the standing part of the pendant with two half-hitches. He said to Jim, "These last turns are to hold the leach down, but if the pendant is dry like it is now the turns should not be hauled too tight, for if it rains later it will shrink down unmercifully tight."

In the meantime, the light breeze had shifted to due south and the whole western half of the sky had become very dark and ominous. The air was noticeably oppressive and a sailor would feel quite certain of what was coming, although there was no other sound than a distant rumbling of thunder. Weldon now began to work quite fast. He took from his pocket the two lines of reef lacing which were about ten feet long and, giving one to Jim, told him to make one end fast forward with a square knot and then work aft passing the lacing through a reef eye in the sail and then around the foot of the sail, making a spiral as he worked aft. Weldon started aft and worked forward. As they came near each other in this work, Jim asked why the *Rozinante* did not have reef points, but his uncle was so busy he only replied: "I will tell you tonight."

Fortunately, the lacing had progressed quite rapidly as it often does when the foot of the sail is hauled aft enough to bring the reef eyes in line. Weldon had just hauled the lace lines tight and tied them together with a square knot when little Dan called: "Oh, Uncle, look! There's a white streak along the water ahead of us!"

Instead of looking, Weldon dived for the jib halyard and cast it off while he hauled on the downhaul. At the same time, in a calm voice, he told Jim to take in the mizzen as quick as he could. He then hurried forward with a sail stop and took two or three turns around the lowered jib close to the forestay. Before he got back to the cockpit, the squall had struck.

Fortunately, the first blast was without rain so he had time to take the helm from little Dan and get the *Rozinante* settled on a course toward the westward which helped Jim muzzle the mizzen. Weldon sent Dan in the cabin for sou'westers and oilers. Before he returned, the *Rozinante* was enveloped in a cloud of spindrift and horizontally traveling rain that was borne by roaring wind that screeched in the rigging and knocked the *Rozinante* on her beam ends. For a few seconds, they could neither see nor do anything, and Weldon in speaking of it afterwards said he did not know why the sail was not torn out of the roping. Fortunately, the reef had been well tied down and it stood.

This was the boys' first squall and they were too excited to be scared and so occupied in holding on that the few minutes of heavy wind passed like seconds. Finally, after a flash of lightning accompanied by very loud thunder, the rain let up enough for them to see ahead a few lengths. They were astonished to see a power boat hove over to about forty-five degrees with her awning torn to shreds and some very scared looking people clustered along her weather rail. Fortunately, they cleared this craft and left her in the swelter behind as the *Rozinante* righted slightly and began to gather way. At first, the wind had leveled the surface of the Sound in its mad rush but in a matter of minutes angry little waves began to strike the *Rozinante* as she scudded along on a close reach. By this time, the rain had stopped although the wind was still blowing so hard from the northwest that it was difficult to talk. Soon the whole west was tinged with gold and, almost before they knew it, they were bathed in sunlight again. The Sound seemed covered with white horses racing to leeward. Little Dan now came out of the cabin with the sou'westers and oilskins but his uncle only waved him back as he said to himself that they would only hold the water in now. He called to Jim to get the bilge pump going. As the boys took turns at the pump, they were surprised at the amount of water that had been shipped and called to their uncle to inquire if they had taken water in to leeward.

"Yes," he called back, "we took it in to leeward, to weather, and from above."

The wind was now noticeably lighter and the leeward shrouds no longer shook violently, so Weldon called Dan back to take the helm while he set the jib and mizzen. After this, the *Rozinante* danced along close-hauled under a dazzling blue sky as the storm clouds passed to leeward and the whitecaps raced by. It was certainly exhilarating sailing and the *Rozinante* had all the canvas she could stand, though her mainsail was reefed. However, by about five o'clock they began to get under the high land of Nashawena Island where the wind let up and seemed to come more from the westward, so they took a few tacks and at times came very close to shore. The boys were much impressed with the beauty of the rolling hills covered with brown and green shrubbery for, although the hills may not be 150 feet high, they seem to tower above you when close in shore. Way off to leeward, Gay Head was more vividly pink than usual for the western sun seemed to throw its rays directly on the cliffs that had just been drenched with rain. As they changed into dry clothes, the feeling of contentment was greater than can be described for the sun seems to shine with a redoubled brightness to those who have just passed through a tempest.

It is a short way from where they were to Canapitsit Channel which separates Nashawena from Cuttyhunk, and almost before they knew it they were abreast this opening. The northwester was blowing almost straight through the channel so that a deeper or less weatherly boat than *Rozinante* couldn't have made it. But after careful study of the detailed chart and planning their tacks, they passed through in two tacks, one of which carried them quite close to a rock that was awash in the ground swell. Altogether, it had been an exciting day.

As they swung to the westward, they could see ahead of them the *Viator* in a perfectly landlocked harbor. Their troubles, however, were not all over yet for this harbor has a long narrow entrance beside a jetty or breakwater. The channel ran slightly higher than the *Rozinante* could point, while it was not wide enough to tack ship in. Weldon overcame this difficulty by sailing the *Rozinante* with a good rap full until she neared the lee shore and then momentarily brought her in the wind and shot to windward almost to the other bank. So, in two long and short hitches, he passed through and dropped anchor a little beyond the *Viator*. We must say, however, that this maneuver can only be made with a boat that carries her way well and turns easily. Also, she must have good lateral resistance and the helmsman must bring her around easily or she will lose headway. It is a very useful maneuver at times, but should not be attempted without practice. You will find the length of the course with full sails should be about eight times the distance shot to windward, or else you will make excessive leeway when the sails are full.

Soon after the anchor was down, Goddard came rowing over to invite them all aboard. Weldon thanked him, but said there was too much to be done on the *Rozinante* and, besides, he and the boys were all tired out so Goddard came aboard to help them. The first thing they did was to take the reef out of the mainsail. Goddard explained to the boys that a nice sail should never be furled when reefed because there were generally puddles of water in the rolled up part where the reef was which would shrink the foot rope all night and perhaps stretch the leach at the reef cringle.

Sure enough, when the reef lace line was unrove, several cups full of water fell from the sail and the wet sail was severely wrinkled where the reef pendant had passed around the boom.

It was blowing one of those clear northwesters that will dry things out even after sunset and as there were still several hours of daylight, Weldon hoisted or tied in the rigging every piece of clothing or bedding that was damp. In the meantime, Jim had bailed out the *Sancho Panza* which had three or four inches of water in her.

At the first pause in these occupations and after the men's pipes were drawing well, Weldon inquired how the *Viator* had weathered the squall.

Goddard replied: "We had been going under power for some time, as you know, and luckily had the sails furled and stopped down. Of course, I thought the sky looked threatening but, still, I would not have seen the squall coming if it had not been from dead ahead. When the white streak appeared, I had just time to get Mrs. Goddard and the girls below and into oilskins. I believe it was the hardest squall I ever was in. I'm surprised it did not split your sail, for it stopped the *Viator* dead. She swung off beam to it and was knocked down nearly to the rail. I imagine it must have been alarming below in such conditions with the hatches all closed, but the girls stood it O.K."

Weldon remarked: "I have heard they have these twisters every few years off this coast as well as in Narragansett Bay and Buzzards Bay. The worst thing about them is that you can't recognize them as they approach. Sometimes, the black bank of clouds will only amount to a change of wind and sometimes it will amount to nothing, but when they strike they strike hard and I imagine the strong wind is in a comparatively narrow strip. Most meteorologists agree that these squalls are the strongest winds we have in New England and have estimated the wind velocity as much as 90 miles an hour. It is very fortunate they do not usually last long or they would be worse than a hurricane. What do you suppose is the answer to this squall problem?" he asked.

Goddard replied emphatically: "When you are off this coast

and see a black sky to the westward, be prepared for the worst. I have often seen people in unseaworthy boats laying back in perfect oblivion as a squall was gathering. If they had known a lion's paw was poised above them, they would have acted quite differently."

Just then Goddard got a hail from the *Viator* and when he looked at his watch, he said: "My, this day has passed quickly. It's time to eat again." After he had cast off, Weldon went below to start supper.

The cabin seemed very pleasant in the cool dry northwester, so he decided to make sort of a goulash as he thought the boys would appreciate a warm supper. After a little water was boiling in the saucepan, he cut about a dozen thin slices of salami and put them, together with some sliced onions, in the pan and let this combination boil for about ten minutes. It certainly gave off an enticing odor. Finally, he emptied a couple of cans of vegetable soup into the pan and after it had come to a simmer he stirred it carefully and called the boys. The boys were already sitting as close to the cabin bulkhead as they could, so after handing out some hard tack he gave them the steaming bowls with the advice to take it easy, for it was hot.

After this a general silence prevailed that was only interrupted by the flapping and snapping of drying clothes in the rigging.

Finally, Jim said: "Is there any more?"

"No," said his uncle in a tone of exasperation, "you each had twice as much as I did. I thought I would fill you up this time, but it seems to be like filling a bottomless pit." Weldon then smiled and added: "I will open a can of peaches for you boys. You can have them with some evaporated milk and triscuits, so rinse your bowls over the side and wipe them with these paper towels." After the drying clothes were taken in and the cabin put in order they all went below, for the northwester had a hint of fall and Weldon remarked: "Thank God we will not have any mosquitoes tonight."

As he settled back in his easy chair, he thought the boys would be too tired and full of food to even stir. But before he could open his book of poetry, Jim said: "Uncle, just before the squall, you said you would tell me about reef points tonight."

"Oh, did I?" sighed Weldon, putting down his book. At first, he seemed a little annoyed but the last cup of tea had made him talkative and good natured, so he began: "In the first place, I am very glad we had that strong squall, for I think you will remember it all your lives and always be prepared for the worst when you see a squall coming. You boys certainly behaved well and I am glad of it, for there is no use in getting scared or panicky in a squall. Instead, you should hang on and think calmly so you can do the right thing, always remembering that the worst of a squall will soon pass by. Do you remember the power boat we passed just after the worst of the squall? Well, her crew were all hanging to the weather rail, panic-stricken."

"What should they have done?" inquired Jim.

"They at least should have stuck to their stations," Weldon answered. "I think she was a boat with power enough to keep head to the wind. If they had done this, she probably would not have lost her awning or heeled over at all. However, on many power boats the rudder is too small for the amount of top hamper they have nowadays."

"Could we have helped them?" inquired Dan.

"No," said their uncle, "for at the height of a squall nearly all boats are so unmanageable that they will only make matters worse if they come together. However, a very deep boat like a tugboat can be maneuvered in strong wind and an auxiliary under bare poles, if she has a deep keel and powerful engine, can be somewhat manageable if handled properly. But if the usual power boat gets side to a strong breeze the only two things you can do is to go full speed ahead and head into it, or go astern moderately when the bow will invariably swing off. But that is not practical if there is a sea running. I suppose we should have run back when the squall let up to see how they were faring, but I was sure they would be all right when it moderated. Besides, it is not customary for a sailboat to offer assistance to a power boat.

THE COMPLEAT CRUISER 289

"Now to get back to reefing. The usual method of tying down a
reef seems to be at least three or four hundred years old, and perhaps much older. Although there have been innumerable mechanical arrangements to simplify reefing, such as the roller yard, the
roller boom and the various tackle line and batten rigs of the sailing canoes, few of them have been popular with the sailor. Perhaps the principal reason for this is that the sailor prefers to
handle ropes and cords rather than ratchets, pawls and cranks. Let
that be as it may, the early fore-and-aft sails were loose-footed as
the square sails had been. The square sails reefed from above, or
at the yard whereas the fore-and-aft sail reefed at the foot which
very much concentrated the strain at the ends of the sail, particularly at the after end or clew. At first, cutters and sloops used a
clew reefing tackle which was normally carried hooked under the
boom. In taking a reef, the tackle was swung above the boom and
hooked into whichever reef cringle was desired. This arrangement,
however, had the disadvantage that if a deeper reef was required,
some sort of temporary seizing had to be clapped on the clew to
hold it in place while the reef tackle was shifted or hooked to another cringle. So eventually, and particularly on the smaller boats,
the simple reef pendant was adopted. It consists of a rope which
had its standing end secured to a cleat on the starboard side of the
boom, from whence the pendant was rove up through the reef
cringle and down on the port side to another cleat with a hole in
it. After the clew was hauled down, some turns could be taken
around the boom near the reef cringle and well secured. Some old
time boats carried their reef pendants all the time. I can remember
when most Cape Cod cat boats did, but the smaller of these craft
used a single parted pendant that was spliced into the leach and
rove through a cleat on one side of the boom. It is a nuisance,
however, to carry the reef pendants rove for they often catch in
things, particularly in hoisting sail, so that the standard way to
rig the reef pendant or outhaul is like this." Weldon took the
Rozinante's slate and drew a boom end as seen from starboard
from above and from aport. While he was drawing, he remarked:

"It is a great comfort to a newcomer on a boat if the reef cleats are rigged correctly, for if he has to put in a reef at night he will know how to proceed."

Jim asked why the cleat to starboard only had a hole in it while the cleat to port was hook-shaped.

The star board cleat acts as a stopper for the standing end of the pendant, while the port cleat is made hook-shaped simply because it is easier to hook the bight of the pendant over a hook than to reeve its whole length through a hole."

Dan then asked why it was that lace lines were better than reef points. His uncle explained that with the old loose-footed sail, perhaps the reef points (or nettles as they used to be called in England) were better, for their use then was only to keep the rolled up foot of the sail in place. But with a sail laced or secured to the boom, the condition is different. Then, if one reef point is tied tighter than another it will stretch the sail or even tear it. It is always bad for the set of the racing sails. Weldon continued: "With the old up-and-down cut sail, where the reef points were secured at the lap of the cloths, it was still tolerated but with the advent of the cross-cut sail nearly all progressive sailors used the lace line because it renders enough to make the strain even all along the foot. Then, too, it was found in racing that a reef could be tied down quicker with lace lines because instead of stopping to tie a knot at each sail grommet the line was simply rove through. On the larger yachts, the lace line was usually in four or five lengths so that four or five people could be lacing off, but in smaller boats it is usually only in two parts."

Poor little Dan was getting drowsy and confused with reef points and nettles, but as this was one of the points of seamanship that Weldon was a little hipped on, he continued: "As a general rule, cruising men and beginners prefer reef points, but racers always use reef lace lines. The points have several disadvantages besides being hard on the sail. At times, and especially in light weather, they make a tiresome, continuous rustle, rattle and tap on the sails. The reef points often become frayed or weakened near the sail and are not reliable. They hold dampness in a furled

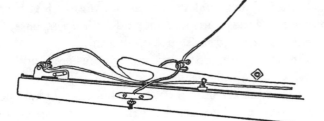

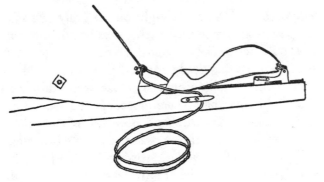

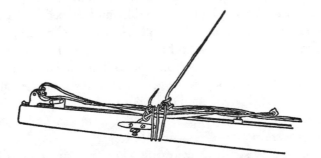

From top to bottom: Reefing the clew of a sail with a reef
pendant and reef cleats.

sail which often shows mildew where the damp points have laid. The lesser disadvantages are that they add a little expense, a little weight, and a little wind resistance to the sails."

Even Jim was getting drowsy but he mustered up strength enough to ask why a little weight was bad in sails.

"In a breeze it makes little difference, but in light weather if a sail hangs down and loses its draft it seems to lose all driving power. You know, a light balloon jib will fill out and draw in very light airs, but if it were even a few ounces heavier per square yard it would be dead. So any weight on the belly of a sail is bad, although there is no reason why the headboard, luff rope, foot rope, etc., should not be as heavy as desired."

The boys were getting ready for bed now and Weldon moved out into the cockpit to enjoy his last smoke while they were turning in. Finally, as darkness began to settle, he went forward to hang the riding light. The sun had been down some time but as he faced the west he saw the sky was still tinted a salmon pink that gradually changed to yellow, then green, and finally a cold bluish steel gray overhead where the stars blinked in the clear westerly wind.

Yes, he said to himself, every day, every hour, every minute is different on a cruise. How different this cool, bracing evening is from the last several nights. When he regained the cockpit and sat leaning against the cabin bulkhead he had a spell of yawning in which each long breath of the cool bracing air seemed better than the last one. At last such a comfortable drowsiness settled over him that he went into the cabin and to bed. Before falling into oblivion, his sense of contentedness compelled him to thank the Almighty and he said to himself how glad he was to be here and not in some resort overrun with oil men, movie actors, and cowboys, or the type of females who trail after these creatures.

Weldon had thought the boys would go to sleep right after supper, but it seemed that the boys had become so used to cruising that they were no longer exhausted after a sail.

While Jim was still chewing his bed time snack of strawberry jam on hard tack, he said: "Uncle, you promised us that when we got to anchor you would tell us about the West Island Boats."

"Well, did I?" Weldon queried as he chuckled to himself and kept cleaning up around the stove. He was pleased that the boys showed this interest in the old sail boats.

"You know, most of the boats I have told you about were double enders, as most of our early fishing boats were, and, although the West Island Boats were of a much later date, they too stuck to the sharp stern. Perhaps this was because they fished and sailed in rough water, and perhaps because their fishing ground was between the areas used by the No Man's Land boats and the Block Island boats, so that maybe the West Island boats were simply a later generation of these fine earlier types. However, most of our early small boats were of lapstrake construction but by the time the West Island boats were in vogue the smooth seam (or square calked seam) had become popular among boat builders."

Jim spoke up to inquire if a lapstrake planked boat was better than a square seamed one.

"That question has never been satisfactorily answered, although it has been argued back and forth for some thousand years. My answer to it is that both types of planking have advantages which cannot well be combined unless we go into double planking.

"Most of our early boat builders had learned their trade in England where lapstrake construction had been the usual thing for centuries—perhaps since the Danish invasions, or before the time of William the Conqueror. The old English way of building a lapstrake boat was also easy for those who were accustomed to it. They simply set up two or three molds, or 'shadows' over the keel and planked up the vessel without any frames. The way they made both sides of the boat somewhat similar between the molds was to use each plank after it was fitted and taken down again, as the pattern for the opposite plank. Of course, the stem and stern post were well braced in place during the building so that as each plank was fastened to its neighbor along its lap, the skin of the vessel in itself became a very stiff structure that could not easily be sprung out of shape. In fact, the skin of a lapstrake boat has so much inherent strength that the framing can be very light so that the whole construction is lighter for its strength. After the boat was completely planked up and the laps or seams fastened with rivets or clinch nails, the frames were put in from the inside. You see these early boats were not laid down on the floor, or as far as is known, had any designs. This was a good easy construction in that case but the builder had to be an artist and be his own designer as the work progressed."

"How could they fit the frames to match the planking?" inquired Jim.

"This is an easy matter with steam bent frames. While the boat was being built, the builder had a great many frames already bent into approximate shape which he kept sprung over traps or nailed down on the floor. You see, the old time builders had wonderful eyes for shape so these frames only had to be bent slightly when riveted in place. This was done with what was called a persuader; a piece of wood which held the frame in place during the fastening. When sawn frames or natural crooks were used, the old time builder could get out the approximate shape by eye. Then, after the frame was laid in the boat nearly in place, he transferred to it the exact shape of the planking by using some transfer scribers that were particularly made for that purpose and are practically unknown today. At any rate, the old time boat builder could quickly get out a frame that would exactly fit in place including the notches where the laps in the planking occurred. The frame would also be correctly beveled for the curves of the planking at the bow and stern. All in all, the old lapstrake construction was light and strong while it could stand shrinking and swelling without leaking.

"The square seamed planked boat was a quite different proposition. The frame complete was made first and the planks were fastened to the frames as the planking advanced but as each plank was a separate stave, later separated from its neighbor by the calking, this construction lacked the diagonal strength that is inherent with lapstrake construction. The main frame had to be strong enough to take almost all the twisting and hogging strains that the vessel would be subjected to. Also, the frames had to be strong in order to resist the spreading effect of the calking which ran the full length of every seam and amounted to a terrific pressure. However, the square seamed calked construction of planking is the oldest and was used by the Egyptians some 3,000 years B.C. It is the cheapest construction for a boat that has been previously designed and laid down and it's about the only construction that the modern carpenter understands. The square seamed construction is vastly the best to stand the abuse of lying alongside wharves, or any other chafing. On the whole, it probably lasts the longest, although it may need periodic recalking.

"To get back to the West Island boats . . . They were generally between 25 and 30 feet long, but I believe a few were built a little larger for use as yachts right here at Newport. These boats were mostly built at Westport, Rhode Island, and planked up with native soft pine. In model, they were quite similar to an old style Narragansett Bay cat boat, if the stern of the latter had been carried out to make a double ender. They, too, were like the cat boats in having a good sized deckhouse and roomy cabin, even if there was not head room." Weldon began to draw the sail plan of a West Island boat on the slate, but he had not gone far when little Dan, who was watching the drawing carefully, exclaimed: "Gee, she's a cat schooner isn't she?"

"No, Dan," his uncle replied, "there isn't such a thing as a cat schooner. The name of a rig which has two masts of about the same height and no head sail is sometimes called a 'periauger.' It is a very ancient rig that was much used in Holland some three hundred years ago. It was also a rig used around the mouth of the Hudson from Dutch times, until perhaps 1830. They were used for ferry boats running to Staten Island and towns on the Jersey shore, and were sometimes called 'pirogue' ferries. It might interest you to know that the original Cornelius Vanderbilt started that family's fortune in a periauger that he sailed out of Staten Island around 1810."

The periauger *Periwinkle,* owned in Newport, R.I., about 1900.

Dan mentioned that a yawl is called a cat yawl if she has no head sail.

"Yes, you are right," his uncle agreed, "but a sloop and schooner are both rigs with head sails, and it is as ridiculous to call a vessel a cat schooner as to call one a schooner sloop. That reminds me of the nonsensical poem that says, 'The good ship was a racing yawl,

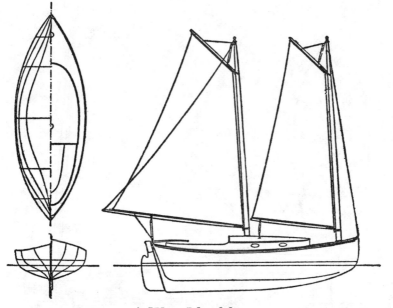

A West Island boat.

a square-rigged schooner sloop,' but I don't blame you boys for not knowing the name of the rig, for the periauger is seldom seen to-day. The West Island boats and the Block Island boats were pure periaugers, and I suppose the Isle of Shoals boats could be called the same for they usually sailed without a jib."

By this time, Weldon was drawing the lines of a West Island boat and he showed her with a keel and no centerboard, so Jim asked him if a periauger was always a keel boat.

"No," said Weldon, "and it is told that the earlier ones built by the Dutch at New York had lee boards, and the later ones there had centerboards for there were many shallow inlets where the early New York periaugers sailed. The Block Island boats and earlier Newport cat boats that sailed in deeper water, however, used a keel, but I have no doubt that some West Island boats used a centerboard for that arrangement became popular in cat boats after 1860 or so. The West Island boats were very much liked by

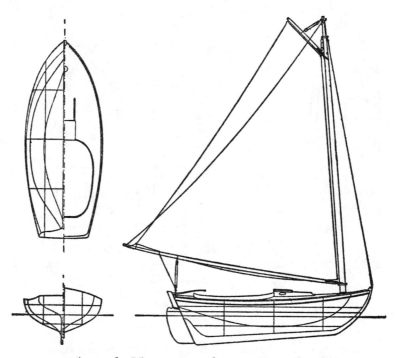

An early Newport cat boat or Point boat.

those who sailed them, and it is said that their only particular disadvantage was that they turned slowly on account of their sharp bow and stern."

Weldon had no sooner finished the sketch of the lines of a West Island boat than Jim said: "Now tell us about the Newport cat boats you have spoken of so often."

"In Newport there is a neck of land that is now called Long

Wharf, but before it was built up and filled in (which happened many years ago) it was simply called The Point and it is my belief that the cat boat originated there in colonial times. Of course, I do not mean to say there had not been many types of single masted boats before that, but apparently they had lug sails, lateen sails, or square sails. Of course, there had been rowing boats for centuries that stepped a single mast, but it is likely the first boats of a fixed type for sailing alone with a single gaff sail were developed on that neck of land once called The Point, and the boats were called Point boats. It seems there was a colony of boatbuilders there in early times, and when Newport became a summer resort these boats were much in demand for sailing parties. The Point boats were also used for fishing and shooting for in those days there were many ducks in the bay. Most every harbor in the bay had one or two of these Point boats, so that even before 1800 there were races at Newport for this type of boat.

"After this, or perhaps around 1830, this single masted type of boat became popular for racing at the head of Long Island Sound where they were built with a centerboard and called cat boats. By 1850, these centerboarders developed into the racing sandbaggers that were raced both sloop and cat rigged. While I have told you that you should never use the words 'cat schooner' to describe a rig, it is true that the words 'cat sloop' were sometimes used to describe a cat boat which had a bowsprit and at times set a jib, but this description was limited to boats which had the mast stepped near the stem.

"After the Civil War, the cat boat became popular from Newport to the Chesapeake, and by 1870 or so they came into vogue on Cape Cod where the centerboard cats were so popular that many people speak of them as Cape Cod cats. In England and Europe, they are usually referred to as Una boats because one of the Newport cat boats named *Una* was sent to Cowes, England in 1852, as a present to the Marquis of Coyningham from William Butler Duncan. The *Una* proved very popular in Europe and many copies of her were made for the lakes and shallow water regions of England and the continent. At the time the *Una* was built, many of the Newport cat boats were using the centerboard which was a New York influence, but the original Point boats were like this." Weldon drew the lines and sail plan of a Point Boat on the slate. Before the drawing was completed, little Dan was overcome by the sandman and they turned in as the distant noises of the city and its shipping mingled with the ripple of the waves alongside. The boys were asleep before Weldon finished undressing and as he doused the light he said to himself: This is a happy ending of a very pleasant day.

8

The Story of Newport / Making Johnny Cakes

A Foggy Passage / Block Island

The morning after their arrival in Newport Harbor following the short passage from their last anchorage at Cuttyhunk they were awake quite early on the *Rozinante*, for the slight bobble from the distant ferry boats and other moving craft gave her, at times, quick little pitches and half rolls, but at other times she was quiet for a minute or two. The hum of the city could be heard below, but somehow the presence of the city could be felt, and while these things had not been noticed in their sound sleep after yesterday's sail, now they crept into their consciousness as they awoke completely refreshed. *Rozinante* was headed toward the westward in the dying northwester, and, as the sun rose above the city on its circuit to the south, it shone directly into the cabin. At first Weldon simply turned over on the bunk to have his eyes in the shade, but finally the heat of the sun made the blanket uncomfortable, so he quietly squirmed out of the berth, and dressed.

Weldon liked to swab the deck and chamois the brightwork in the morning dew, for, as he said to himself, this thin covering of pure, fresh water is a blessing and it is too bad to let it dry before it is used. He had not proceeded far before Jim was beside him in the cockpit, and as he greeted Jim, Weldon said he was surprised to see him up so early. Jim only yawned and blinked his eyes, as he asked in a sleepy way what time it was. Weldon replied: "About half-past five, but if you wash your face while I make some tea, you will then feel quite awake."

Weldon had found that the South American tea, called Maté was a good early morning drink, and to be sure after Jim had taken a few swallows of the warm beverage, he felt very comfortable all over. Perhaps a tumbler of warm water would have aroused Jim nearly as gently, but it would not have soothed the nerves of an empty stomach nearly as well as the Maté. However, some people think it best for young ones to be aroused with a sudden shock, like diving overboard. But if they have a long day before them, you will find they will do best with an awakening that is not a shock to the nerves. In other words, the boy who has had the early morning dip is apt to be tired, listless, and even cranky before the morning is over. Nevertheless, the cold dip is best for late risers or the boy who will not have enough exercise during the day. Weldon was quite aware of the little comforts that can make or mar a cruise, and was always careful to have the nerves well rested with sleep, the inner man well looked out for and the mind constantly employed with interesting thoughts.

After they had moved out into the cockpit again the sun was drying up the dew so that Weldon hurried as much as he could, wiping off the brightwork, while Jim, who was now fully awake, asked him why he liked to chamois the morning dew so much. He explained: "The dew has been settling on the brightwork all night and has softened up the films of dirt, salt and gum that are on the surface of the varnish." Weldon then chamoised a place in the shade where the dew still remained and it came out as smooth as a piece of amber. Then he wiped a place where the sun had partly dried off the dew so that there were drops between dry places. Here the surface was mottled after wiping, for in the dry places the film of dirt and gum had dried on again. Weldon explained to Jim that the spots where the drops were would show indistinctly all day unless the brightwork was rubbed hard for, as he said, where the dew drops were the surface is clean, but where the surface has dried the film of dirt has stuck on again.

When Weldon did this early morning chamoising he kept a hand basin of fresh water near him, and occasionally rinsed out the chamois. The water in the basin was black by that time, so Weldon commented: "You would not think all that dirt was on the brightwork, but it is just this sort of wiping off that makes a boat look yachty, while the one which is wiped off with salt water, or even if done later in the day with soap and water, always looks grimy."

"Why do soaps make the varnish work look grimy?" inquired Jim.

"Most of the soaps have a fine abrasive in them which is hard to get all off unless you go over the work the second time with clean water. Some of the soaps have chemicals in them that make the varnish dull before the season is over. So for the easiest day-after-day cleaning, the dewy surface wiped off with a well rinsed chamois is best."

There were several yachts anchored near them, and Weldon pointed out to Jim the chamois they had drying over deck houses and hand rails and mentioned that the sailors take good care of chamois because good ones are very expensive today, but a small one like ours is good enough for a small boat.

Jim then asked if a wet rag or a piece of waste wouldn't do just as well, but Weldon said: "No. The rag seems to give off lint and the waste doesn't seem to absorb water well, but some of the new synthetic sponges and 'miracle' cloths are quite satisfactory, but will not stand hard wringing out as well as a good chamois." Weldon added that he thought it was time for breakfast, and Jim said he thought so too, so as the tea kettle and frying pan began to rattle on the stove, little Dan gave a couple of stretches and a yawn and muttered something quite inaudible.

Jim asked: "Where are you, Dan?" and he replied: "I don't know, but something smells awfully good."

"That's right," his uncle answered, "and if you get up you can have some right off."

Weldon gave the boys some bottled tomato juice first and then their regular breakfast of bacon and eggs, but before they were through the colors gun had sounded, so there was an interruption until the club pennant and private signal were hoisted. The boys were elated because they had the flags mastheaded before some of the yachts.

Weldon remarked that they would soon see some life on the *Viator* now, but as it turned out only Goddard came on deck and, after making colors, rowed over in the dinghy. When he got alongside, he said, "I don't know if I will ever get my womenfolks going today, for they seem to be primping and dressing as if they were going to the opera."

Weldon answered: "Maybe they don't want to go ashore early for, as you know, about this time of day about all there is to be seen are swill wagons, street sprinklers and navy boys returning from leave, who look as if they had been keel-hauled. In the meantime, you'd better come aboard and tell the boys something about Newport."

After tying up the dinghy, and everyone getting settled in the cockpit, Goddard commenced: "The southern part of Rhode Island was to a great extent settled by English gentlemen who had the means to build good houses and lay out country estates. They were, as a class, more like some early settlers in Virginia and were quite free from the religious prejudices which dominated most of New England in its early days. It is said that they came to southern Rhode Island for the purpose of raising horses for the English army and in the early years developed a breed of horse called the Narragansett Pacer. But, while the first pursuits of most of these country gentlemen were of an agricultural nature, there were some who took to the water and in a generation or two they became by far the wealthiest and most influential. This was mostly because they took to privateering which was very profitable in colonial times. It has been said that Rhode Island sent out more of these craft that fought under the British flag than any other of the colonies, but with Newport's fine harbors she went into all sorts of shipping. This included foreign commerce, whaling, running slaves and, last but not least, coastal trading, so that soon after 1700, Newport was an important seaport, perhaps only second to Baltimore, New York, and Boston.

"During the Revolution, the French fleet made Newport its headquarters and one of the French admirals pronounced Newport's outer harbor one of the best places in the world to anchor a squadron of war vessels. Some people say the social life of Newport was started during the stay of the French fleet, but about this time some of the southern aristocracy, or plantation owners, were in the habit of visiting Newport annually for the summer season. They came north and returned on the sailing vessels that traded between Newport and the South, so that Newport has been a fashionable summer resort since colonial times."

As Goddard stopped for breath, Jim spoke up and asked if the French fleet did any fighting when they were here.

"Yes," replied Goddard, "they were in one quite heavy engagement that is not generally recorded in history. This was near the close of the Revolutionary War, when the French fleet was leaving Newport and had stood out to somewhere southeast of Block Island where they happened to run across an English fleet which had sailed from New York and was on its way home. They mauled each other considerably, but the battle was interrupted by a change of weather and nightfall without either side gaining an advantage."

Jim then asked if the French Navy helped us much in the Revolution, and Goddard replied: "Yes, very decidedly, though the usual small school history speaks much more about the French Army under Lafayette. But without the French navy, we never could have achieved independence. I think they had three fleets here at one time. The siege of Yorktown, and the surrender of Cornwallis never could have been accomplished if the French fleet had not prevented Cornwallis from receiving reinforcements. It might be said we had no navy in the Revolution, so if sea power is the most decisive factor in warfare, the French navy is given too little credit for the work it did.

"Now, to get back to the story of Newport. As I have just said, social life started here in colonial times, and Newport is really our oldest summer resort if you disregard various hot springs or locations attended for medical reasons. The waters around Newport were ideal for sailing so that for the last 150 years, Newport has been considered our best place for yachting, which had started with the Newport cat boat or Point boat.

"As soon as the New Yorkers began to build yachts of some size, Newport was usually the destination of their cruises and, as the racing conditions at Newport were ideal, the New York Yacht Club for the last seventy years or so has held its most important annual regattas here."

Weldon had an old New York Yacht Club handbook aboard the *Rozinante,* and after he brought it out into the cockpit, said to Goddard: "If you will excuse me for interrupting your narrative, I will read to the boys a list of some of the cups sailed for off Newport. Among the early challenge cups were the Gordon-Bennett trophies given in 1871; then the Goelet cups were raced for, between 1882 and 1897. In 1899, the famous Astor cup races were started which run to the present time. Then, there were the races for the King Edward VII cup between 1906 and 1911 when his son, King George V, gave a cup that was raced for from 1912 to the time of his death. At the present time, there are two or three other annual awards which are generally raced for off Newport and since 1930 the races for the America's Cup have been held here. If in some years Marblehead has had the greatest number of yachts in its races and Larchmont the largest aggregate tonnage in its regattas, the yacht races off Newport were for much the most valuable trophies, for most of them were valued at a thousand dollars and often have been of solid gold, while the winners at Marblehead or Larchmont were apt to get a pennant, a twenty dollar trophy, or perhaps only so many points toward the season's championship. So you see Newport has been a very important yachting center for a long time."

Little Dan spoke up to ask why there were so many naval ships in the outer harbor, so Goddard told him that Newport was the official northern U. S. Navy anchorage. "What does that mean?"

inquired Jim, so Goddard went on, and told him. "When ships come back from a cruise or some practice maneuvers they usually go to one of the navy yards to have repairs and alterations made, also to refuel. But while waiting for the next steaming orders, they usually anchor in an official anchorage, and for years Newport has been a favorite anchorage for these stand-by ships. Sometimes there is a large squadron of them here that reaches for several miles in different directions.

"While the waters of New England have been the favorite naval practice areas in the summer, Guantanamo Bay, near Cuba, has been the usual winter practice grounds.

"The entrance to Narragansett Bay, and Newport Harbor, has been protected with forts of some kind or other since some time around 1800. At first, there was a round fort named Fort Dumpling on the north side of the entrance, but around Civil War times the large fort at the south side named Fort Adams was built. This remained an important fortress until after the Spanish War, but as its guns could only be trained on ships in the opening, Fort Dumpling was rebuilt. This time it was armed with disappearing guns of considerable range, that were supposed to keep an attacking vessel out of range of the anchorage here."

"What are disappearing guns?" asked Dan.

Goddard explained: "They are guns that rise up on their trunnions just at the moment of firing; the recoil of discharging the projectile throws them back and down again out of sight where they can be loaded and trained back of the emplacements. In most cases, disappearing guns were not mounted in a fort but back of a natural cliff, or sunken in the ground, so before the days of the aeroplane, the enemy had difficulty in locating them."

"How could such guns be aimed if they were back of a cliff or in a hole out of sight?" inquired Jim, while Dan listened with his mouth half open.

Goddard continued: "These guns did not have sights but the gun mounts were finely graduated so when the gun pointers were given the angle of elevation and the direction to train the gun, this could all be done safely back of the natural fortress. These guns usually had two sighting stations which were some distance apart and as the sights in each were like large surveying instruments, by the use of a telephone the observers could tell the chief gunner the bearing of the target. As there were two sighting stations, this gave him the distance as well as the direction. Few yachtsmen, as they went in and out of the entrance to Newport Harbor, realized there were heavy guns on the north side of the channel, but since the aeroplane these disappearing guns are a thing of the past for the modern gun must be hard to spot from overhead as well as on the horizon, so the practice is to have them spread so that if one is bombed, the others may escape. Perhaps, in the future, guided missiles will take the place of the heavy guns, for their launching ways can be well camouflaged and thus hard to see from the air.

"However, what I am trying to say is that this entrance to Narragansett Bay has usually been fortified with the best guns of the time to protect our fleet when anchored here. When the torpedo came into use as a weapon, that island over there was selected to be what was called the Torpedo Station, and not only were our early torpedo boats kept there but a great deal of the testing and developing of the torpedo was done there. Forty years ago, there used to be some of the earliest torpedoes on the island which included models that were propelled by a flame squirting out their stern like the modern jet planes. These torpedoes were called rocket torpedoes, and I think were tried about 1870. Then there were the towing torpedoes and the ones which had a boat-shaped float on the surface, some of which were developed soon after the Civil War. But while the automobile, or self-propelled, torpedo (that was then called the fish torpedo), was invented by Mr. Robert Whitehead of Fiume, Austria, this country developed its own torpedoes independently and much of the work of perfecting and proving them was done right there on the Goat Island torpedo station. Since the torpedo business has expanded, it has been moved to several locations."

Weldon here broke into the conversation to remark: "I am surprised that torpedoes were used so many years ago."

"Oh, yes," replied Goddard, "they were used in one form or another quite a lot in the Civil War, mostly by the Confederates, and they started that practice first, for they formed a secret service torpedo corps in 1862. In those days, the stationary torpedoes or mines were classed with the movable ones, but about the first important action with a spar torpedo was carried out by Lt. Cushing of the Northern Navy when he sank the Confederate Ram *Albemarle*. Cushing used a steam launch that had been rigged up with a torpedo or bomb on the end of a spar. When this exploded, it not only sank the *Albemarle* but also swamped Cushing's launch. It was befitting that our first steel torpedo boat was named *Cushing*, and she was built at Bristol, R. I., just ten miles north of the Torpedo Station."

Goddard then went on to say: "Another interesting institution that was started at Newport soon after the Civil War is the Naval War College. Perhaps one of the reasons this organization got off to a good start was that one of its first commandants was the famous Captain Mahan, who wrote several books about sea power, and naval strategy. The Naval War College is a post graduate school for naval officers who have had some service and it has been attended by most of our progressive officers of various ranks and ages.

"Just north of the War College is the Training Station that was built up soon after the Spanish-American War. Here the enlisted man or boy receives his first naval training. Now that the navy is so mechanized, the Training Station is much enlarged and gives instruction in many subjects. Its buildings and training fields now cover much of the north part of Newport that was farm land before World War I."

Goddard stopped for breath and laid down his pipe which had been out for some time while the boys looked around with renewed interest, for to know history of visited places, greatly increases the pleasure of cruising.

Goddard began again: "It wasn't until about 1890 that the wealthy New Yorkers began building the fine summer residences that we see along the ocean side of Newport. Then the horse and carriage was at its height of popularity, so that a famous drive called The Ten Mile Drive was developed. This drive wound its way along the cliffs and coves south of Newport and went by many of the fine estates, so that most anyone of consequence drove over part of it almost daily in the summer time. This was long before the income tax and several of our wealthiest citizens made Newport their summer home. They liked to call these houses 'cottages,' although the stables of the places, alone, might be large enough for an inn and there may have been as many as 20 servants attached to a place. The matrons of these establishments vied with one another in giving sumptuous dinner parties and, if short of male diners, always had the Naval War College to draw on for interesting fill-ins. So, together with yachting and navy establishments and the Ten Mile Drive, Newport was a stirring place in the gay nineties. However, there was another life here before recorded American history, and that seems to me the most interesting thing in the whole place."

Jim spoke up to say: "I suppose you mean the Indians."

"No," answered Goddard, "there was a remarkable stone tower at Newport when the early settlers came here and as the tower is undoubtedly of European workmanship or style, it is sometimes spoken of as the greatest mystery in New England."

"What did the early settlers think of it?" inquired Dan, and Goddard went on to say: "The first settlers around here had all come from places where the ruins of stone buildings were so common that they took no interest in it. The first mention of it seems to be in a man's will where he left it described as 'my old mill,' and this statement seemed to have thrown most historians off the trail of the old tower for the best part of 200 years."

Goddard stood up and reached for the dinghy's painter, and, as he boarded the tender, said in an exasperated tone: "The principal reason I came to Newport was to show Mrs. Goddard and the girls this tower, but they seem to think that getting dressed up and going around the Ten Mile Drive is the thing to do."

As he rowed away, Weldon called to him to say: "The boys and

I want to see the tower anyway, so we will accompany you if you don't mind."

When Goddard boarded the *Viator,* Mrs. Goddard and the girls were ready; in fact, they rather turned the tables on him when they said they had been waiting for him for some time. By now, the sun was well overhead and gave promise of a scorching hot day, but as the dinghies approached the shore they found a good place to tie them at a small wharf just north of the ship yard. In a matter of minutes they were walking up Thames Street with the boys lagging behind to look in the windows of the interesting stores on that street, many of which had such nautical aspect that even the men had to stop occasionally. Goddard remarked that the stores of that street were famous a hundred years ago and more, for they then had all sorts of foreign merchandise as Newport ships traded with all parts of the world. One shop which traded in oriental curiosities was said to be quite remarkable in old times.

After asking for directions, they turned up a side street which soon brought them to a small common with seats in the shade of elm trees, while before them was the old tower. The common was deserted with the exception of a few old codgers who sat with folded newspapers in hand as they gazed at nothing.

The children soon began to ask questions and gathered around Goddard, so he tried to tell what little was known of the tower:

"Some people think this tower was built before Columbus's time and others think soon after. It is interesting that most every country between Spain and Norway has been credited with it in the last 200 years. However, the men who are acquainted with the history of architecture say its construction is similar to some early Christian churches that were built in the part of the Scandinavian peninsula that is now Sweden, but was then ruled by a Norwegian king. These early fortified round churches were built to resist the anti-Christian marauders of the time and were supposed to be somewhat fireproof strongholds. The readers of the sagas say King Magnus Ericson, who ruled Norway and Sweden, sent an expedition to this country in 1355, so it would have been quite natural for them to build a stronghold of the type they were used to, particularly if one of their leaders were a priest or missionary. The building of this tower, or round church, must have been quite an undertaking in those days. No doubt it was a royal or government project and probably was surrounded by a settlement of wooden houses. Just why the colony was given up, probably we shall never know but if a supply ship or two were wrecked, then communication with the mother country would have been interrupted enough to terminate it.

"There were two other tokens of this early settlement that our forefathers neglected to thoroughly investigate. One of them was a skeleton in light armor which was found on the mainland twenty or so miles north of the tower. It is said these remains were simply interred without examining the armor which, though it might have been much rusted, should have given some light on the matter. But the people of that time were not interested in these things. However, this find has been immortalized by Longfellow's fine poem, *The Skeleton in Armor,* which to a great extent is about the tower. Another old Newport tradition is that in early times there was the keel or backbone of a vessel sunk in the mud in a cove on the island of Conanicut, near what is called Dutch Island Harbor; in other words, within about three miles of the tower. This cove would have been the best place in the neighborhood to lay a boat or ship up for the winter and the old time Newporters believed the remains were those of a Viking ship. At any rate, if this tower had been built in 1355, it must be nearly 600 years old, or some 250 years older than Gosnold's temporary settlement on Cuttyhunk."

Goddard stopped for breath while the boys and Weldon walked around the protective iron fencing of the tower. After they had all sat on some of the park benches, Weldon remarked: "I believe this is one of the most impressive things I have ever seen. The more you look at it the more it grows on you." The boys were so awed by the sight that they even refrained from asking questions, but before long Mrs. Goddard and the girls became restless and

Miss Prim said: "Yes, Pa, but when are we to take the Ten Mile Drive and see the Newport villas?"

"Oh, very soon, now," Goddard replied, as they all rose and walked to Perry Square, which was nearby. Here the two parties separated, as Goddard hired an automobile for their excursion and Weldon took the boys for a walking trip which included Long Wharf, the government landing and the New York Yacht Club station.

On their way back they did some shopping on Thames Street, for there are some good grocery stores there. Among other things purchased was some salami that a certain store is famous for and keep particularly for the Greek fishermen of Newport. Last, but not least, was some Rhode Island johnny cake meal, which Goddard had asked them to purchase for him.

The afternoon was very pleasant when they reboarded the *Rozinante*, so Weldon asked how they would like to have a sail and see Newport from the water. The boys thought it would be great, so Weldon said: "This time, I will not hoist the anchor, but instead, leave the *Sancho* at the anchor with the warp coiled aboard her."

The anchor warp of the *Rozinante* was usually carried in the cockpit, but now Weldon tucked his arm through the coil and went forward with it. At the same time, he told Jim to bring the tender under the bow at the same side that the anchor was streamed, and told Dan to set the mizzen. When the tender was abreast the *Rozinante's* mooring cleat, Weldon cast the warp aboard her, so that it landed in a neat coil in her bottom right side up. This was easy to do, because the warp was stopped up with three or four seizings, tied with half bow knots. Weldon then took the tender's painter and bent it to the warp between the mooring cleat and the bow chock. By this time, the tender was abreast the main shrouds so Weldon told Jim to keep her off until he cast the warp out of the bow chock, and then to climb aboard smartly. Jim not only did this but also gave the tender a shove away as he boarded, so the whole maneuver was done without the tender touching the *Rozinante*. There was not much leeway astern of them, but as Weldon hoisted the main halyards, Jim ran up the jib, so they had a rap full before sagging astern more than two or three lengths.

The wind was still light from the northwest and as they took up a northerly course through the inner harbor, the questions of the boys popped quicker than Weldon could answer them, so he had to say: "Pipe down until we get by the government landing."

Weldon was always good natured, but there were so many launches, ferry boats and yachts going in different directions that he had all he could do to keep clear.

Jim said: "I thought a sail boat always had the right of way." By this time, they were clear of the worst of the traffic. Weldon answered: "No, for in the congestion around a city, the law of 'might is right' has to prevail for many of the longer power vessels cannot turn quickly. If they are required to stop, they may become much embarrassed if they are in a maneuver which will bring them to a certain place. Around a city, small boats of every kind should keep clear no matter what rights they may have. I am sure that if you were the captain of a ferry boat, you would think so. Besides, the small boat can turn quickly and run into shallow water. So I hope you boys will remember that it is the duty of the small sail boat to keep clear even if she has the law on her side."

By this time, they were between Goat Island and Long Wharf. Weldon got enough ahead of the questions to say: "While I prefer cruising along uninhabited coasts, like back of the Cape, the contrast of visiting a city is certainly a pleasant change. I must say, one can get a much better idea of the layout of a city when he sees it from the water. The aeroplane has to rush over a city; the automobile is constricted to one-way streets; while the pedestrian is fatigued. But here we sit in comfort and safety and can stop and turn almost as we please as we sit here, away from the dirt and dust to enjoy the sights at a distance."

The northwest wind kept them quite close to the shore along here, so they could look up the streets which ran at right angles to the water. Weldon told them that there were some fine old houses along those streets that were built before the Revolution. Finally they came to the Naval Hospital and had to tack to the westward to clear Coasters Harbor Island where the War College is. They came about again and resumed their northerly course until they were by the Training Station. There were a great many naval craft of all kinds in the bay here, and as the boys were so much taken with these craft, Weldon thought it well to spend the remainder of the afternoon sailing around them. As he had served in the Navy in World War I, he could answer many of their questions except those that had to do with radar which seemed to have a prominent place on the newer vessels.

He did, however, tell the boys something that does not seem to be well known: that is, it is rather dangerous to round the bow or stern of large anchored vessels closely, because there may be a launch or boat on the other side, coming around, which will not be seen soon enough to avoid a collision if either is going fast.

After this, Weldon took the boys over to the Dumpling Rocks off Jamestown, and told them the bottom there ran off very boldly, so that about where they were sailing, it was 175 feet deep—the deepest place for several miles around and one of the deepest places close to shore in New England. Jim asked him why that should be so, and he supposed the tides running in and out of the bay for thousands of years have scoured out the channel. It is fortunate there is great depth here, otherwise the tides would be too strong for safe navigation, and it would be rather rough at times.

The westerly wind was dying as they ran back, wing and wing, to the anchorage, and the boys thought this had been the most interesting sail they had ever had, while Weldon remarked that Newport had always been considered a grand place to sail. As they neared their anchored tender, Weldon had the boys take in the jib, and mizzen, and instead of shooting for the *Sancho Panza*, he approached her, heading a little higher than a close reach, but with the mainsail only slightly full. In this way he could control their speed very exactly for if he wanted more way on, he pulled in the sheet; if he wanted to stop, he paid out more sheet. When they were close to the *Sancho*, Weldon told Jim to go forward, jump in and hold her off, while he hauled the anchor warp aboard. When Weldon went forward, he had a boat hook and, after hooking on to one of the stops, hauled the warp aboard without any tangles. In the meantime, Jim had unbent the painter, and taken the tender astern. This was all done quicker than it can be described and was in great contrast to the mess that some yachtsmen make in picking up an anchored tender. More often than not, the yacht will get the tender under her bow to the detriment of both.

As they were putting on the sail stops, Jim called: "Mr. Goddard is rowing over, Uncle!" and in a matter of seconds, he had swung alongside with his near oar and rowlock removed.

"How did the sight seeing excursion make out?" inquired Weldon.

"No worse than I had expected," replied Goddard. "However, what I came over for was to get the johnny cake meal and salami, and invite you all over to supper, for I intend to make some Rhode Island johnny cakes."

After the packages were handed over, Weldon asked, "Are you sure there will be room for us all?"

"Yes," answered Goddard, "it is a fine evening, and the young ones can eat in the cockpit." As he shoved off, he remarked: "We will expect you between six and half-past."

There was now more than an hour to while away, which the boys spent by sitting on the after deck, jigging their bare toes in the water as they trolled their models back and forth in absentminded contentment. Weldon took advantage of the opportunity to shave. As he paused in his lathering and looked out at the boys, he was in a very happy mood but just then one of the modern motorboats went by, that fetched a wave under the counter that wet Dan's seat. As the *Rozinante* gave a lurch, away went Weldon's camp mirror, shaving brush and hot water. This was too much, even for the good nature of Weldon, and as he stepped out in the cockpit to shake his fist at the retiring motor boat, he was such a queer sight, with his lathered face, that the boys burst out laughing. But all difficulties were finally overcome, and they rowed over to the *Viator*.

The girls had changed back to their slacks, and sat in the cockpit to receive them, while Mrs. Goddard stood in the companionway to offer her welcome. It was quite evident that something unusual was going on. As soon as they had boarded, a pleasant, strong, steamy odor announced to them that a large supper was in preparation. Mrs. Goddard had been standing in the companionway with her head above deck in the clear air but ready to carry out the chief steward's orders for, as you know, when a man undertakes cooking he becomes very dictatorial and demands instant action from his assistants. But now, feeling that she was about to be relieved, Mrs. Goddard went on deck with a sigh of relief.

As Weldon went below, he was nearly overcome by the combination of smoke and steam that filled the cabin. He saw that the table was set and, as Goddard opened the oven door, the sight of a platter full of johnny cakes greeted his eye.

Goddard was now frying some eggs, together with slices of salami. He said to Weldon: "There, now! you hold one plate after the other while I serve up the chow." There were seven plates in all, and by the time each had its knife and fork, as well as its cup of tea, the cabin table was loaded.

In the meantime, the children were very busy tying knots in the ends of the sheets and halyards for there was a friendly rivalry in seamanship among the two crews. Miss Prim certainly knew the most knots but little Dan with his quick fingers could tie and untie a Tom Fool's knot the quickest of all. Just as Jim was constructing a jar sling around the cedar bucket, they heard the welcome cry: "Chow coming up!"

When the children were served, Goddard asked his wife if she were not coming below, but she replied: "No, thank you, I am quite comfortable up here." So the two men sat at the cabin table with plenty of room.

By this time, the smoke had cleared away and soon after Weldon had finished his first johnny cake, he said: "By Jove! That *is* good! I wish you would tell me just how you make them for my trials have generally been somewhat of a failure."

Goddard was quite pleased that someone liked his cooking, so he went into considerable detail about johnny cakes. "There are several little points about making them that make quite a difference, and while there are many ways to make them I proceed as follows:

"First, you should use a heavy crockery mixing bowl to mix or raise the meal in. The reason for that is the heavy bowl holds the heat. Well, I proceed something like this: While the tea kettle is heating on the stove, I pour the desired amount of meal in the bowl and dry mix it with a little salt and perhaps one-twentieth part of brown sugar. I am not giving you exact quantities for that varies with the number of mouths you have to feed. But remember, the meal will swell quite a lot.

"Next, I put the bowl and its contents in the oven until it gets as warm as the hand can stand. Then when the water in the kettle is boiling furiously, I pour a little of it at a time on the meal mixture and stir it very briskly. I must say, a great deal of the success of the johnny cakes depend on this hot water mixing. That is why the bowl, and all, should be hot, otherwise the scalding water will not do its work in this first cooking or swelling of the meal. The old timers used to say you should beat air into the mixture, but it is the real hot water which does the work. When properly done, the meal turns to a heavy, creamy mixture which will even taste good at this stage. However, no matter how much hot water you add, the batter will not thin out properly. When it has properly risen, or expanded, then it must be thinned with either cold water or milk, which will at once make it pour from the mixing spoon in the right consistency to make cakes about one-quarter inch thick on the griddle. I must say that this thinning with cold water is where most cooks fall down and do not succeed in making thin cakes."

During this explanation, the frying pan has been heating. "It can be greased," Goddard went on, referring to the skillet, "with either bacon fat or butter and as soon as it starts to smoke slightly you can pour on the meal mixture in cakes about three or four inches wide. The cooking, after that, should proceed leisurely, for the slower johnny cakes are cooked the better. The cakes should not be turned over until they have formed a good, firm crust on their lower sides. This can be seen around the edge of the cakes as they are cooking."

Weldon wanted to know if the cakes did not sometimes stick to the pan.

"No, not very often, but it is necessary to use a well broken-in cast iron skillet that has a good coating of carbon to hold the fat, for even the well broken-in aluminum frying pan seems to stick at times."

Weldon inquired if the different varieties of meal made much difference.

"Some people think so, and some Rhode Islanders go so far as to think all meal not grown and ground in Rhode Island is no good, but my opinion is, that some of the corn meal from the south is just as good."

"Why do you speak of southern meal?" asked Weldon.

"There are two principal varieties of corn—one is called flint corn and is grown in the north; the other is dent corn, and is grown in the south. The flint corn has a rather round, full kernel, and is called a '90-day corn,' for it takes 90 days to grow or mature. The southern, or dent corn, has a long, thin kernel with a dent in its end and takes 110 days to mature."

"Well, isn't the dent corn planted in the north?" asked Weldon.

"Yes, it is invariably planted for fodder and silage, for it has the largest leaves and stalks and sometimes on good soil it will reach 12 feet in height, but the frost will get it before its 110 days of growth are completed. The flint corn, which generally only reaches a height of seven feet, matures quickly enough for our climate. The thing that makes the big difference in johnny cake meal is how it is ground. It should be very fine, or else it will not swell so well with the hot water. To grind it fine without heating it is the problem, for if the meal is overheated in grinding it isn't much good for anything, even feeding to cattle. This is probably the reason the meal, ground between stones in the old fashioned windmills got its good name."

"How about the difference in color of meal?" pursued Weldon.

"That is a lot of bunk. There are varieties of both flint and dent corn which make white and yellow meal. Some people think the yellow meal is the richest and some think the white meal the purest but right here on the Island of Rhode Island, their best known old varieties are called Rhode Island White Cap and Rhode Island Golden Cap. They both make equally good johnny cakes when ground and cooked properly. If you have some white meal and want to make golden colored johnny cakes, you can mix the yolks of some eggs in the meal after it is scalded."

By this time, everyone had finished supper and felt very comfortable. The ones on deck handed down their plates, while Weldon and Goddard washed and cleaned up below. It was now commencing to get dark and there was a fallish feel in the air. Now that the smoke had cleared out of the cabin, and the lamps were lit, the children and Mrs. Goddard began coming below one at a time.

After they were settled around the table, Mr. Goddard, who liked to read aloud, said: "How would you children like to hear Longfellow's poem, 'The Skeleton in Armor'?" Although there was not much enthusiasm shown, Goddard started the poem. Before long, all were spellbound, for Goddard could read well and the dimly lit cabin seemed to lend enchantment. Of course, having seen the old stone tower referred to in the poem during their Newport sight-seeing had its effect. As Goddard finished the poem, everyone was wrapped in silent reverie for a few moments.

Although all the others had been attentive to the end, little Dan had become soothed with the even rhythm and now was sound asleep with his head on Jim's shoulder. When Weldon noticed this, he remarked: "I guess sight-seeing, sailing and a good supper has been too much for our young friend. Now we will have a job to get him aboard the *Rozinante*." But after they gave him a glass of water, he could stumble up the companion-way with little help. The fresh air on deck revived him enough to make the trip over but the next morning, as they teased him about the affair, he could remember nothing of the latter part of the evening.

That night the crews of both boats slept in a happy dream. They awoke the next morning to a world much changed, for the harbor was wrapped in fog while the distant sounds of fog bells and fog horns were their most conscious connection with the surroundings.

Although the next morning was foggy, the southerly breeze which had sprung up during the night was pleasantly warm. There was no need that day to hurry with the morning swabbing for the deckwork promised to be damp until noon, so Weldon decided to have breakfast first.

As the boys seemed reluctant to leave their downy nests, he sat in his built-in easy chair and started two cans of Sterno in the stove. One was under a kettle, for the morning tea, while the other flame was warming water in a saucepan for the boys' morning washup. Under ordinary circumstances, this small fire would not give a perceptible heat, but now it seemed to radiate a sense of dryness in the cabin, as one heard the drip on the deck. By the time the tea kettle began to murmur and chortle, Jim sat up in bed and said good morning to his uncle. In reply, Weldon only put his fingers to his lips and pointed to Dan, so Jim squirmed quietly out of the bunk and the two of them confined themselves to whispered conversation. But when the bacon was being tried out, Dan became restless and finally, with a wide yawn, joined the others. First, they had a cup of tea all around. Then, while Dan was washing with some of the warm water in the hand basin, Weldon served up the bacon and eggs on paper plates. Now, with a second cup of tea, they all felt very contented.

Weldon remarked that it was a wonderful thing to get under way comfortably in the morning. It was strange how few cruisers knew how to do it. If both the inner and outer man are comfortably aroused with tea and warm washing water even the worst disposition is sometimes made agreeable.

"Some people think it is hardening to be awakened suddenly with a cold dip, and perhaps it is, but on a damp morning like this, it is certainly agreeable not to go on deck until the spirit moves." He might have gone on for some time about the comforts of cruising, but just then they were hailed by Goddard, as he came alongside in the dinghy.

Jim jumped out into the cockpit to grab the painter, while Weldon called out: "Come aboard, sir!"

Goddard had on an oilskin jacket and sou'wester, so he preferred to sit in the cockpit. As soon as he sat down, he asked; "Well, what do you think about it?"

Weldon replied: "It is only a little over 20 miles to Block Island, so we can wait for it to clear a little if we want to."

Goddard answered: "Yes, I know, but this fog is a sort of challenge to me and I get a thrill out of navigating in it. Although there is, no doubt, quite a ground swell outside still, as you know, it seldom blows over six or eight miles an hour when it is foggy. If we keep out of the steamers' tracks we should be safe enough. The wind seems to be a little south of southwest, as it often is on these damp mornings. If we tack out close along the shore until we get to Castle Hill, we should be inside steamer traffic. You know you can go as close to shore as you like all the way."

"Let's have a chart out here to look at," said Weldon, so Jim brought out the chart of Newport Harbor.

After it was spread on the cockpit seat, Goddard continued: "You see, there are bells to guide us all the way. First, the one on Fort Adams Wharf, then the one on Castle Hill Lighthouse, then the bell buoy off Butter Ball Rock. After that, if we go on tacks of about equal intervals we shall soon hear the whistle on Brenton's Reef Light Vessel. On the way out here you will hear the seas breaking on Brenton's Reef, but don't let that worry you even if you see long streaks of spindrift, for you can approach Brenton's Reef very closely on its western side. As long as there is no broken water you are safe. After we get to the lightship, we can start tacks of about a quarter hour duration. After about six miles of sailing we should hear the whistle off Point Judith, and I expect it will be clear by that time."

"All right," replied Weldon. "I am ready to start when you are. These changes in weather, and their problems, are what make cruising fun, for variety is the spice of life."

Soon after Goddard boarded the *Viator*, the girls came on deck in their oilskins. Although the *Viator* was gotten under way quickly, the *Rozinante* swung under her stern with a good rap full, as Weldon sang out: "I'll beat you to the Butter Ball buoy!" Then he lowered his voice and said to Dan: "Now I want you to keep very concise memoranda of our times of passing marks. While I may need the slate for quick calculations, you'd better take one page of the log book and write in pencil what I tell you. For instance, put down now, 'Torpedo Station bell bears North at 9:37."

By this time the *Viator* was following in their wake and the boys were very much on their toes with a queer feeling of mingled interest and we might say, fear, for a thick fog is somewhat scary to the best of us. There seemed to be bells, horns and whistles on all sides of them now. Although they sounded close, they could not be seen. In this interval, Weldon told the boys in a very reassuring voice that a small sail boat with way on was a comparatively safe thing in a fog, for she is perfectly noiseless and you can hear other craft at some distance. Still, she can turn quickly.

During this time, of course, both the *Rozinante* and *Viator* were blowing their foghorns at intervals of about one minute. This had been done by Weldon on the *Rozinante*, when Dan asked his uncle why he blew two short blasts on the horn.

"That is the fog signal for a sailboat on the port tack. I must tell you boys that a sail boat has the great advantage of letting any nearby vessel know about how she is standing, for she blows one blast on the horn if on the starboard tack, two blasts for the port tack and three blasts when running. In this way, and knowing the direction of the wind, the other fellow can tell approximately which way you are heading. If he is a quick witted person, he can guess from the direction of the sound if you will clear or not. In this way, in old times, sailing boats often kept in close company in thick weather with little danger of collision. After the steam and power boats came in, things were not so simple for they might come out of the fog headed in any direction, which was very disconcerting to the old fashioned sailor."

By this time, they could hear the measured clang of the bell on Fort Adams Wharf and finally that forbidding granite pier loomed through the fog. There was a back-draft of wind here, and the *Rozinante* nearly lost headway, while they heard a motor boat's horn, faintly, but close-to. Just when the bell, which was now nearly overhead, gave a resounding clash and ring, a power boat appeared out of the fog headed right for them. Weldon gave a strong blast on the horn, and tried to head up, but he was right in the lee of the wharf so the boat only came in stays. Fortunately, the power boat sheered off to leeward and as she passed, Weldon pointed astern to warn her of the *Viator*.

However, as the *Viator* had stood further off shore here, she now passed to leeward with her sails full, while Goddard gave them the cheery hail: "Who's ahead now?" They both stood to the westward for a while, with the *Rozinante* a little to weather of the *Viator's* wake.

The fog seemed to come over in streaks, as if it were undecided whether to clear a little or become thicker. As the *Viator* drove on ahead, she looked like some sort of a wraith or spirit of the fog that gave off its two blasts as it proceeded. The bell off Fort Adams now seemed far astern and the low blast of a steamer mingled with distant sounds of bells, horns and whistles, while the dampness settled with a chill that made the rigging drip. The *Viator* sailed well now, and gradually pulled ahead so that she was occasionally out of sight. On the *Rozinante* they redoubled the vigil of the lookout, but finally they heard a single blast of the horn a little to weather, when Weldon said: "By Jove, he has come about, and now has the wind over his starboard side."

Then he jumped up and rather startled the boys, but all he said was: "We have forgotten something!"

"What is it?" asked Jim.

"In the excitement, we forgot to write down our time off Fort Adams, so get the log book, quick!"

After looking at the clock, and seeing that it was nearly ten, he said: "Well, write down 9:45." Then they tacked inshore, with the horn at single blasts, and could plainly hear the *Viator* ahead of them on the same tack.

They had not stood that way long when all of a sudden the *Viator* came in view tacking ship. When they crossed her wake, a high, pebbly beach appeared ahead with fog above. Weldon stood on a length or two and told the boys there was good water all along that shore. He wanted to keep inshore of traffic when he could, but as they came about the beach looked very close at hand to the boys. They stood on, tack and tack, for some time now, and saw nothing but the shore at the end of their starboard tacks, but the bell on Castle Hill was now giving its cheerful clang more plainly. Soon the ground swells were very perceptible and even before the shore came in sight, the wash and gurgle of the seas could be heard.

As they rounded Castle Hill, Weldon went way in close to the miniature white lighthouse which, as the fog shut out all else, seemed close at hand as its bell rang out its warning. Weldon said: "This shore is remarkably steep here and very likely our topsides would strike before the keel would." Nevertheless, the boys were relieved when they stood out again and the wisps of fog gradually shut out the land. They were now in the region where the friendly tinkle of the Butter Ball buoy seemed to chime with the measured clang of the lighthouse bell and where the *Rozinante* rose with the ground swells, only to plunge in the hollow beyond.

At first, it seemed quite rough to the boys for a fog seems to accentuate the movement of a boat, but they were soon used to it, and felt the thrill that is imparted by the motion of a good sea boat. Each starboard tack now brought them to where the roar of the seas on Brenton's Reef was very audible. The breakers on these rocks seemed to add to the general dampness and saltiness of the air, as they sailed on through patches of spindrift and an occasional long strip of floating kelp. But if the on-shore tacks were a little disconcerting to the boys as they struggled on in their little world surrounded by fog, the off-shore tacks were a worry to their uncle, for somewhere to the westward the low tones of a steamer's whistle were becoming stronger and stronger. They had not seen the *Viator* for some time but the occasional weak blasts of her horn came down the damp wind only to inform them what an insignificant thing she was to the oncoming steamer. The lightship's whistle was of a higher tone and as they were to leeward of her, it had been strong for some time.

Weldon told the boys that the steamship was probably a tanker, feeling her way in and trying to pick up the lightship. But after both whistles bore well to the westward, there was a slight rift in the fog and Dan sang out: "There she is!"

For an instant, the masts and stack of the lightship came in view as the steam of her whistles plumed up, but the fog soon shut her out. Weldon at once said to Jim: "Write down, B. R. lightship, bears West one-eighth-mile at 11:37."

After that they went on quarter-hour tacks with the crew changing station at each tack so that they alternated as helmsman, lookout and horn blower. It would have been a dreary, monotonous sail if this change in duties had not occurred and the horn blower certainly would have been winded. However, they all learned to blow the horn with little effort and as one of them at least had to watch the clock while the others were occupied as lookout and helmsman, the time soon passed until a little grumbling of the inner man made them think of eating.

The seas out there were longer and flatter than inshore, so the *Rozinante* seemed to ghost along well in the light weather for as only the nearby sea could be seen, it appeared to glide by rapidly. No other horn than their own now could be heard. They seemed to be gliding along in a world of their own with no other sound than that of the lee bow wave.

Weldon went below to make sandwiches and soon returned with a plateful of them, made with canned tongue with a little mustard on it. The boys had unusual appetites, for the constant occupation as lookout and hornsman in the damp air had done its work. Weldon took over both the helm and the horn while the boys refreshed themselves and washed down the sandwiches with ginger ale. He could not help smiling at the boys' enjoyment of the food, and said to himself: Yes, a little is always better than too much for real satisfaction.

Weldon was again at the helm at two that afternoon. As he steered by both the wind and compass, he noticed that the breeze had shifted a little toward the west. Soon after this, a white, silvery line appeared on the horizon west of them. Gradually it increased and as it rose it became broader, until the curtain lifted. In the few feet visible, the sea turned a transparent blue, faint at first, then brighter until a robin's-egg-blue streak was beside them. As the light continued to approach, it became vivid and the curtain of fog rolled away as if it had been gradually furled. As it noiselessly swept to leeward, the warmth of the sun was welcomed by all and the fog horn was thankfully placed under the after deck. The breeze now ruffled the water as the *Rozinante* heeled with a change of motion. As they looked around, it seemed a different world.

"My, how bright and pleasant it seems!" exclaimed Jim.

"Yes," his uncle agreed, "it is always so, for after one has emerged from some sorrow or worry or the fog has cleared away things seem clearer than usual."

As they looked around them, they saw the curtain of the fog a mile or two away, in slowly moving vertical folds. There was nothing else in sight, so Weldon mused aloud: "Alone, alone, all, all alone; alone on a wide, wild sea!" But little Dan who gazed around unaffected by these sentiments, asked: "Oh, uncle, what is that?" as he pointed toward the southeast.

At first, Weldon saw nothing, but soon a smile passed over his face as he replied; "Dan, that is a nautilus, or what the sailors call a Portuguese Man-of-War. I will tack ship and stand in that direction so that you can see it." He then went on to explain: "These little creatures are very plentiful in the warm waters of the south, but only reach these regions in warm weather when the wind has been southerly."

As they neared the nautilus, the boys were fascinated by the light rainbow colors reflected from its "sail," as it scudded along toward the northeast. Weldon continued: "It is supposed that the sailors of olden time called them Portuguese Men-of-War because of their varied colors, for about 500 years ago Portuguese war vessels set brightly colored sails." By this time they could see many other nautiluses scattered to seaward. Then they came about and stood to the westward again in the coming breeze.

As the horizon cleared, distant vessels appeared one after the other. There were swordfishermen in various directions with lookouts aloft. Away off to the South, two destroyers cruised along in company. As it cleared to the westward, the *Viator* appeared bearing west-northwest and astern of her the high light and whistle buoy off Point Judith. Although the *Viator* was three miles distant, Weldon remarked that she was no more than a mile or two ahead of them. He then asked for the tide book, and after some study, he said: "I think we will beat her yet, for the tide will soon be running strong to the eastward through Block Island Sound. If we stand off away to the South now, we can later tack up under Sandy Point, out of the tide."

The afternoon breezes now hardened to a nice sailing strength, and a slight sea seemed to make, but the boys were so occupied with trying to catch up with the *Viator* that time passed quickly. Block Island had been in sight for some time, but it seemed very distant until, apparently all at once, it appeared close by and they could see the rolling hills and the cliffs of Clay Head quite plainly. The *Viator*, seeing them headed toward the east side of the island, stood between the *Rozinante*, and the finish line.

But when the *Viator* came to the bell buoy off Sandy Point, she tacked to the westward.

"Now," said Weldon to the boys, "we've got her!" The boys looked puzzled, thinking that the *Viator* still had a good lead. Weldon took the *Rozinante* well in on the northeast side of Sandy Point before swinging to the westward. There was no ground swell in there; in fact it was as smooth as a mill pond although there was a good afternoon breeze coming off the island.

The *Viator* was now right in the full strength of the tide which set her to leeward so rapidly, that she soon changed her bearing from dead ahead, to as far off the *Rozinante's* lee bow as the rigging. This was partly because the *Rozinante* was being set to weather by the tide's back eddy behind the point. But now there was a very angry looking tide rip ahead of them, which was more than a mile long. It was a strange looking affair, perfectly smooth on their side but where the ground swell of the other side struck, it boiled up in white water. Beyond the rip, the sea was a placid mixture of blue, brown, and green, but in the rip the water was decidedly lighter colored. It certainly looked very shallow there, and Weldon had to look at the chart repeatedly to convince himself that it was not. Finally, they entered the rip half way between the buoy and the land. The rip is very narrow but, nevertheless, if it had not been for the good land breeze they would have been set back and to leeward by it. However, as they ran into the ground swells on the other side, the boys could see that they were nearly up to the *Viator*.

From here on it was a very pleasant sail in the dying southwester and after the *Viator* tacked inshore, they were in close company. It is thrilling to most of us to approach any island, but now as the two yachts rose over the swells and darted forward in their race to the finish, everyone seemed animated with the sailor's natural love of competition.

As they tacked inshore, the higher land and sand dunes gave a sense of security which, though not analyzed or admitted, certainly was a relief after their long vigil in the fog. It also must be remembered that the *Rozinante* was little more than a sailing canoe, with the heads of the crew a little over three feet above the water as they sat in the cockpit. No doubt, the *Rozinante* was much safer than some boats that were larger, deeper, and had explosives aboard but her small dimensions always gave one an extra thrill when making harbor.

As they approached the breakwater, they crossed tacks for the first time, and, although the *Viator* was on the starboard tack, the *Rozinante* crossed her bow with several lengths to spare, whereupon, Weldon stood up and called: "Who's ahead now?"

The *Viator* may have answered this hail, but if so it was not heard aboard the *Rozinante*. Weldon, in his excitement, overstood the mark or was too much impressed by the outer black buoy (which is really a guide buoy), while the *Viator* took the much shorter course inshore toward the second black buoy, so that as they ran into the smooth water back of the breakwater the *Viator* had a substantial lead. As the girls stripped off their oilskins they were very cordial in their waves at the *Rozinante*, but this time the boys were looking anywhere but ahead and only half-heartedly returned the salutes.

As they ran up the harbor, their eyes were directed toward a long, double-ended power boat that was anchored off the water dock in the southwest part of the harbor. It is true there was the usual number of auxiliary cruisers and sport fishing crates there but these unfortunate craft only gave one the impression that the Salt Pond was a dumping place for refuse. In contrast, the long white double-ender stood out like a Venus among these misshapen tubs for, though either sail or power, their principal object was to crowd the most complication in the least length and their crews plainly showed the hardships they had encountered in cruising. Most of them were dressed as if they had recently escaped from some sanitarium and acted as if panic-stricken at being twenty miles from a motel.

The *Viator* and *Rozinante* ran way to the south end of the harbor and dropped anchor near a place where the chart showed several boulders under water. They were very close together, and as the sails were being furled, Weldon called over: "Well sir, I guess you beat us after all!"

Goddard replied: "It was a pretty close finish and I would not have passed you if I had not cut inside you at the breakwater."

Weldon chuckled. "I never would have caught you if I had not cut inside the Sandy Point buoy. This cutting inside buoys is one of the most exciting parts of our cruising races, and it's good training for navigation."

It was about quarter-past six by that time, so after things were straightened out on deck the boys and their uncle sat in the cockpit looking at the chart of Block Island.

Dan mused: "I wonder why they call this harbor the Great Salt Pond."

His uncle replied: "It *was* a great salt pond until the Government cut the channel through to the sea in about 1893. Block Island is famous for having many ponds. Like Plymouth County in Massachusetts and several other places, it is said to have three hundred and sixty-five ponds—one for each day of the year. While this is called Great Salt Pond on the chart, the Block Islanders call it the New Harbor." Weldon then pointed on the chart to a place named Block Island Harbor where there were quite extensive breakwaters and said that the natives called this place, "Old Harbor." He went on to explain: "Block Island had no enclosed harbor in the old days, but near where the breakwaters at the Old Harbor are there was a somewhat sheltered cove when the wind was southwest. That was the place where most of the Block Island boats were kept in olden times."

"Did they anchor in that unsheltered place?" asked Jim.

"Yes, and no," replied his uncle. "They did not anchor, but tied up to long oak poles that were driven in the bottom. After the first small breakwater was built there, these poles were so plentiful that at one time that place was called the Pole Harbor, for the story is that there were several hundred poles there. The older Block Island boats were smaller and, at the approach of bad weather, the boats were landed on a sandy beach and their cobblestone ballast thrown out. Then they were hauled ashore by oxen, for the old Block Island boats were quite light when the ballast was removed."

Weldon remarked that it was getting time for supper, but if the boys came into the cabin he would tell them more about Block Island boats while he was getting supper. Weldon had a way of talking about the old fashioned boats that fascinated the two boys. While they had the same interest in aeroplanes and high speed motor boats that other boys had, these talks about the local craft that had been in the waters they cruised made every harbor much more interesting.

Weldon heated some chicken soup and was making some bacon and eggs, for the boys seemed to like this breakfast dish at any hour of the day. It certainly is a good cruising meal. Another advantage of the bacon and eggs was that Weldon had cooked this meal so often that he could do it automatically while carrying on a conversation, so he continued to talk about Block Island, and its boats.

"Block Island was discovered or claimed by Adrien Block in 1614. It seems that right after Hudson discovered Manhattan, the Dutch were in the habit of sending a fleet of ships there annually to trade for furs with the Indians. But in the fall of 1613, one of the ships named *Tiger* was so badly damaged by fire that she could not return. Her captain Adrien Block and his crew spent the winter of 1613, and 1614 on Manhattan, where they built the second boat built in this country.

This vessel was named *Onrust,* meaning restless, and in the *Onrust* Block went on an exploring expedition, passing through Hell Gate and Long Island Sound and discovering Block Island.

As this was six years before the Pilgrims settled at Plymouth, you can see it was very early. However, the Dutch had a permanent settlement on Manhattan from 1624 until New Amsterdam, or Manhattan, was finally ceded to the English by treaty in 1674. So the Dutch colonists had many years to visit Block Island and the Connecticut and New Jersey shores.

I only speak of it now because the rig of the Block Island boats was identical to the rig of the Dutch yachts and boats of around

1600, so the experts say the Block Island boats are of Dutch descent. They, no doubt, were similar to the periaguas that are often mentioned in early accounts of New York. While I believe it is true that the first settlers of Block Island were English, still it is perfectly possible that they adopted the type of periagua that the Dutch had used for fishing in this region. But as all this

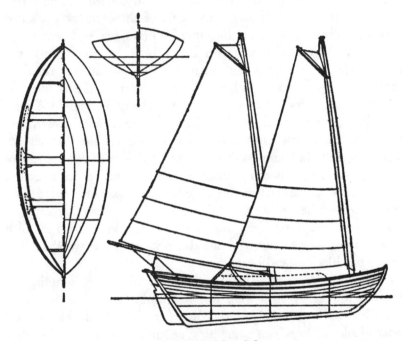

An old Block Island boat.

happened before 1700, there is no definite proof of the origin of the Block Island boats. About all we know now is that the Block Island boat had developed to a very definite type by 1840 and remained much the same until about 1880. The only great variation was in size; the smaller ones were all open, while the larger ones had a very small cuddy and stove forward."

By this time, they had finished supper on the *Rozinante* and as the boys lay back on the berth, Weldon cleaned up, stowed the utensils and lit his pipe. After he had settled in his easy chair, he continued.

"The Block Island boats are principally famous because they usually returned home safely, which cannot be said of any other fishing boats the world over. This must have been partly because of the remarkably good seamen that the island bred. While there were usually about 50 boats at the island, only two were lost in about half a century. One of these struck a sunken rock off Point Judith and the other went to sea and was never heard of. Perhaps she was run down by a steamer. This is a remarkable record for open boats used in about the roughest region along our coast. When you consider that the island had no good harbor for many years, it seems almost incredible. I have said before that the Block Islanders were excellent seamen and some of them still alive have such a remarkable instinct for direction that they can navigate night or day without the use of a compass. Their homing instinct is only second to a carrier pigeon or a salmon. Even the advent of the gasoline engine has not entirely killed this remarkable fifth sense. They are capable, hardy and very intelligent but the best man in the world must have a good boat to survive around Block Island, so we shall look at the old Block Island boats.

"They ranged in size between 20 and 40 feet in length over all, but the larger ones were few in number and generally were used for carrying mail and passengers to the island. The typical boat of olden times was something about 30 feet over all with a beam of 11 1/2 feet, but as they had very flaring sides, the beam on the water line was very much less, perhaps under 9 feet. The principal characteristic of these boats was their great displacement, for they were very heavily ballasted for open boats. The model was very much alike at both ends but, as they were generally ballasted by the stern, there was the most freeboard forward and most draft aft. One, 30 feet long, would have a draft of about 4 feet. The Block Island boats had considerable sheer and have been criticized by some for their low freeboard amidships, but low freeboard at some place or other is a characteristic of most fishing craft, large or small, for it makes hauling nets, shipping dories, etc., much easier. However, the Block Island boats usually had removable washboards which increased the freeboard when desired for the winter season or when hand lining. But the Block Island boat was not only famous for its seaworthiness, it was also very fast under certain conditions. It is said none of the yachts of their size could beat them to windward in a strong breeze and choppy sea. It was not until yachts had adopted outside ballast and scientific rigging that they could beat them under these conditions."

Weldon took the slate and drew a Block Island boat while the boys looked on with rapt attention. He had something to say with almost each line drawn and as he was finishing he said, apologetically: "The only reason I have drawn the boat out for you boys is that the usual drawings and models of Block Island boats represent the larger and later ones of this type, such as the *Island Belle, Roaring Bessie* and *Dauntless* which were all about half decked and used to carry mail, freight, and passengers.

"You see, some of the peculiarities of the rig were that the main mast was stepped amidships or even slightly forward of the middle. They had long, tapering masts and many rows of reefs in the sails. In light weather, they set high, narrow sails almost like our modern ones for their gaffs were little more than enlarged headboards. But when it came on to blow, they could reef down so the sails were only on the large lower part of the masts. The foresails of these craft had unusually deep reefs and it is said they could beat to windward under this sail when all other craft, large or small, had to lay-to or scud. This was because they had large displacement and ample lateral plane. Also, they carried their ballast quite concentrated aft of the middle and, being double-enders, rode the waves like ducks as they forged to windward, while the large-sterned craft which wallowed and dove had so much resistance that they could not make good to windward under a small sail."

When Weldon stopped to light his pipe, little Dan spoke up to inquire why they were such good sea boats.

"I suppose it was on account of their good sheer, and high ends. They also had flaring sides all the way around, and were of lapstrake construction. Both of these things keep the sea and spray down. Then, too, as they heeled the weather rail raised quickly as it does on a wide boat."

Jim then wanted to know if a model like a Block Island boat would make a good yacht.

"No, not particularly, because, if outside ballast is combined with sides that have flare or flam, the motion of the yacht becomes sudden or, as the sailor would say, the motion is 'corky.' But with some of the ballast inside and strong rigging this motion could be controlled. The Block Island boats are too low amidships for good cabin accommodations and they would turn too slowly to suit the modern yachtsman who is used to craft which are cut away at both ends. On the whole, the modern yacht is pretty good and it is interesting that Captain Nat Herreshoff, the principal developer of the modern yacht, lived within a day's sail of Block Island and was a great admirer of the Block Island boats."

The boys were getting sleepy by that time but as Jim studied over the sail plan on the slate he could not help asking how they managed a gaff with one halyard. Weldon told him they did it in different ways; some had a rather triangular span with one end made fast near the gaff jaws, and the other end secured near the peak, while others simply secured the halyard on the gaff where experiment showed it worked best.

It was now quite dark and the wind began to make the rigging moan and sing, so Weldon stepped out in the cockpit to see what was up. When he came in again and was lighting the riding light, he said: "The wind has shifted to the southeast, and the barometer is falling, so we may get a storm tonight but we are in a snug anchorage and you boys might as well turn in."

The wind soon rose to a good breeze and was accompanied by heavy rain but the cabin seemed very snug, indeed, for before

Weldon turned in he lighted a lantern which he hung in the cockpit just aft of the partition. This threw a faint light into the cabin. They were all soon sound asleep, as the rain beat on the deck close overhead and the sea outside gave a seething sound. As they were anchored close under the lee, all these sounds only gave them a comfortable, thankful feeling.

9

A Stranded Motor Boat / The Lampooner

On Towing / The End of the Cruise

On a small boat like the *Rozinante,* one is usually conscious of changes in weather, whether on deck or below. Though the boys slept soundly that night, Weldon tried to keep a sort of reclining watch with one eye open but, somehow, the steady drumming of the rain on the deck and the moan of the wind in the rigging got the best of him and the next thing he knew it was beginning to be light in the east.

The rain had stopped, though gusts of wind were coming over stronger than ever. When they struck, the *Rozinante* seemed to quiver all over as she swung to her anchor and the ripples alongside gave a very businesslike sound.

Weldon turned over for another nap, but before long occasional bursts of sunlight streamed over the cockpit coaming and made dancing patches of light in the cabin. At first, this did not register much on his mind but as he grew more alert it dawned on him that there had been a change of wind and they were now tailing out toward the northeast. So he got up for a look around.

It was a fresh morning with a strong west-southwest wind and patches of blue sky between moving clouds. When he looked where the fleet of motor cruisers had been anchored, he saw most of them had dragged clear across the harbor and had fetched up close to the harbor entrance. One was ashore there, so he called the boys and started an early breakfast for he thought they would like to see the fun. While breakfast was cooking, he told the boys to pump out the bilge. When they lifted the hatch in the floor boards, they were surprised at the amount of rain that had fallen in last night's storm. Weldon told them that southeast storms struck Block Island with their full force and were sometimes almost like a tropical storm where heavy rain and wind are combined, but he expected the wind would soon shift to the northwest.

Little Dan said; "Gee, it will be some job to pump out this bilge. Why don't we wait until after breakfast?" His uncle merely replied: "I expect to get under way soon after breakfast."

Luckily, about this time Goddard came over in the dinghy. After boarding the *Rozinante,* he said: "Phew! There is a good breeze blowing this morning."

"Yes," replied Weldon, "but I intend to get under way after breakfast and plant an anchor for that motor boat that is aground down by the opening. If he has an anchor out when the wind shifts to the northwest he will float clear."

Goddard only remarked: "I think it will be some job in this wind," but Weldon suggested: "If you come along with us and we talk it over first, I believe we can make light work of it."

"Well," replied Goddard, "I guess I like being a Good Samaritan as well as you do. As soon as we get the water out of the bilge you can tell us your plan for the maneuver."

Weldon suddenly looked up at Goddard and asked: "Have you had your breakfast?"

Goddard hung his head and answered: "I must confess I have not, but if we are to do a good turn it is of no consequence."

Weldon remarked, simply, that he liked to have his crews well fed and passed Goddard a steaming cup of tea and a plate of bacon and eggs. Then he put more water in the kettle and fried two more eggs for himself.

While the others were eating, Weldon said: "My plan is

something like this. We will hang my big spare anchor over the stern of the dinghy and coil the warp down on her floor boards. Then we will sail over to something like a cable's length to weather of the stranded motor boat when we will drop off Mr. Goddard in the dinghy. When he drifts down to within thirty fathoms or 180 feet of the motor boat, he can let go the anchor and carry the bitter end of the warp to the boat."

By that time, breakfast was finished and Goddard said: "I like your plan first rate excepting towing two dinghies. I suggest, first of all, that I go aboard the *Viator,* leave my dinghy, and you can come over in the *Sancho* to pick me up. That will also give me a chance to tell Mrs. Goddard what we are up to."

The men were soon off in the two dinghies and, almost before the boys got on their oilskins and had taken the stops off jib and mizzen, they were back in the *Sancho Panza.* The first thing Weldon did was to go forward and take the anchor warp out of the chock and carry it aft to the main shrouds where he lashed it with a sail stop. This made the *Rozinante* ride partly side to the wind and allowed the dinghy to lay quietly in the lee while they transferred the anchor and warp.

At first, they coiled the warp down in the bottom of the *Sancho,* using loops as large as they could. When they came to the end of the warp that had been shaken well to take the kinks out, they bent it to the anchor with a fisherman's bend or anchor knot. Then they lowered the anchor carefully over the side of the *Rozinante* so that it was just under water, whereupon Goddard got into the dinghy and brought her stern up alongside so the scull hole was right at the anchor warp. Weldon then handed the warp to Goddard who pulled the anchor up so that its stock was just above water and across the dinghy's stern. Goddard, who was facing aft, then sat down on the amidships thwart still holding the warp in his hand. As the knot in the warp came in the scull hole, it took little strain to hold it, so he simply held it for the next few seconds by putting his foot on it where it went over the after thwart. He next bent a piece of cord to the warp with a rolling hitch and took the cord around the thwart where he was sitting, fastening it with a half bowknot or slip knot. All this time it had been blowing too fresh to carry on much conversation and if this transfer of the anchor had not been done just about as described there would have been considerable confusion with tangled warps and dented topsides. Now, as the Sancho Panza was let astern, she had a very businesslike appearance with the anchor well secured.

Weldon did not want to have his sails flapping long in such strong wind, so he told the boys to be ready to hoist the mizzen when he ordered it. The two men then went forward and hauled in Rozinante's anchor, hand over hand. Just before it broke out, Weldon called to them to set the mizzen. The boys succeeded in doing this very quickly while the men were bringing the anchor aft to the cockpit with the warp leading outside the shrouds. The jib was now run up and sheeted home while the Rozinante swung off on her course, wind abeam. The strong puffs of wind made her heel some, even with only jib and mizzen set, but the Rozinante was well balanced and they all had the elated feeling that they were about to accomplish something.

It was but a short sail to the stranded motor boat, but Goddard chuckling said: "It is strange for a sailboat to be going to the rescue of a power craft."

Weldon replied: "Yes, but when there is no propeller to think about or tangle with ropes, there are some advantages. I suppose most of the rescues of the past were made under sail."

They were now close to the stranded power yacht and did not have much time for conversation, but Weldon did say: "You had better take a watch tackle, or handy-billy, along with you in the dinghy for you can never tell when they will come in handy. Dan, you get the watch tackle and be ready to throw it in the bow of the dinghy when she is alongside."

They were exactly to windward of the power boat when Weldon headed the Rozinante well up in the wind, let go the tiller and took the weather jib sheet in his hand. The Rozinante lay very quietly this way for the mizzen was forcing her ahead and heading her up but by hauling in or slacking out on the jib, which was partly aback, Weldon could control the boat very exactly although she had no way on. It was not rough in the pond where they were, nevertheless the wind was still strong. As the *Rozinante* lay partly side to the wind with no way on, it was easy to board the dinghy when it was hauled under her lee, so Goddard sat on the after deck ready to swing his legs into her. Jim hauled the *Sancho* in smartly; Dan tossed in the watch tackle. Goddard slid onto the middle thwart in a matter of seconds and called out: "All right! Cast off!" Jim put the coiled painter in the bow and shoved the nose off.

Goddard had his oars out almost before the *Sancho* swung around, but as the anchor under the stern acted like a drogue she headed and drifted to leeward very steadily.

He sat looking over his shoulder trying to gauge the distance accurately. Finally, he took both oars in one hand, and put his feet up on the thwart stringers. With his free hand, he pulled the end of the half bowknot and the anchor warp ran out without any more fuss than the slight rising of the stern.

Goddard now took in his oars and leisurely paid out on the warp but, unfortunately, he came to the bitter end before he reached the stranded power boat. This made Weldon on the *Rozinante* pass some remarks that startled the boys, but Goddard kept his wits about him and bent the dinghy's painter onto the warp. This let her swing down so the man on the power boat could heave him a rope. Though there was a good deal of spray flying and the tender became partly swamped, Goddard succeeded in hauling the *Sancho* back to the anchor warp where he made the rope fast to the warp with a double sheet bend. This knot or bend is a good way to secure two ropes which are to be under a strain and still untie easily afterwards.

Then Goddard took the dinghy to the leeward side of the power boat and, when invited aboard, threw the watch tackle onto the power boat. He climbed up the side with the dinghy's painter in his mouth, for the power boat was one of those high-sided things that the sailor would describe as having three decks and no bottom.

The crew of the power craft consisted of the owner, his wife and two children, all of whom seemed scared and dazed. Goddard said: "Come now, we must haul off by high tide."

"Well, how can we possibly do that?" inquired the owner.

Goddard only replied; "I think the wind and tide will do most of it if we give them a chance."

The power boat was laying with her head toward the west, so Goddard went forward to put a strain on the anchor warp. He found the bow chocks were miserable chromium plated affairs that could not take a side strain and were so poorly rounded off that they would only take a lead from straight ahead. If the craft had had a capstan, instead of a windlass, Goddard might have taken the anchor warp to that. He thought to himself: This poor fellow is hard up, for while all this mahogany and chromium plating looks fine in a showroom, it isn't of much use now. He hove in hand-taut on the anchor warp and made it fast to the windlass. Then he fleeted the watch tackle and made one end of it fast to the base of the windlass. The other end of the watch tackle had a tapered hemp tail, so Goddard secured it to the warp with a sliding hitch which consisted of three half-hitches which he slid out on the warp as far as he could reach. When they heaved in on the watch tackle, the man's wife took up the slack of the warp where it bent around the winch head. After freshening the nip two or three times, or sliding the watch tackle whip along the warp, the anchor finally took hold in earnest and the power boat heeled toward it.

Goddard said to them: "That is about all we can do now but, when the wind gets more toward the westward, you will swing clear if the tide is still high."

After they had all moved aft, the bow gave a little shudder, the boat righted and the warp sagged. So they freshened the nip again and this time the bow swung offshore quite easily. After the bow had swung in line with the warp they put it in the bow chock and after that used the windlass instead of the watch tackle.

When they had a hard strain on the warp, the power boat owner said: "That anchor of yours certainly holds well."

"Yes," replied Goddard, "and you will find there is quite a difference in anchors, for one will let you drag ashore while the other will haul you off." He then suggested going ahead slowly with the engine. When this was done and the anchor warp again hove in, she came a little more and was waterborne. They shut down the engine and swung to the anchor. Then Goddard said: "I advise you to lay to this anchor until the wind goes down and we will come alongside tomorrow and take the anchor and warp."

The owner and his family were so elated at getting off the beach so easily that they beamed all over as they thanked Goddard, but he explained: "The real thanks are due to the owner of the *Rozinante,* for he proposed the maneuver and furnished the anchor and warp." He went on to say: "The anchor will probably break out pretty hard. But if you go ahead and astern a couple of times when the warp is straight up and down, it will come out O.K."

The power boat owner remarked: "Oh, I have one of those patent anchors which breaks out easily." Goddard's only reply was; "I have no doubt of it but, if I were you, I would never go to sleep with that sort of anchor down." And, after saying good-by all around, Goddard rowed off in the dinghy.

The wind had veered to the west and there was a temporary lull, but a bank of northwest wind clouds was gathering to windward and they all knew it would soon blow from that quarter. As soon as Goddard boarded the *Rozinante,* they bore off toward their previous anchorage and soon brought up just where they were an hour and a half before. By this time, the wind was from the west and the sun, as it streamed down between the moving clouds, quickly dried the cockpit seats so that is was very pleasant sitting in the lee of the *Rozinante's* deckhouse. This made a good time for the boys to ask questions for they had been very much interested in the morning's maneuvers. Jim asked his uncle why it was that so many power boats had dragged across the pond during the night.

Weldon said: "If you bring me the slate I think I can explain to you."

When it was brought out, he drew an exaggerated cross-section of the pond and went on: "In the first place, most of the bottom of the Pond is poor holding ground for it is soft mud and sand. In the second place, the water of the southwest shore deepens very rapidly. This makes the bottom lay on an angle with the surface. When a vessel swings offshore there, the angle of her warp and the bottom is too great for the stockless type of anchors to hold. You know, the light-headed or stockless anchors need a scope of almost four to one to hold well. But when a vessel swings offshore where those power boats were anchored, the scope, as compared with the angle of the bottom, may be as little as two to one. I think if we row down by those boats this afternoon we will find all of those which dragged had stockless anchors." Weldon then illustrated this condition on the slate and showed that as the anchor passed over the parts of the pond that were fifty feet deep, the warp tended nearly up and down.

Goddard then spoke up: "The chap on the power boat which we pulled off the beach seemed to be proud that his anchor was of the type which breaks out easily, but I think if he saw the illustration you have just made on the slate he might change his mind."

Just then, there was a hail from the *Viator*. Mrs. Goddard and the girls appeared on deck, dressed for going ashore, so Goddard made a quick departure, saying: "I suppose now they will make me change some of my clothes, but I'll see you when I come back. I want to row down the harbor with you this afternoon to see that long double-ended power yacht."

The boys had an itch to go ashore, too, so Weldon told them that if he remembered correctly, there was a narrow inlet in the southeast part of the Pond that would allow them to row almost half way to town.

They started out with Weldon amidships doing the rowing and a boy at each end. After passing the steamboat wharf, they

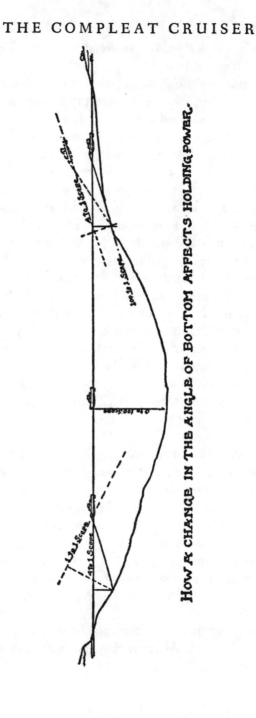

HOW A CHANGE IN THE ANGLE OF BOTTOM AFFECTS HOLDING POWER.

entered a landlocked sheet of water called Trims Pond. It is mostly very shallow but in the eastern part there was a narrow entrance into another pond. When they got to the head of this second pond, they were right beside the roadway. This little row was very amusing to the boys because almost all the way they could see bottom and in places the channel was narrow. However, after securing the *Sancho Panza* they only had a short walk to the Old Harbor.

There was still quite a sea running in from last night's south-easter and occasionally the spray of a wave would fly over the breakwater, making a flash of light over the somber spectacle. As they came closer, they could see there were many fishing boats in and they all seemed to move back and forth as the ground swells came in the breakwater entrance.

Finally, they arrived at the old inner basin which is built of red sandstone. Here the boats were thickly clustered, while the fishermen gathered in groups around the wooden platform, basking in the sun as they smoked their cigarettes, turned back their oilskins and turned down their boots. No doubt, there were some good stories being told but the boys were mostly interested in seeing the fish which were being weighed in. Among them were a couple of swordfish which seemed as big as a man, although their swords and tails had been cut off. There was a tuna, or horse mackerel, that was said to weigh 350 pounds. Some of the fishermen were drying nets and everything around smelt very fishy and salty. In fact, the wharf platform and walks were coated with a crust of salt and fish scales. This, together with the fresh westerly wind that was blowing, began to make the boys hungry so they went to the dining room of one of the several hotels a few steps away. They were among the first of the diners, so the change from the bustle and mess of the wharf only a few minutes before to the long, quiet dining room was very agreeable. The dinner was good and the boys quite equal to it, so as they started back over the road they all were contented. Weldon told the boys that there were a great many small hotels or boarding houses scattered over the island. Some of them were named for the nearby cities in Connecticut and Rhode Island and people from those places often spent weekends there, for there used to be two steamers running daily. Unfortunately, Block Island used to be quite a drinking place, and during prohibition times the Block Islanders did considerable rumrunning. One reason for that was that the high seas limit, or borderline, came close to Block Island, so the rum ships could anchor quite close off the island.

Weldon went on to say: "Block Island is a very pleasant place on summer evenings, and the saying is: 'Every night you will have to pull a blanket over you before morning.' In hot weather, many people used to come here from places like Providence and New London."

When they got back to the pond beside the road, they found that two Block Island boys were out rowing in the *Sancho Panza.* When Weldon called to them they came ashore promptly and said: "We didn't know that was your but."

He gave each of them a dime and after they had gone away Jim said with a chuckle; "Did you hear him call a boat a but?"

"Yes, the old Rhode Islanders used to cut some words short and would say cut for coat, flut for float and, as you just heard, but for boat. One might say: I put on my cut and got in my but, and put her aflut.' I suppose these old pronunciations have persisted longer out here than on the mainland."

Little Dan said, "They looked like pretty tough boys."

"Well," said his uncle, "the Block Island boys are tough and they're famous for using bad language. But almost all island-bred boys are good-hearted like their fathers before them."

When they were rowing out they passed a dory being rowed by an old man, and Jim noticed that he was only using one thole pin to an oar. He noticed this, perhaps, because the oars were making no noise, which is unusual in this sort of a dory. He called his uncle's attention to it, but Weldon said: "Many Block Islanders used to prefer to row with one thole pin in calm weather, and it is sometimes the best way although it takes some practice to do it easily. You know, with two thole pins, the oar can't be swung as much as in an oarlock. In rowing by an object, or coming alongside, the oar must be taken in or it will certainly break one of the thole pins. But when only one pin is used the oar can be swung way around, or quickly shipped or unshipped."

"But I can't see how he does it," pursued Dan.

"If you watch carefully, I will show you." He lifted the looms of the oars out of the locks and placed them on the gunwale right aft of the locks. Of course, it was easy to take the stroke with the oars that way. But on the recovery, he swung the blades forward quite slowly while very gradually feathering the blades. It was this rolling of the loom that held the oar against the lock. When he got to the end of the recovery, he did some wrist work which was hard to see, for he did not unfeather the oar again until it was in the water. Besides, he held the oars forward with a twist of the wrist which is hard to explain but is easily learned.

Weldon rowed that way a short time when Dan asked: "How can you back up?"

As quick as a flash, Weldon lifted the looms over the rowlocks to their forward side and backed up so suddenly that the boys slid on their seats. He soon put the oars back in the locks because this sort of rowing rubbed the varnish off the gunwale and had a tendency to raise the locks. He told the boys that the old Viking ships only had a hook shaped wooden block on the gunwale to hold the oar in place. Probably, the oar was held against this single thole by a thong or rope when there was any wind.

By this time they were back to the *Rozinante*. The first part of the afternoon was spent by Weldon drying sails, and the boys in whittling models. The dory Jim made only had one thole pin to a side.

Along toward four o'clock, the crew of the *Viator* came out and soon after Goddard came alongside the *Rozinante* saying; "How about that row down the Pond?"

"That's just what we are waiting for," answered Weldon, so in a few seconds they were rowing down the Salt Pond with a boy in each dinghy.

By this time, most of the power boats that had dragged were reanchored along the southwest reach of the harbor, so it was easy to pass them one after the other. The ones which had a spare anchor on deck were passed quickly, for they took it for granted that the planted anchor was a similar one. But when they came to a craft with no anchor on deck, either Goddard or Weldon would say to the man on deck; "I guess it blew some last night."

The power boat man would answer: "I'll say it did and we dragged clean across the pond."

This would usually be the opening, when they could ask what sort of anchors the power boat had. The answer, more times than not, would be: "She's got the regular kind of anchor most power boats use. They are what they call navy anchors, so they ought to hold all right."

After they rowed away, Goddard would say; "You see? Almost none of them know the difference between a stock or a stock-less anchor, or even call them by those names."

Finally, they came to one of the boats that had dragged and she had a fair looking stock anchor on deck. This was a puzzler but, when they asked her owner if that was the type of anchor which he dragged last night, he replied, "No, I had down one of those patent anchors which are very light but will hold in a hurricane, and yet you can break them out easily."

"That sounds like a very useful combination," replied Goddard, "and it certainly must have blown hard to start you."

"Yes," replied the motorboater, "it must have been more than a hurricane."

This time, after they rowed along, Goddard said: "That is one of the typical powerboaters; he will believe everything he sees in advertisements and nothing taught by his own experience."

By that time, they had arrived abreast the long white double-ender, and they lay on their oars as they drifted slowly by. This vessel had a bow very much like the modern destroyer; that is, her flare was very moderate so she could run in a seaway without jumping, while her beautifully shaped stern would not force her bow under when both ends were in a wave. Jim asked his uncle if such a long, narrow hull would not be apt to roll a lot?

"No. It is the sea that makes a vessel roll, and the wider she is the more hold the sea has on her. The reason the long, narrow boat is steadier than a short, wide one of the same weight is that different parts of the long boat are in different parts of a wave. At the bow, the wave may be trying to heel her to starboard when the stern is trying to tip to port. The shorter and wider boat is more often under the influence of one part of the wave only, while her great beam gives the wave a greater lever arm to work on."

Jim remarked that she certainly looked like some of the destroyers. His uncle agreed: "If the destroyers were not just about as they are, they never could be driven in rough water."

The name of the double-ender was *Lampooner*, and Jim was curious to know what the name meant. Weldon said: "I suppose it means a joker, or a maker of satire. This long double-ender certainly makes a joke of the large sterned boats with their full deck lines forward that rear, plunge and snort when trying to run in a seaway."

There was a man sitting in the pilot house of the *Lampooner* and he, seeing the interest the men and boys were taking in his craft, stepped on deck and nodded. After taking a second look, he said: "I think you are the men who put the anchor down for the stranded power boat, and as we both seem to prefer double-enders won't you come aboard and shake hands?"

Weldon replied, "There is nothing we would like so well, sir, particularly the boys."

So the owner let down a short Jacob's ladder that was between two removable boarding stanchions. As they climbed aboard, he said: "My name is Townsend."

Little Dan, who was below the age of embarrassment, answered, "Yes, we know, for we looked the *Lampooner* up in our Lloyd's."

This served to break the ice, so Townsend said with a smile: "Won't you come forward to the pilot house?" The men went

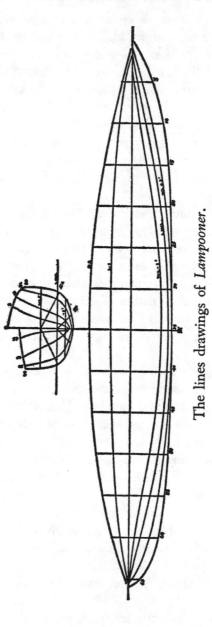

The lines drawings of *Lampooner.*

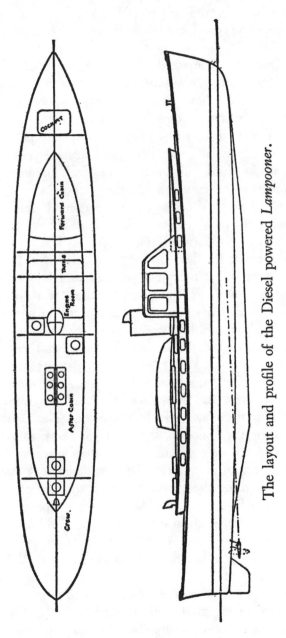

The layout and profile of the Diesel powered *Lampooner.*

with him, but the boys had to take a walk around the deck first, and when they got to the sunken forward cockpit they had to try the seat there.

Mr. Townsend remarked: "Our forward cockpit has an irresistible attraction for young ones. When one is seated there only the head is above deck and there is nothing forward of you but the stemhead, some rather neat bowchocks, and a small capstan. We find this bow cockpit very useful. Not only is it a safe place for children where you can have your eye on them but, when handling the anchor, the deck becomes waist high and supports one so he can lift the anchor in and out without danger of slipping. We also carry our ground tackle on the forward part of the cockpit floor, so it is all off the deck."

The men looked forward, when Weldon said: "I must say you have the neatest foredeck I ever have seen. But, don't you take water in the forward cockpit if you run your bow under?"

"Yes, but only a small amount, for there is a canvas cover for the cockpit which has two strongbacks under it and, as the cockpit is self bailing, a little water is of no consequence."

Goddard remarked; "I see you have no hand rails around the deck."

"That is right," answered Townsend, "and there are several reasons for it. In the first place, you can pass from forward to aft all the way below deck. In the second place, there are grab rails all along the housetop, so that if you move along in a sitting position you are very secure even in rough weather. Hand rails, of course, are unnecessary when at anchor. I have tried to arrange everything the simplest way on the *Lampooner,* not only to reduce the first cost and upkeep, but principally because I like the looks of straightforward simplicity. You hear people talk about streamlining as if it were to add queer looking things to the upper structure, but the best streamlining of all is to do away with exposed parts."

Pointing to a nearby power boat, he said: "You see that vessel with its bent-over mast and flagstaffs? Well, although she is smaller than we are, I suppose she has four times the wind resistance because of her deck complications. The way I make a mental estimate of wind resistance is to visualize a boat turned upside down and towed through the water. Perhaps you know how hard a fish net tows through the water? If so, you can see how the multiplicity of junk on most power boats would cause resistance. For instance, that bent-over mast there, of I-beam construction, including its lightening holes, will have from two to three times the wind resistance of a plain round spar."

When Townsend stopped speaking, Weldon asked him if he thought wind resistance on a yacht was of much consequence.

"No, not on a slow one but, when you go twenty miles an hour against a head wind it is of some consequence. Also, it is worth considering when laying at anchor in a breeze like last night."

This, of course, brought up the question of anchors and when Goddard asked what sort of ground tackle the *Lampooner* had, Townsend said; "She has stock anchors of the yachtsman type, and the one we had down last night weighs about sixty pounds. It was used with a nylon warp which has a short length of chain at the anchor to take the chafe of bottoms."

When they asked him if he had dragged last night, he said; "No, why should I? We haven't got much wind resistance."

Weldon mentioned that one of the men on a power boat they passed said it blew more than a hurricane last night and that was what broke his anchor out. Townsend remarked that it was customary to get a breeze like last night about every two months along the New England coast in the summer, and stronger ones about every month in the spring, winter and fall.

By this time, the boys had come aft to the pilot house so Townsend asked them if they would like to look around below, and invited the men along. They went down forward by a companionway beside the steering wheel. This brought them to a double stateroom which had its own toilet room and over six feet of headroom everywhere over the floor. The boys were quite impressed by this light, airy room for it had several opening windows along the deckhouse side.

Goddard spoke up and said; "I see she is built on the longitudinal system of construction."

"Yes," replied Townsend, "that seems to be the lightest, strongest and cheapest way to build a vessel of this model. A long boat so built does not require any special bracing to stop her from hogging."

They then climbed the companionway again and, when back in the pilot house, Townsend paused to say: "The fuel tanks are under the forward part of this floor while the forward part of the engine room is under the after section. The after part of the engine room is aft of the pilot house (with full headroom) so we will go there next."

He led the way down a companionway which was in the dummy smokestack and they saw that the engine room here had good headroom, light, and ventilation. Townsend's only remark was that having the engine room partly under the pilot house simplified the controls and made the engines quick to get at. Then they passed through the door in the engine room after bulkhead and entered a long compartment which was all open excepting a toilet room. This compartment was made up of a combination galley and messroom, and had three folding berths.

Townsend said: "This is where my son and his friend generally hang out, and it is a comfortable place to cook and eat." Pointing aft, he continued: "Aft of that bulkhead is the crew's quarters with a hatch opening on deck."

Goddard who was usually rather uncommunicative, now said; "As a general rule, I detest the modern power boats that have lounges above breakfast nooks and flying bridges above all, for there is nothing nautical or useful about them. But when I see a vessel like this with light, air, and usefulness throughout her length, it makes me take a new interest in power craft."

By the time they got back to the pilot house and had sat down Weldon remarked: "I see you prefer two-cycle Diesels." Townsend answered; "My engines both develop a little over 100 horsepower and in that size of engine there is little to choose between two- and four-cycle. In smaller sizes, the four-cycle is usually the simplest and cheapest, particularly those which will explode their charge at lower compression on account of special shaped heads or turbulence chambers. These types are now highly developed for trucks and traction engines so I suppose will soon be more reasonable in price. But all Diesels and semi-Diesels will be somewhat expensive on account of fuel-injection systems and speed-governing apparatus, both of which are difficult to simplify. However, in the sizes of over 100 horsepower, more and more of the builders both here and abroad are turning to two-cycle, so that in a few years the larger engines will practically all be two-cycle."

"How do you suppose that has come about?" inquired Weldon.

"Well, I suppose it was something like this. In the gasoline era, an engine was throttled or slowed down by allowing less mixture to enter the combustion chamber so that at slow and moderate speeds the intake chambers were in a partial vacuum. This seemed to work all right with the four or Otto cycle. But with the crankcase-charged, two-cycle engine, it was never a success for they ran so unevenly at different throttles that they were not satisfactory for automotive purposes. In other words, when a two-cycle engine was throttled down there was not enough pressure developed in the crankcase to pass a charge into the combustion chamber."

"Yes, I understand that," remarked Weldon.

"This was all changed when two-cycle crankcase-charged motors were used as Diesels or compression-ignited engines, for then there was no throttle and the intake was always under atmospheric pressure. You see, the speed of a Diesel is controlled by a governor which makes the fuel distributor meter out more or less fuel according to the power that is wanted. The crankcase-charged Diesels were made for many years in Sweden and Denmark and acquired a fine name for reliability. But as much as thirty years ago, the designers of large Diesels for ship propulsion began using two-cycle Diesels charged by air pumps which were generally called scavenging pumps. The early ones were of the piston type, but of late years rotary scavenging pumps have been developed that seem as if they were to make the two-cycle the best arrangement in all large engines for marine and stationary work."

When Townsend stopped, Goddard said: "I thank you for explaining to me why the two-cycle engine has again come into use, for I never seem to keep up with the mutability of the internal combustion engine. Modern advertising, instead of explaining something about the product, usually shows a girl in a bathing suit and a captain's hat, or in some other way tries to divert your attention from the truth of the matter."

Weldon, who was an engineer by profession, knew all that had been talked of, but now inquired if the *Lampooner* changed her trim much when running.

"No, not much," answered Townsend, "and sometimes I wish she did more, for a boat which raises her bow when under way does not need so much freeboard forward."

"Does her stern settle?" asked Weldon.

"Very little, indeed. The double-ender of the past has usually acquired a bad name for settling aft, I know, but that has been because the lines aft have swung up to the waterline or swung up to give room for a single screw. But when twin screws are used, the lines at the centerline do not have to be swept upward so the stern has little cause for settling.

"The *Lampooner* can go about 25 miles an hour when wide open, and at that speed the bow may rise six inches and the stern settle three and, while she is not a quick turning craft, still she banks just right on the turns."

Goddard asked how she acted in a seaway, and Townsend told him that running in a sea was the *Lampooner's* best feature, for she usually could cruise along at 20 miles an hour when the short wide-sterned craft has to slow down to eight or ten miles an hour. She was really extraordinary in a following sea, for she seemed to have no tendency to yaw.

"How about your cruising radius?" asked Goddard.

Townsend chuckled and replied: "She seems to go about two miles on a gallon at the rate of 20 miles per hour, and her tank holds around 500 gallons, so you see we can run about 1000 miles on a tankful and it will take us a little over two days to do it. You see, a Diesel engine uses about 25 per cent less fuel than a gasoline engine. When that is coupled with a long, light, easily driven hull, the results are remarkable. As far as I can make out, our cost of fuel, as compared to short, wide gasoline craft of the same accommodations and speed, is four to one in our favor."

"How can there possibly be that great difference?" inquired Goddard.

"Well," replied Townsend, "did you ever try to row one of the wide-sterned outboard motor boats?"

"Yes, I have," acknowledged Goddard, "and I think I now see the difference."

Townsend continued: "Now, if you add the difference in fuel consumption between the gasoline and Diesel engine and consider the difference in cost of the fuels, the *Lampooner's* performance is reasonable."

Weldon then asked him if he thought the difference in cost of fuel between the gasoline and Diesel engines in a boat of this type would ever make up for the difference in first cost of the two power plants.

"That would be hard to figure, but there surely would not be much difference between the two in three or four years. However, with the Diesel power plant, the cruising radius would be greater; the freedom from explosion and fire a very great advantage for the Diesel; and, last but not least, the exhaust gases of the Diesel are not poisonous even if they are disagreeable."

Weldon inquired as to the *Lampooner's* dimensions, and Townsend said that her length was 66 feet, beam 10 feet, and draft 3 feet 6 inches.

Goddard remarked that the *Lampooner* interested him the most of any power boat he had ever seen and, if it were not a rude question, he would like to inquire how she compared in cost with other craft of her accommodations.

Townsend said that, as far as he could make out, the *Lampooner* cost about as much as the usual power boat of 45 feet length, and that the 45 footer might have as much room if she were two or three feet wider than the *Lampooner*.

"You see," he said, "length is only one of the five or six factors which influence cost; the other ones are beam, depth, weight, quality, and simplicity. As far as cost is concerned, the *Lampooner* loses out in length and maybe weight, but more than makes up in the other factors. As for speed, economy and seaworthiness, she is certainly far superior."

Weldon inquired why the *Lampooner* was so full on the deck line aft. Her owner replied: "It is only for propeller protection and to give room for the steering gear below deck." He said her stern was of the type usually called a cruiser stern, and at the present time was much used on large steam and motorships.

"Why do they call it a cruiser stern?" inquired Jim.

Townsend laughed: "Why, sonny, that is the type of stern generally used on the naval craft called cruisers and battle cruisers."

By this time, the sun was nearing the western horizon and the captain of the *Lampooner* began making culinary sounds in the galley, so Goddard arose and said to Townsend: "Sir, I want to thank you for showing me this fine vessel and giving us all a pleasant time, but we must be getting back to our own little ships."

Townsend answered: "I am sorry you must leave so soon, for I had hoped you would meet Mrs. Townsend and my son, but at present they are on shore looking at the several old burial grounds on the island. Mrs. Townsend is an ardent antiquarian and much interested in genealogy, and our son goodnaturedly accompanies her on these expeditions of research. I must say, cruising is an endless joy to people who have such a hobby, but sometimes the *Lampooner* is loaded with antiquarian objects before we get back."

The boys had brought the dinghies to the gangway ladder for the men to disembark. As they rowed away the boys' heads were turned, for the model of the *Lampooner* kept them spellbound. On the way back, Weldon stopped for the anchor and warp which had been lent to the power boat. This time, instead of slinging it under the stern, the anchor was lowered into the bow on top of the warp that had first been coiled down there.

The owner of the power boat was very profuse in his thanks for the use of the anchor. He had evidently had a hard time in breaking it out for he ended up his talk by saying he would never have an anchor which broke out so hard.

Weldon could not resist answering him by saying: "Did you ever stop to think that an anchor that breaks out hard would also hold well with a steep scope?"

The powerboater's only reply was that the advertisements don't say anything about that.

By that time, Weldon was rowing away and muttering to himself. He finally said to Jim; "I sometimes wonder if it is worth while to help those powerboaters for they never seem to learn seamanship from experience. They will believe the moon is made of green cheese if it says so in an advertisement."

Goddard had already left Dan on the *Rozinante* and, as it was now quite late and the boys were hungry, they had supper as quickly as Weldon could heat some soup and make sandwiches. After supper, the boys seemed tired so Weldon took the spare anchor apart and stowed it in the bilge and recoiled the anchor warp and stopped it down. It was a pleasant evening with a dying northwest wind, but the boys had had quite a day of it and they turned in, leaving Weldon in the cockpit enjoying the island twilight.

Weldon and Goddard had planned to make an early start the next morning, and when Weldon came on deck the sun was just rising out of a gray mist in the east, but before the deck chores were done the sky overhead would have pleased an artist, and as it approached the horizon it seemed to shroud distant objects in a sort of pearly radiance. Each breath of morning air was charged with well-being, and as the boys yawned in the morning sunlight their bodies responded with a healthy glowing feeling in the solar plexus, but before long little Dan's insides made audible rumbling noises and he said: "Uncle, when do we eat?"

Weldon smiled and answered: "We will have some tea just as soon as we get under way, and if you boys hoist the sails while I am getting in the anchor it won't be long before we have something in our stomachs."

The wind was still from the northwest, but very light, so it would be a beat out of the harbor and also for the first part of their passage for they had planned to sail to New London that day which is a distance of about 27 nautical miles. As they sailed by the *Viator*, Goddard stuck his head out of the companionway and called out; "Well, I guess you have got the jump on us today, but it will be a calm morning so I will soon catch up with you with the motor going."

"I realize that," answered Weldon, "but it is nice to be at sea on a morning like this." By this time they were beyond hailing distance so Weldon turned the helm over to Jim and told him to tack down the harbor as he pleased, but to keep a little off the northerly shores. Weldon then made tea and served it up with some hardtack but even before they had finished this morning snack they were at the cut, or narrow harbor entrance, so Weldon again took over the helm while the boys washed and put away the tea cups. The Block Island harbor entrance is quite narrow so that less handy boats than the *Rozinante* would have had difficulty to pass through in a light head wind, but she did it in two tacks and soon bore off to north on a tack just outside some rocks near the entrance. Weldon would have stayed on this 'northerly tack' way over to the mainland if he had not wanted to cross the *Viator's* course later, for the northwest wind holds longest under the shore. But after standing north two miles, he fetched about and took up a course toward the westward. There is nearly always some ground swell in this region and the boys would have felt squeamish if they had not had their morning tea before coming out, but now, as the *Rozinante* rose and fell over the undulating sea in her course toward the western horizon, the boys again began to be hungry.

As it neared eight o'clock, Weldon went below to make breakfast and although there was some motion there was little heel from the dying wind. This time he made cocoa for a change, and the bacon and eggs were done country style, that is, he first put

some strips of bacon on the griddle and let it try out a little which
the slight heel or angle of the stove helped. Then, when holding
the bacon back with a fork, he poured off the excess fat and fried
the eggs among the bacon pieces. This was only a slight change
from their regular morning fare, but somehow or other it tasted
mighty good as they stood to the westward with no other land in
sight but Block Island. Although the wind was falling, it was such
a beautiful morning that they all were in the best of spirits and,
as Weldon lit his pipe and leaned back against the coaming, he
said:

"Some people would be alarmed at the prospects of being becalmed here for an hour or two, but there is no place in the world
that I would rather be, for we can take a nap, eat, or be merry,
just as we want to and if we get too much sun we can move into
the shade. We can read, or find something interesting to talk
about; but the best way to enjoy a calm is to enter a state of almost
utter abandon as far as worldly things are concerned. Sometimes
when you are single-handed these are the happiest moments of
life. You should, however, be conscious enough to keep a weather
eye for squalls. While we have a lot of light weather north of
Cape Cod, we seldom have the flat calms that are prevalent from
here to the head of Long Island Sound. It is interesting that Block
Island has a high average wind velocity while New London, the
next weather station, has a very low average velocity."

"Why do you suppose that is?" inquired Jim.

"I do not know the exact reason for it, but I suppose the fre-
quent calms at New London lower the average while at Block
Island it is seldom dead calm for long, and Block Island is noted
for its hard winds in storms. Some people even say it blows too
hard there for trees to grow well, while some twenty miles north
of Block Island on the mainland trees grow remarkably well."

Weldon picked up the chart and showed the boys how very
level the bottom was in this region for it stretches east and west
here for many miles without generally varying a fathom in depth.
"You know," he said, "it is quite remarkable to have level plains

in New England, but inshore here it is comparatively level, and it is interesting to note that the sea bottom off a piece of land is apt to have the same characteristics as the land."

Just then, Dan spoke up to say he could see the *Viator* coming out of harbor. They saw that she had taken up a course a little to leeward of them so they bore off a point or so, but as the wind had almost petered out they made slow progress even with slacked sheets. After a while, the *Viator* headed toward them and, as she neared, they could see that she was towing a long warp astern.

As she got alongside Goddard called over that while Weldon could hear him he could not hear them, but since it would be calm for an hour or two they had better pick up the towline. So Weldon turned the helm over to Jim and went forward with the boathook.

Although the wind was light, there was considerable ground swell running which usually makes it hard to pick up a towline. However, Goddard now took the *Viator* across the *Rozinante's* bow so that the line ran right under her forefoot and was easy to pick up. In the meantime, Goddard idled his engine so the *Viator* was moving at the same rate as the *Rozinante*. Weldon now hauled in on the loose end of the rope till he came near the end, and passed it through the chock, around the mooring cleat and then belayed it to the mast with a round turn and three half hitches. Weldon had hauled in on the loose end for two reasons; one important reason was that the end of the rope was easy to handle, but the most important reason was that the line would not haul taut while he was belaying it. These may seem like simple points but they are often overlooked in picking up a towline in a seaway.

Weldon now called to Jim to bear way off to the north and this brought the *Rozinante* at about 45 degrees from her course. Thus when the towrope first came taut, instead of fetching taut with a jerk, it simply swung her bow around and gradually got her underway. The towrope was the *Viator's* nylon anchor warp and was very good about stretching as the *Rozinante* forged ahead or held back in the ground swells, but Goddard studied the towrope and finally paid out just the right amount so that both boats held back or forged ahead at about the same time.

After that, they went along quite steadily, considering the ground swell, but Weldon took over the helm and swung the *Rozinante's* bow off suddenly every time the towline slacked, and this took the heavy strain off the line. The *Rozinante* now rolled and her sails slatted around considerably so Weldon had the boys take in the jib and mizzen. He hauled the mainsail in flat and rigged two ropes on the main boom like cross tackles. After the mainsail was hauled very taut, the leach stopped flapping and the rolling became noticeably less, for a very tight sail is an efficient rolling damper, while a loose one does little but strain itself and the gear.

When things were settled down Weldon again got in a talking mood. "Well, we didn't get becalmed after all, and I am a little sorry for I rather like a calm once in a while as it adds much to the contrast when the wind comes again, but I must say a calm is much pleasanter when there is no ground swell."

He then reverted to the problem of picking up the towrope and told the boys he had once seen a Coast Guard launch try to pass a towline to a broken down power boat in a ground swell, and they had proceeded about as follows: First the Coast Guard launch came within about 50 feet of the power boat when the man forward threw a heaving line over with a shot on its end. The first fast fell a little short and the second only smashed a cabin window. At the third cast, the man on the power boat ran away from the shot as it came over, and so was too late to pick it up. The coxswain of the Coast Guard launch then became exasperated and put his launch right alongside to pass the line, but a sea brought them together with a crash that nearly upset the men on both boats. Being in a hurry to get clear, the Coast Guard launch went ahead, but the man on the power boat snubbed the line too quickly and it parted, so they had to go all through the operation again with much hollering on both sides. "So I hope," added Weldon, "you boys will remember that the proper way to pass a line in a seaway is to tow it across the bow of the boat to be towed. If the crews of both boats know their business, a line can be passed this way when it is very rough and both boats can keep well apart. If you have a rope that does not float well you should tie on its end something like a lifering or lifebelt. Then, the whole operation can usually be done quickly without any hollering or jerking of the line."

By this time, land appeared off to the southwest so the boys asked their uncle what it was. He only said: "You just look on the chart, for you will remember these things best that way. If I simply tell you this is Montauk Point, it will go in one ear and out the other."

So Jim and Dan studied the chart for awhile, but soon asked why they could not see Fisher's Island which was, if anything, closer. Weldon replied: "In the first place, the land on Montauk Point is higher, and in the second place there is sort of a mist over the mainland which may denote that a southwest breeze was making up. All over to the northwest, the loom of the land is quite plain, or would be to a sailor, and in a very short time you will see Fisher's Island and the mainland."

Generally, being towed in a calm is rather tiresome but between towing their models and keeping a sharp outlook for new landfalls the boys were very busy until about eleven o'clock when Race Rock Lighthouse and Little Gull Lighthouse were plainly seen. Weldon told them that the stretch of water between the lighthouses was called The Race, and it generally was rough there if there was any wind. It was so rough there in strong wind that small craft usually went through either Fisher's Island Sound at the north side, or Plum Gut, a channel over near Orient Point on Long Island. The boys asked why it should be so rough in The Race, and he told them that nearly all the water that caused the rise and fall of the tides in Long Island Sound had to pass through there. When you consider the Sound is about 90 miles long and nearly 15 miles wide in places, this is a very great volume. The tide in The Race often flows four miles an hour and sometimes five and a half miles. In the northwest gales which often follow an easterly storm, the strong tide here makes a white boiling strip of water that is too rough for any small craft but a lifeboat. "You will find," said he, "that local mariners keep clear of The Race when they can, for even in a calm there are eddies which will swing a large sailboat around in a circle."

"Why?" asked Dan.

"The bottom of The Race is very uneven; in some places it is 300 feet deep, but near the middle of it there is a rock that comes up to within 18 feet of the surface, and it breaks heavily here in rough weather."

By this time, the afternoon southwest wind was ruffling the water, and the mainsail drew steadily so Weldon went forward and cast off. At first, they did not notice this on the *Viator*, but soon there was much waving from the girls as they started to haul in and coil down the towrope. Weldon said: "Look, the girls are coiling the rope down the wrong way," but just then Goddard noticed it too and had the girls pay the rope out again so it would be coiled correctly.

Little Dan remarked: "I never knew there was a right and wrong way to coil a rope."

"Oh, yes; you can tell a sailor at once by the way he coils down, and he always does it, as he says, with the sun."

"What does coiling with the sun mean, Uncle?" asked Dan.

"It means going from east to south to west, as the sun does in our northern hemisphere, or in other words you should coil a rope the way the hands of a clock move."

"Do all ropes have to be coiled that way?"

"No, not all, but more than nine-tenths of them like to be coiled that way. The ropes coiled the other way are cable-laid rope, and some wire ropes, but the best way to coil a stubborn wire rope or a long hose is to make a figure eight of the coil, for then a turn or twist of the rope is thrown in and taken out in each layer of the coil."

Most of this conversation had taken place while the jib and mizzen were being set, and now Weldon showed the boys how to coil down the halyards by holding the succeeding loops of the rope in the left hand while the right hand swung away from the body at the top of the loop. Dan practiced this two or three times with the mizzen halyard and said: "I always make a coil this way anyway, for your thumb gets in the way when you swing the other way."

"Yes," said his uncle, "and that is the reason most ropes are laid up right handed. In old times they used to call a right hand-laid rope a hawser, and a left handed one a cable, but as a matter of fact a cable-laid rope is three or four hawser-laid ropes laid together with a left hand twist. I should tell you boys that a short rope or a dry, old rope can be coiled down either way but a new, long wet rope only likes to be coiled with the sun."

They had a fair tide under them, and now that the beam wind had hardened, they made good progress, and as they neared Race Rock lighthouse the boys said it didn't look rough or seem to boil up anywhere. Weldon mentioned that the upstream side of The Race is often smooth with a beam wind, and the tide was not at full strength then. "But when we get by the lighthouse," he said, "the water may be a little agitated." Sure enough, when they rounded Race Rock they could see that it had made a long wake to the west of it. As they passed through the wake, the Rozinante was unsteady on her course, and all around them were circular patches of smooth water where the undercurrents came boiling to the surface. Weldon told them that these were the patches where seas broke when it was rough. New London Harbor was now straight ahead, and as they sailed along wind on the quarter the boys were much interested to see three or four lighthouses and a lightship at once.

Their attention was taken up by the approach to New London, and they asked questions and pored over the chart, for New London certainly has a picturesque approach as you look up the Thames River and sail through a myriad of buoys. They soon spotted the Viator at anchor in a shallow part of the lower harbor. There were quite a number of large power craft here, but the boys did not like their models after having seen the Lampooner. Dan asked why they all looked down by the head, and Weldon smiled: "That seems to be the modern tendency. An old time sailor would say they were trimmed like a bull going to war, which means they carry their heads down and their tails up. Some of these power boats will come to a proper trim when under way, but most of them never seem to hold a proper trim after their first photograph is taken. The reason for it is that they run at half the speed that was anticipated."

The *Rozinante* came to anchor beside the *Viator* by four in the afternoon, but the young ones on both boats were very busy packing for they were to return home on the train the next day. It had also been arranged that Coridon and Briggs would meet the boats at New London and make up for the deficiency in crews, so that night they had a parting dinner at a nearby restaurant where Goddard succeeded in getting a table for all of them, and they made a very jolly time of it for there is nothing like a well-run cruise to put people in good spirits, and no party is better than where old and young are congenial.

As they were bidding the youngsters good-by the next morning, Goddard said: "I believe this has been the best cruise I have ever had, and it is nice to think that between the two boats nine people have had a pleasant, restful time at little expense, for you see our boats have not depreciated in value at all and the other expenses have been trifling."

And thus ends this overly long story.

An Index of Boating Skills